ABANDONED MARYLAND

RUIN AND RESTORATION

SUSAN TATTERSON

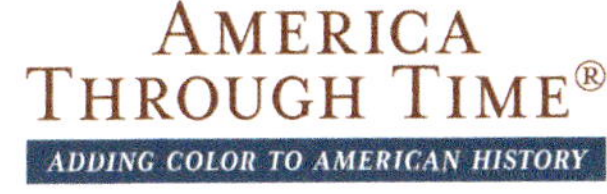

For the Universe. For what is, for what was, and for what can never be again. I am eternally grateful for the mysterious way in which you work. Thank you.

America Through Time is an imprint of Fonthill Media LLC
www.through-time.com
office@through-time.com

Published by Arcadia Publishing by arrangement with Fonthill Media LLC
For all general information, please contact Arcadia Publishing:
Telephone: 843-853-2070
Fax: 843-853-0044
E-mail: sales@arcadiapublishing.com
For customer service and orders:
Toll-Free 1-888-313-2665

www.arcadiapublishing.com

First published 2018

ISBN 978-1-63499-065-3

Typeset in Trade Gothic 10pt on 15pt
Printed and bound in England

CONTENTS

PREFACE

A decade can be an eternity in the life of an abandoned building. Much can happen—ruin or restoration—and *Abandoned Maryland* tells this tale. Most photographs on the following pages were captured a decade ago for my MFA thesis project, "Spirits of the Abandoned." Since then, the journey has continued and encompasses many states and many more abandoned locations, over eighty in fact.

Revisiting Maryland, through these images, for the purpose of compiling this book, has been both a joy and a heartbreak. Just as Maryland is a state of contrast—the streets of gritty Baltimore, where I worked for nine years, to the idyllic countryside of Allegany county — the locations in *Abandoned Maryland* have fallen to contrasting fates. Several historically significant sites have been beautifully and responsibly restored. Equally as many have been destroyed and even more remain as I left them, although undoubtedly worse off.

The most heart-breaking must be the once million-dollar Tome School in the quaint town of Port Deposit. I will never forget standing inside the foyer of the school's show-piece, the majestic Memorial Hall, and gazing in awe at the base of the sweeping marble staircase, with its intricate iron balustrade. I wondered then how such beauty could be ignored and permitted to decay. Memorial Hall was destroyed by fire in 2014.

In stark contrast, the Gunther Brewery leads the way in urban redevelopment. Located in Baltimore's Brewers Hill District, the Gunther building, once abandoned and succumbing to neglect, now boasts 300,000 square feet of sought after residential space. Obrecht Properties LLC has spent fifteen years redeveloping the Brewer's Hill area, and in 2014 Gunther became their crowning achievement.

As dissimilar as their fates may be, the common thread tying the places in this book together is their dereliction and their metamorphosis into light and texture infused-entities. With the complete absence of human existence and intervention they have taken on a life of their own and now possess a mythical quality. They tell their stories with light, color and decay. They inspire us to imagine what went on within their walls and they have led me personally on a wondrous and thought-provoking journey into Maryland's medical, educational, theatrical and industrial past.

I truly believe no creative body of work is created in a vacuum. There are so many people who contributed to the creation of these images. The generous developers who granted me access to their projects: David Knipp, of Obrecht Commercial Real Estate, who, incredibly, gave me the key to Gunther Brewery, before his company had begun restoration, it was like giving a kid the keys to a candy store! I will be forever grateful. Sean McCarthy, the visionary developer who had such grand plans for the beautiful Mayfair theatre, was so gracious with his time and knowledge; it saddens me his dream was never realized. Eric Turner, I will never forget your guided tour of the Westport demolition, and the helpful advice you offered, which will remain our secret, thank you! And a very big thank you to the friends and colleagues at the University of Baltimore and those in the nonprofit sector who sent emails and made phone calls on my behalf.

On a personal note, my friends and family. My wonderful Mum, for teaching me that, sometimes, it's okay to break rules, because not every location I've photographed has come with permission. My little sister, Nicole, who shares my curious nature. And of course, to all the adventurous souls who have accompanied me and broken the rules with me on my explorations, may there be many, many more.

I prefer to photograph alone; I enjoy the solitude these abandonments offer, but I also recognize the danger in my solitary exploits. I smile each time a well-meaning person says, "be careful," and I think of Stephanie, a friend who joined me in exploring some particularly risky locations, and her patience with my antics. We now live on opposite sides of the country but her constant "be careful" is always with me. I'm not careful; it's not in my nature to be so. I often test the limits of sensibility to create the photograph I see in my mind's eye, sometimes they work and are worth it, and sometimes not so much.

Regardless of the risk involved, what I hope for the most is the photographs on the following pages communicate, visually, the rich and varied histories these places share. It is impossible to capture the feeling of standing within their walls. I have attempted, however, to capture their spirit, hence the title of my website *Spirits of the Abandoned.* Many, if not all of them, are off limits to the public and I am grateful to have been given access to them, and to share what hides behind their shuttered facades — may they inspire your imagination as much as they have mine.

Sue Tatterson

Gold Canyon, 2018

My favorite thing is to go where I've never been.
~Diane Arbus

MAYFAIR THEATRE, BALTIMORE

Baltimore's Mayfair Theatre has played as many roles as the actors who once walked its stage: public swimming pool, elegant theatre, ice-skating rink, and a theatre once again, with Turkish baths occupying the basement. Today, only the outer facade of the Mayfair remains.

On June 17, 1880, the Mayfair opened as the Natatorium, a 60 by 244-foot bathing house and swimming pool. In 1885, the Oratorio Society purchased the building, later selling it to James Lawrence Kernan, a Confederate veteran and wealthy philanthropist.

The Mayfair reopened, as the Howard Auditorium, on April 6, 1891, and soon thereafter, became known as the Auditorium. Over the next four decades, Kernan's grand plans continually evolved. In the spring of 1893, he had a 50 by 150-foot ice skating rink called the Ice Palace constructed inside the Auditorium. The Ice Palace attraction included an ice cave—complete with dangling icicles, a gallery, and a roof garden with a promenade and an Oriental pagoda.

Transformation occurred once again in the spring of 1895. Kernan hired New York theatre architect, J. B. McElfatrick, to bring to life his plans for a first-class Vaudeville theater. The ostentatious remodeling was completed by the fall and included 600 alternating double-flashing lights, illuminated and spelling out the name Auditorium, which could be seen from blocks away. Kernan's restless desire to continually renovate the already grand theatre did not stop there. By the time of his death in 1912, he had remodeled and rebuilt the Auditorium numerous times—in 1904, he opened Turkish baths in the basement, and by 1905, with the purchase of additional buildings surrounding the Auditorium, he opened what he claimed to be "the greatest combination of buildings in the world." Although, probably an overstatement, it was without doubt the greatest combination of theatrical buildings in Maryland. Kernan's death in 1912 adversely affected the Auditorium, and future owners never shared his grandiose vision.

By 1932, the Auditorium was struggling. By the late 1930s, the doors were shuttered.

The second phase of its history, as the Mayfair (a movie house), began on January 31, 1941 and continued for forty-five years until April 1986 when, this time, the doors closed permanently.

In 1998, the collapse of the Mayfair's roof made demolition seemingly inevitable. However, the resurgence of interest in the upper west side of downtown, during the early part of this century's first decade, led to renewed hope for the once grand Mayfair. Plans were offered to turn the Mayfair's ground floor into retail space and the upper floors, now collapsed, into apartments, while still preserving the historic facade. It seemed the nineteenth-century Auditorium, now the forlorn Mayfair, had one more starring role yet to play.

Sadly, these new plans never came to fruition. The inevitable demise of the once grand Auditorium, brought about by neglect and lack of foresight, was caused by a fire in what was once the New Academy Hotel. The October 2014 fire in the adjacent building led to it being razed, leaving the Mayfair even more exposed and a greater risk to public safety. The Mayfair's tragic final act; the demolition of all but the facade and thirty-five feet of the lobby, called for the temporary closure of surrounding streets, and took place in August 2016.

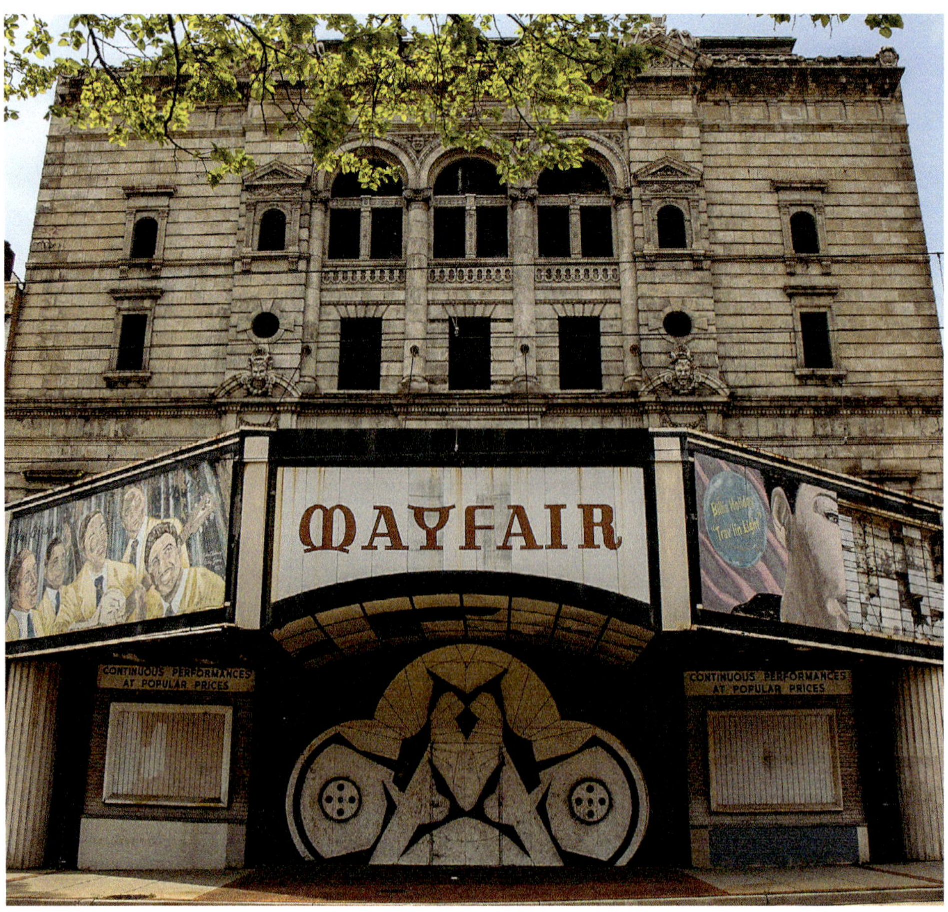

35 feet behind the facade is all that remains of the once grand Auditorium.

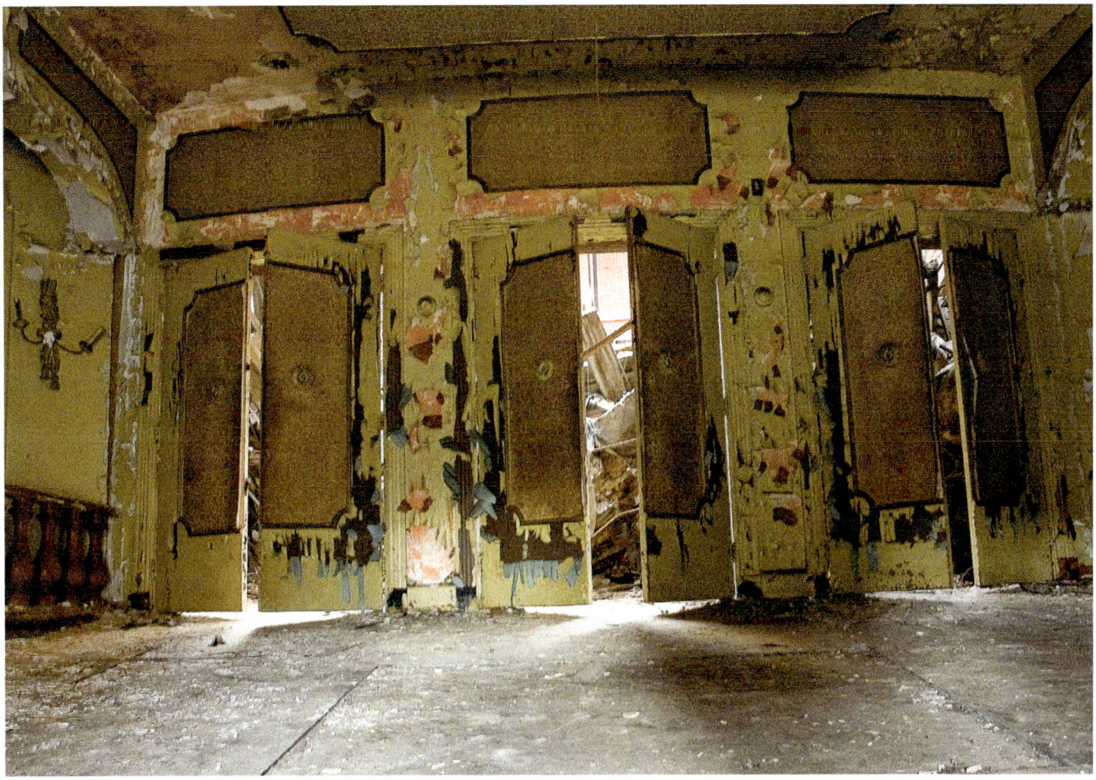

Behind the main theatre entrance doors lie mounds of rubble from the collapsed roof.

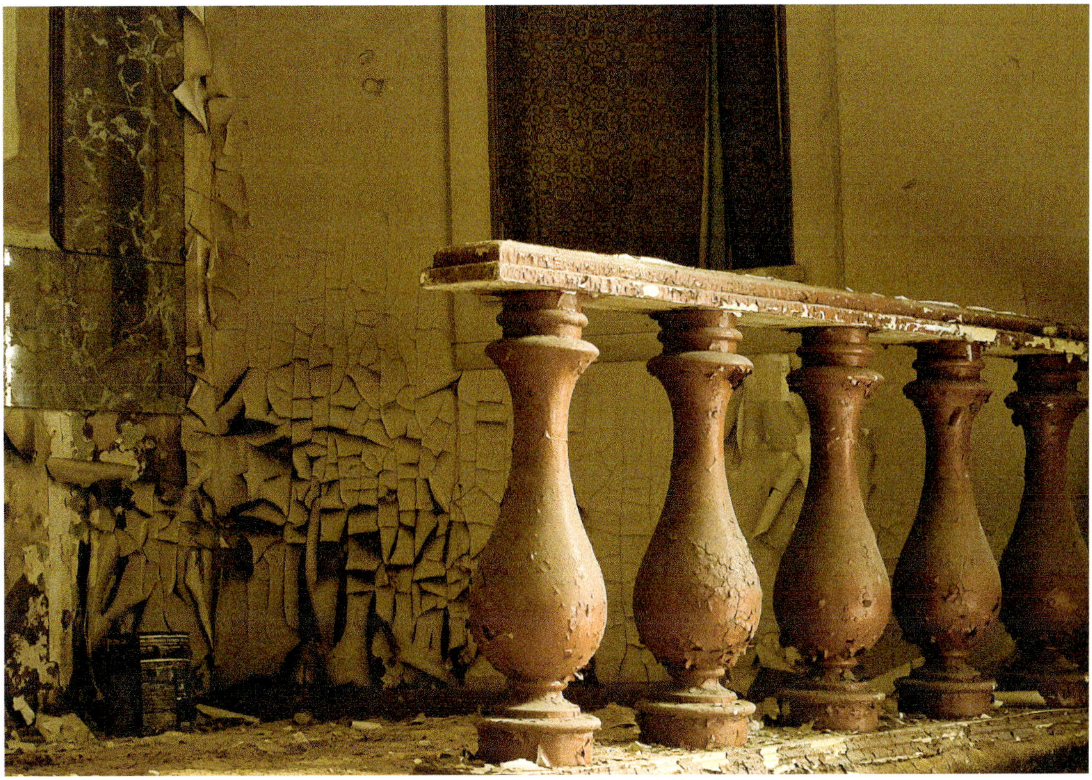

Crumbling pillars in the entrance foyer guard a mirrored alcove.

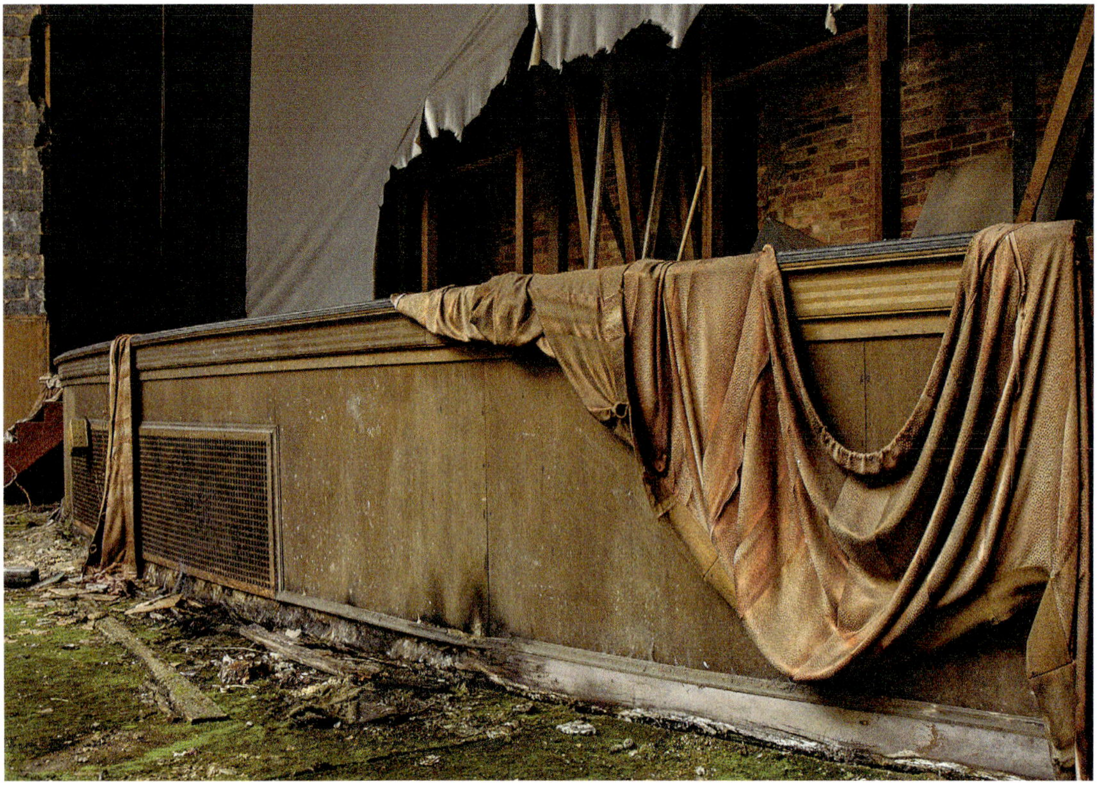

A disintegrating curtain clings to the stage.

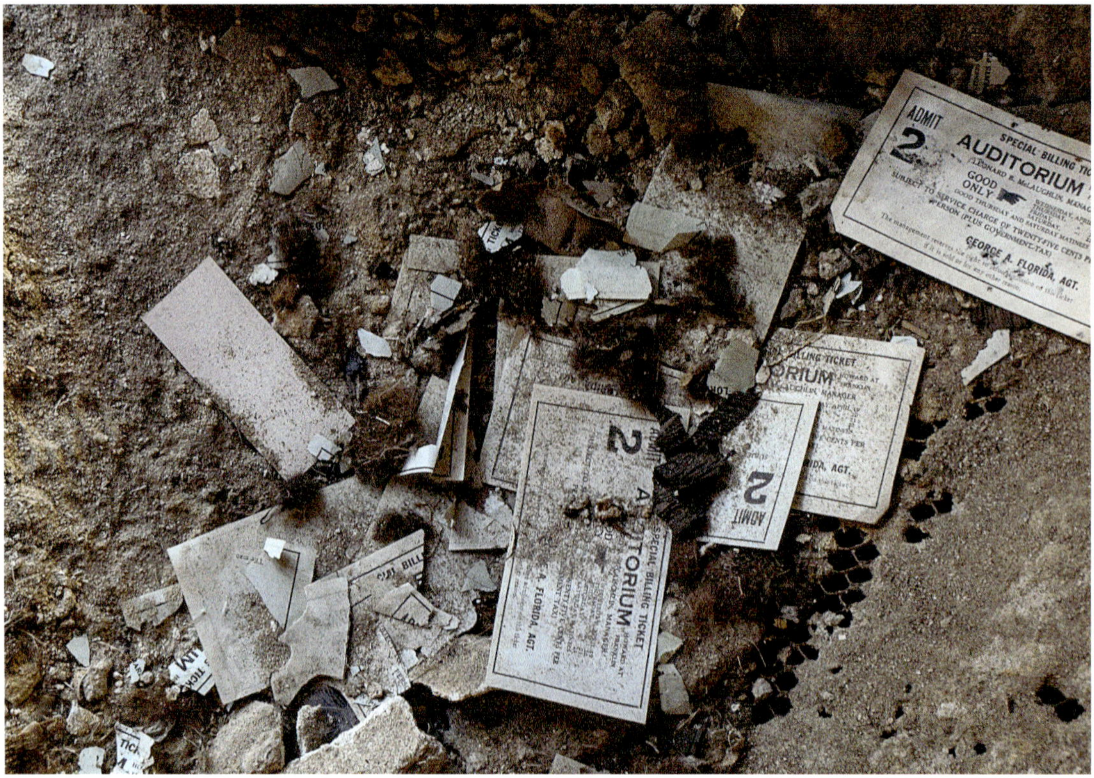

Remnants of Auditorium tickets. Admission was 25 cents per person.

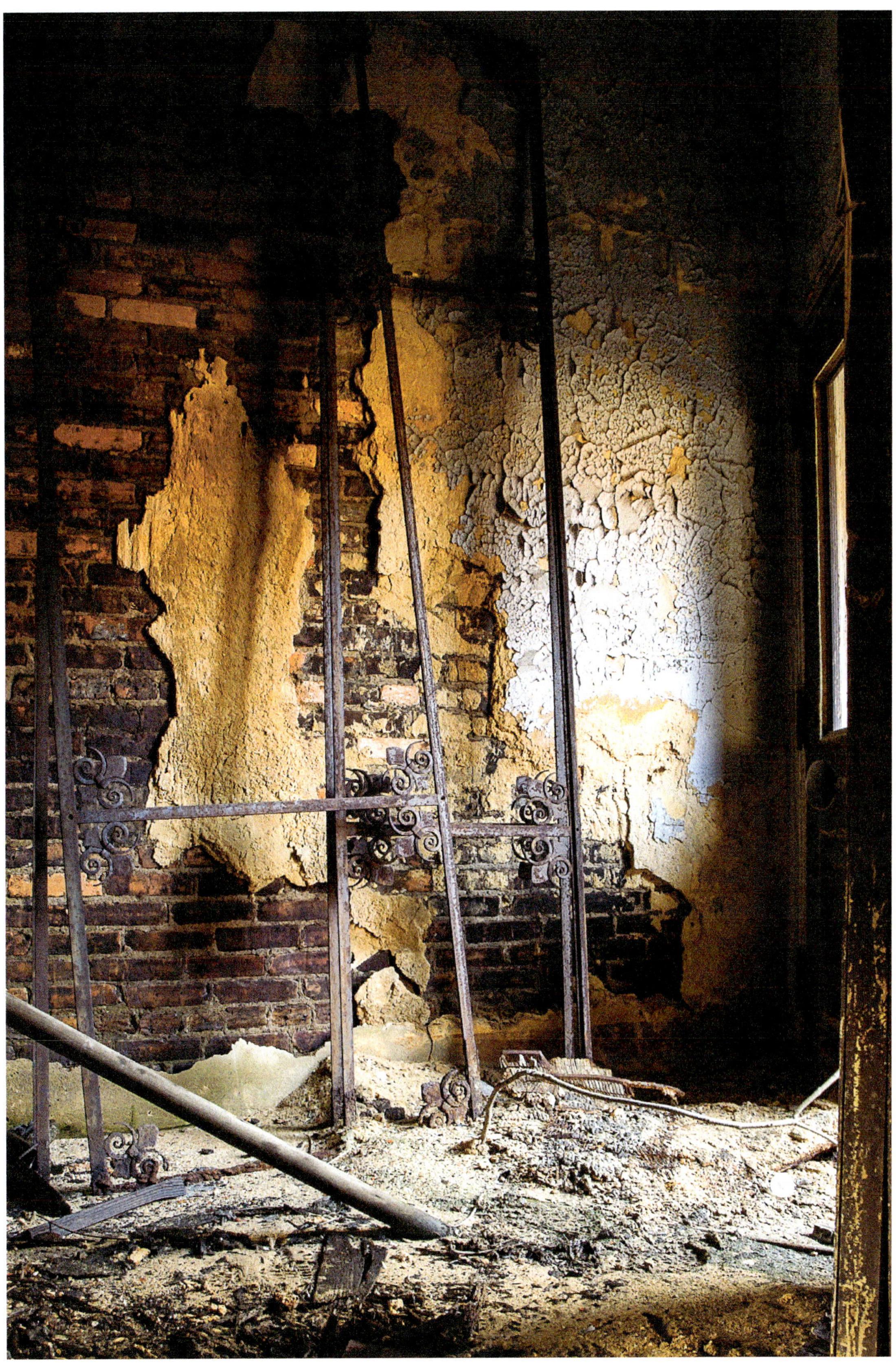

Elaborate ironwork struggles to withstand the ravages of time.

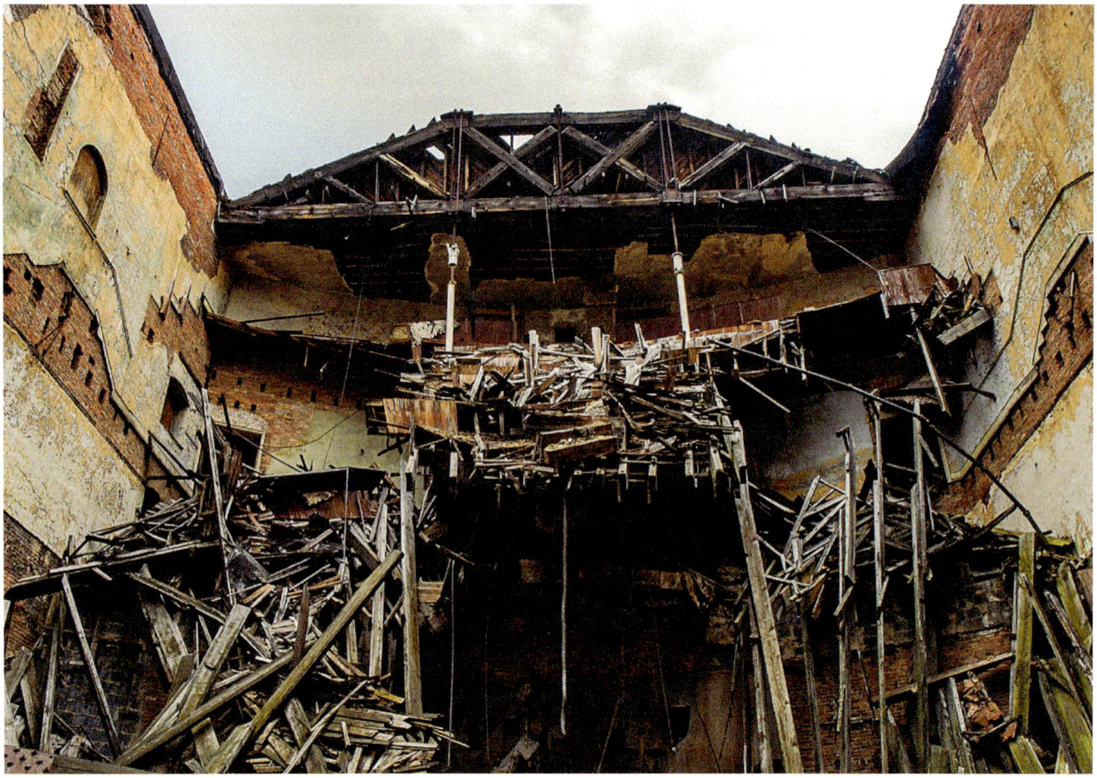

The view from the orchestra, looking up at what remains of the balcony.

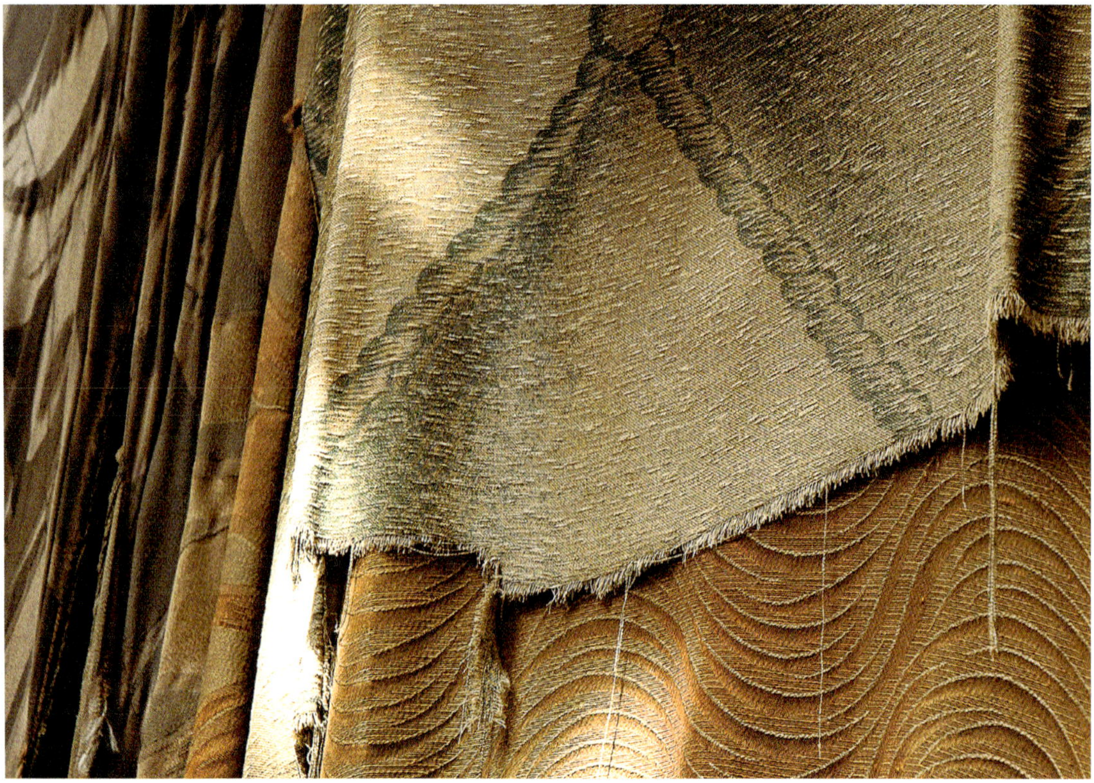

Woven, layered fabric covers the rear wall of the theatre.

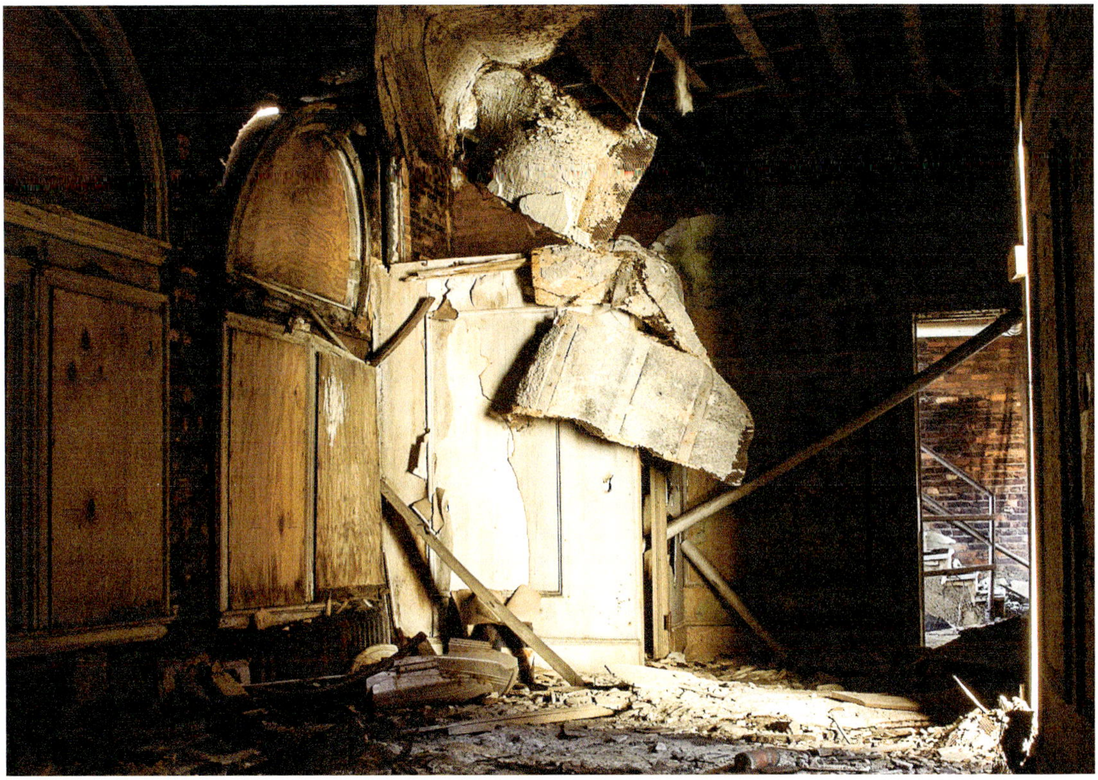

Water damage takes its toll on the ceiling of an upper level foyer.

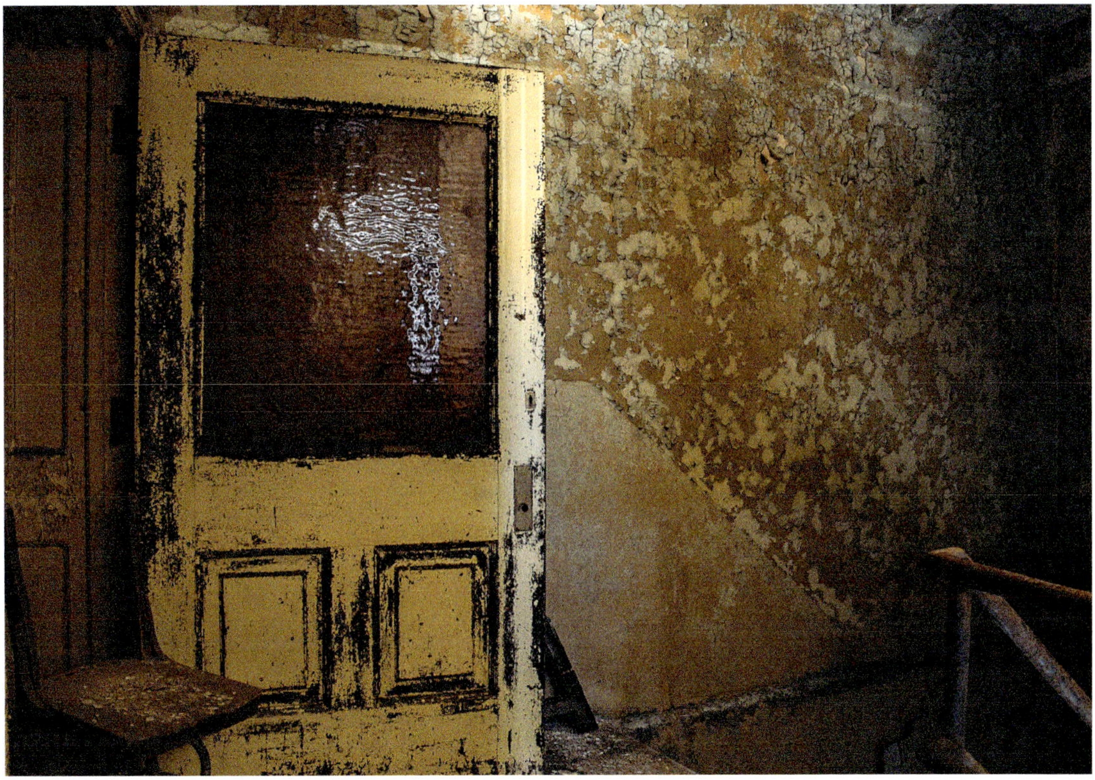

An exit door leads to the deteriorating northern stairwell.

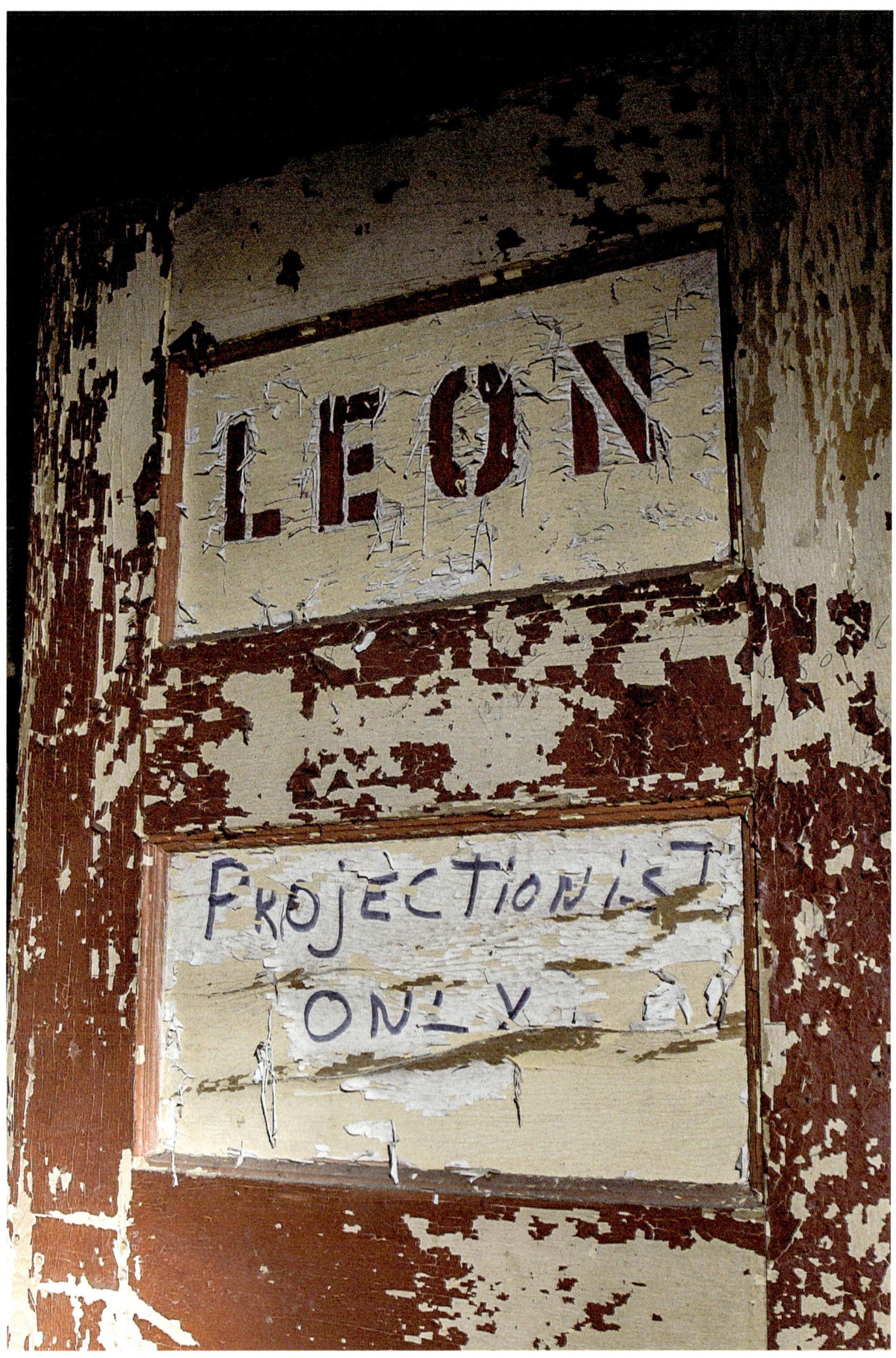

Door to Leon, the projectionist's room.

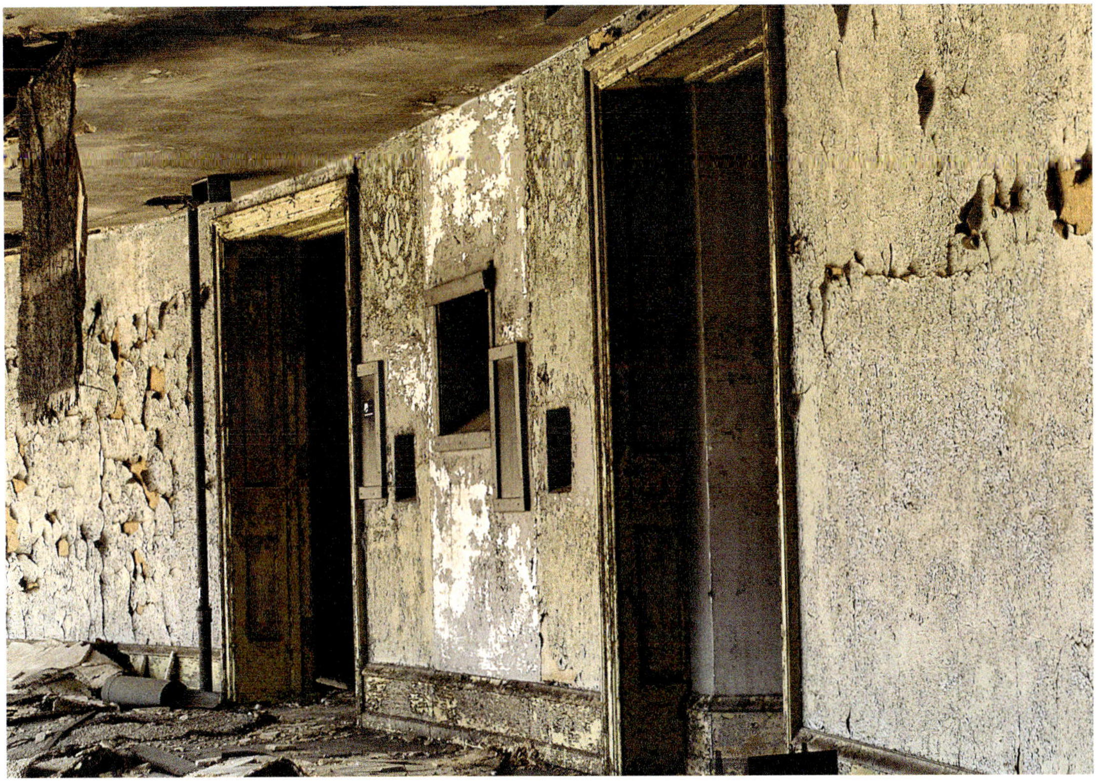

Projection room portholes give a view of the unstable fourth floor balcony.

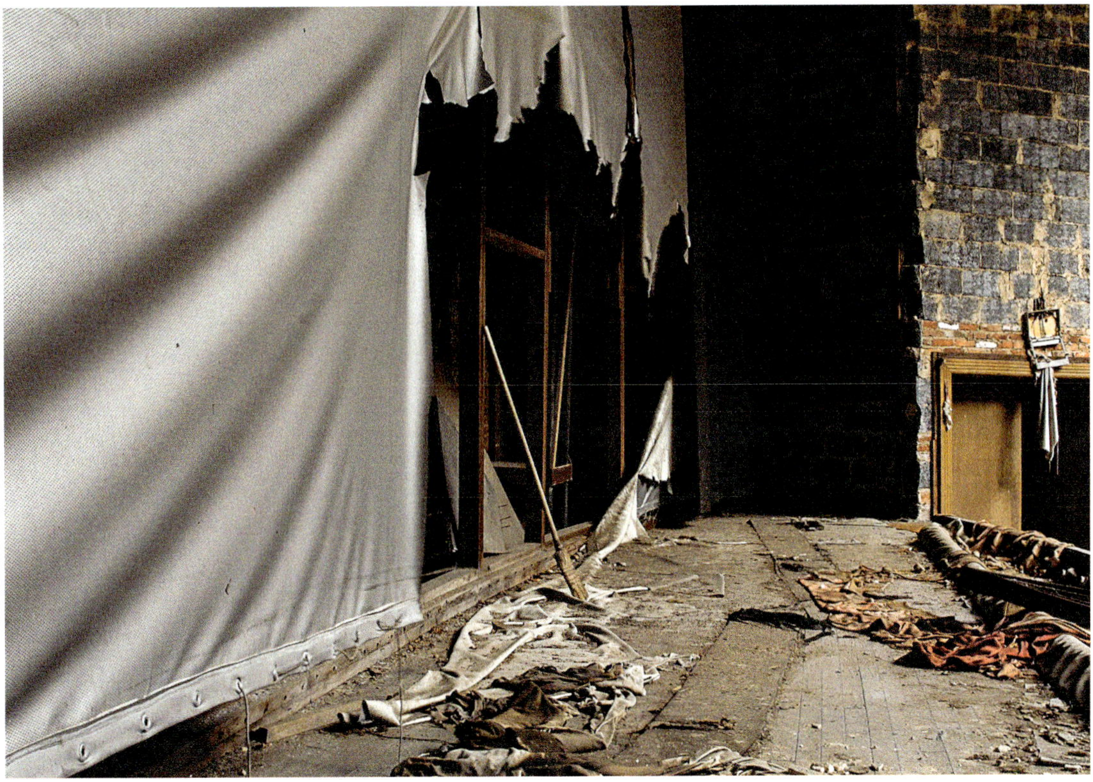

The stage strewn with shredded curtains.

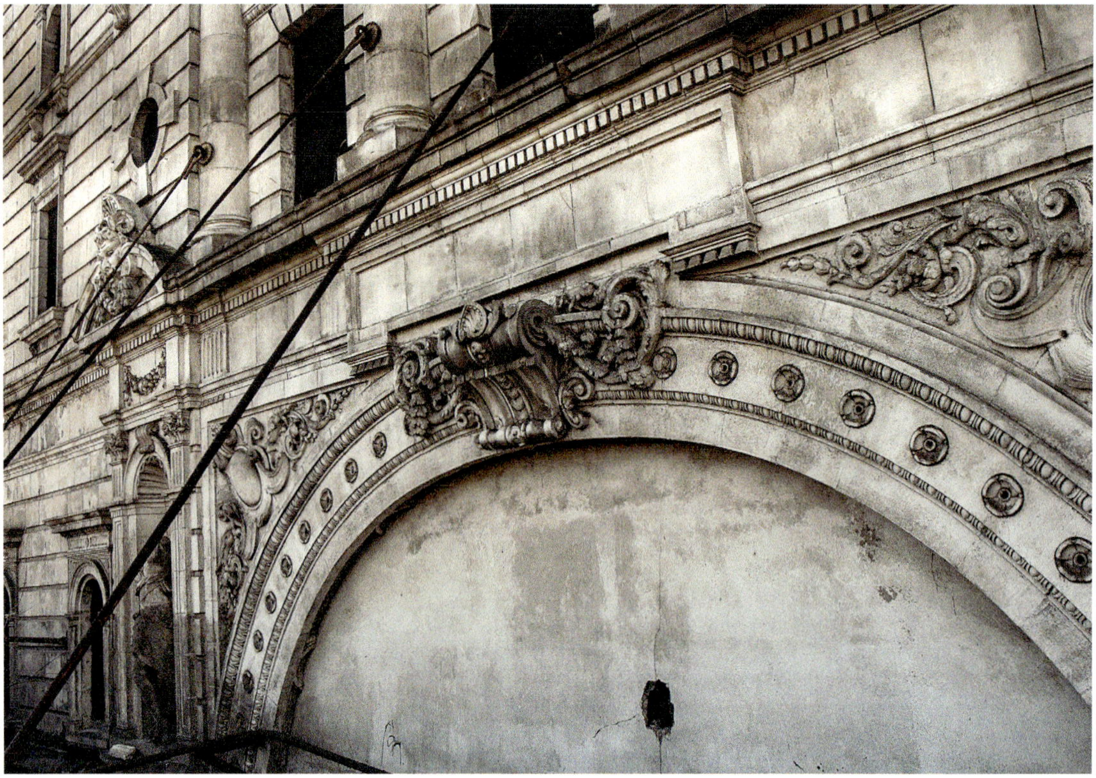

The ornate white terracotta facade of the Auditorium was hidden by the Mayfair marquee for decades.

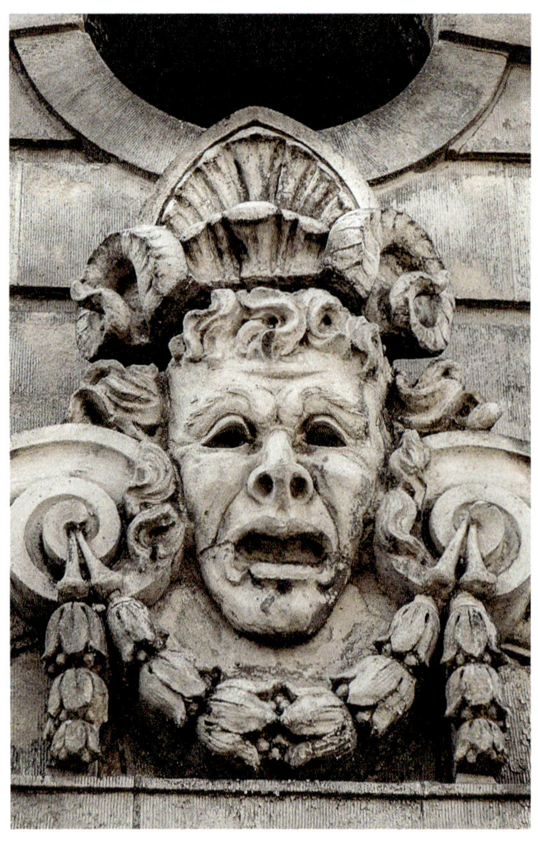

The tragedy drama mask carved from white terra cotta.

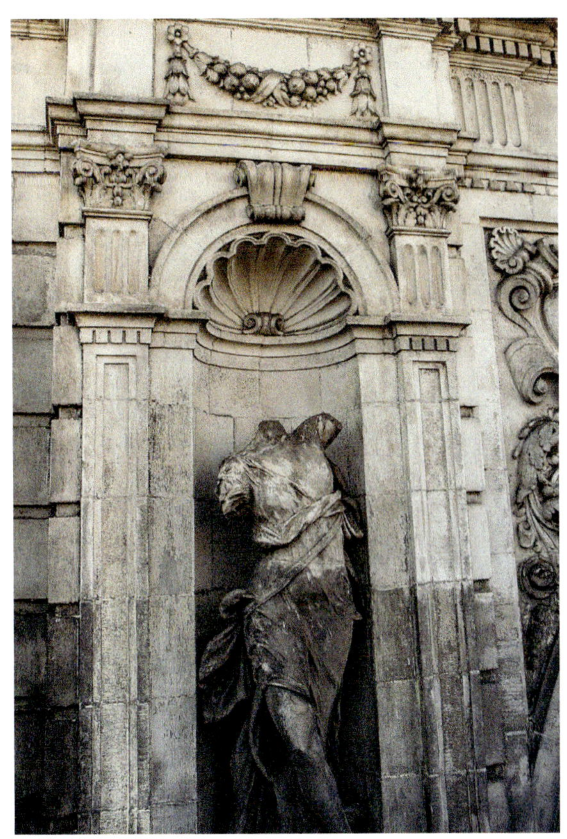

Romanesque style statues of draped women frame the central archway.

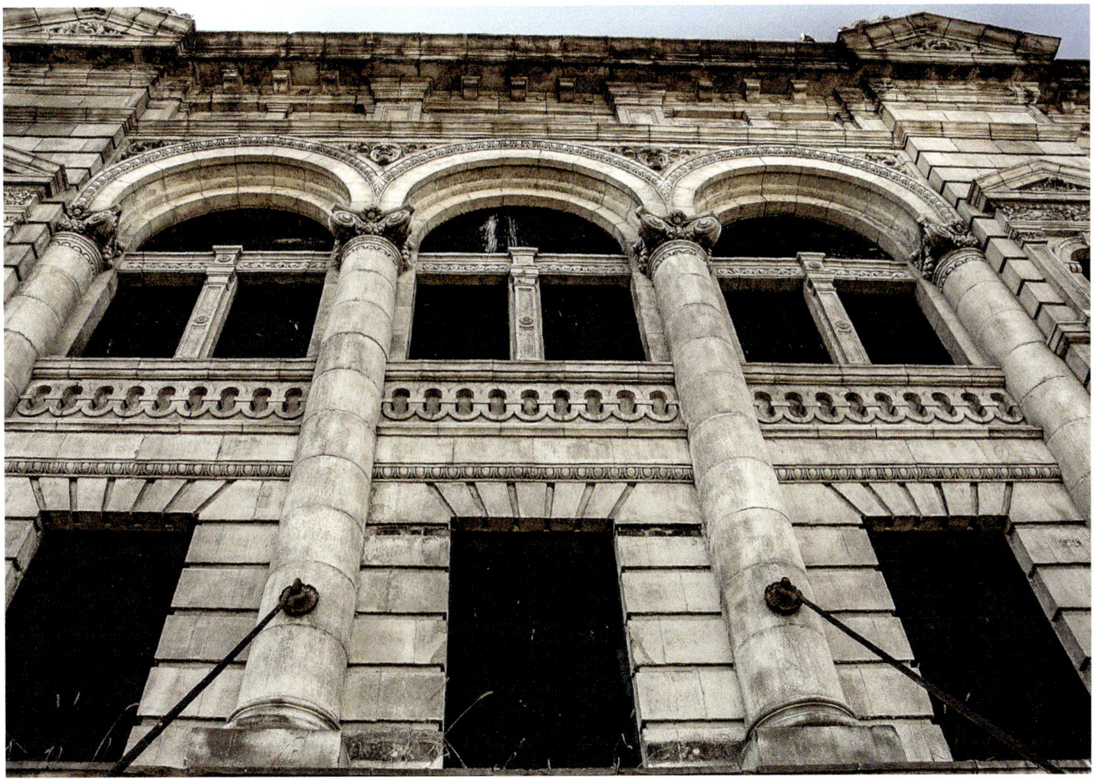

Towering archways and beautifully detailed relief work over the entrance.

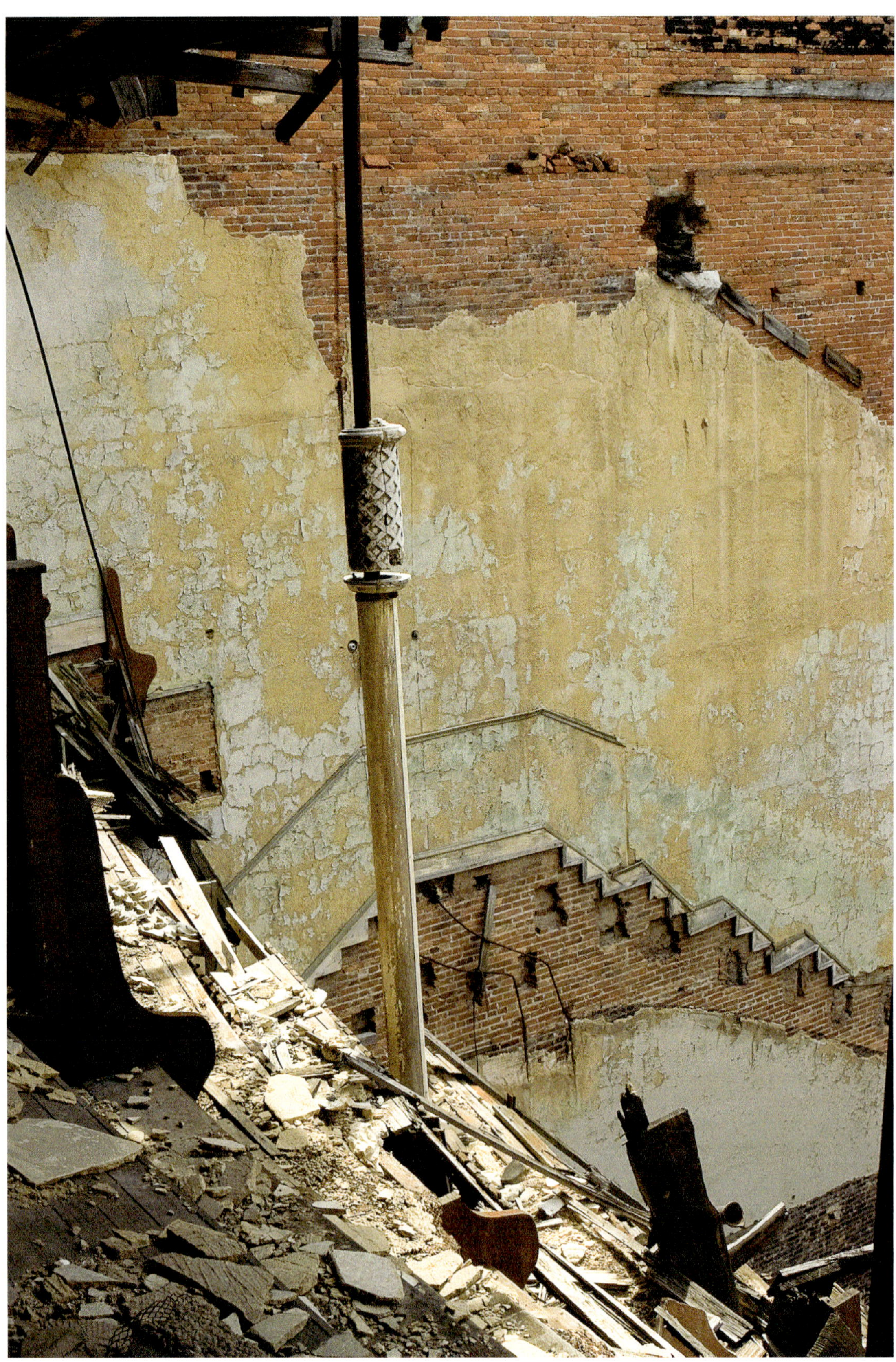

View from what remained of the upper level balcony.

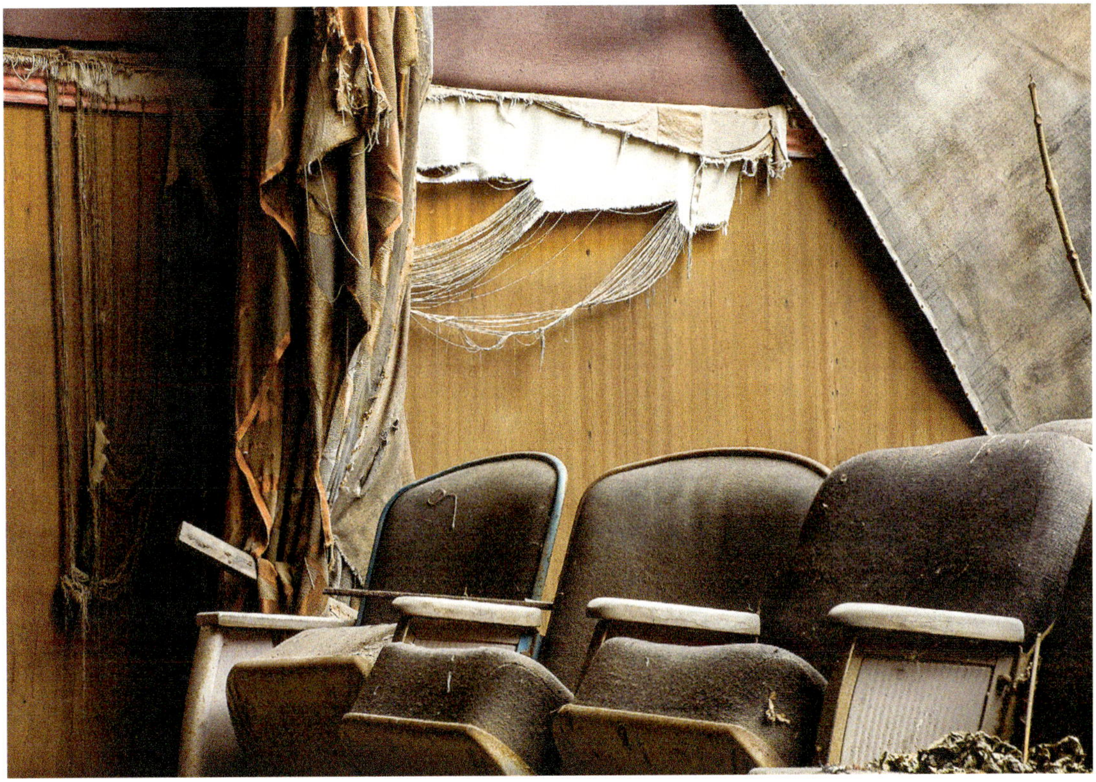

Front row seating before an empty stage.

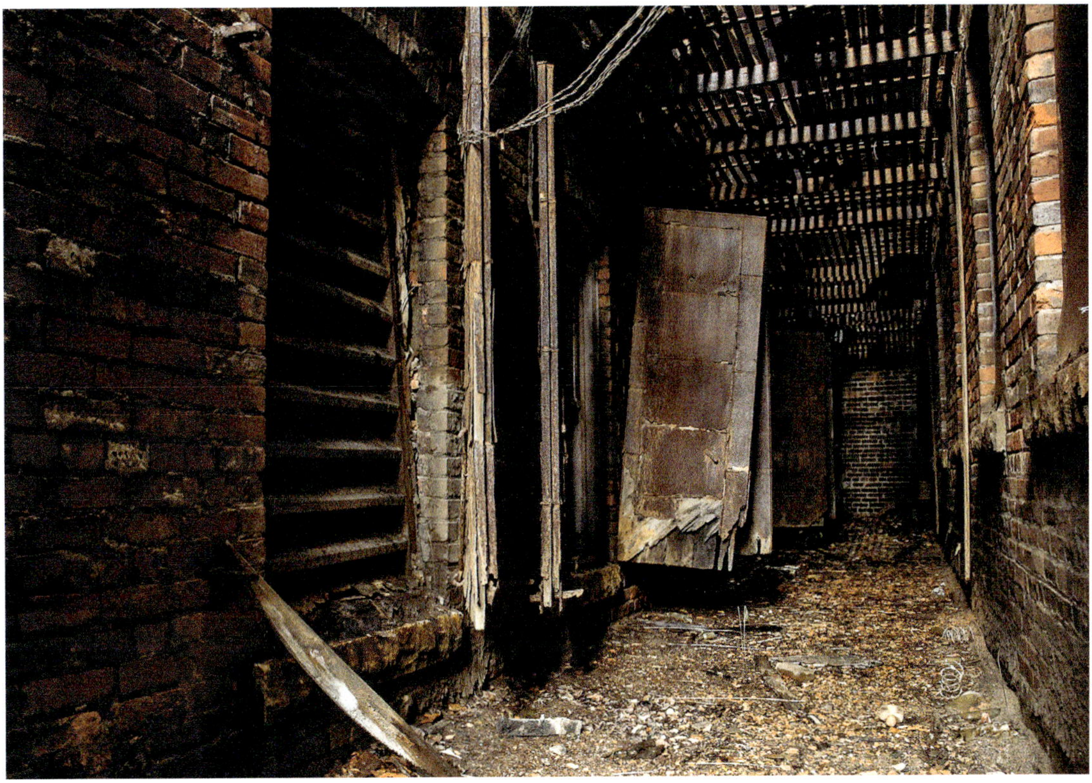

Rusting backstage doors hang from their hinges.

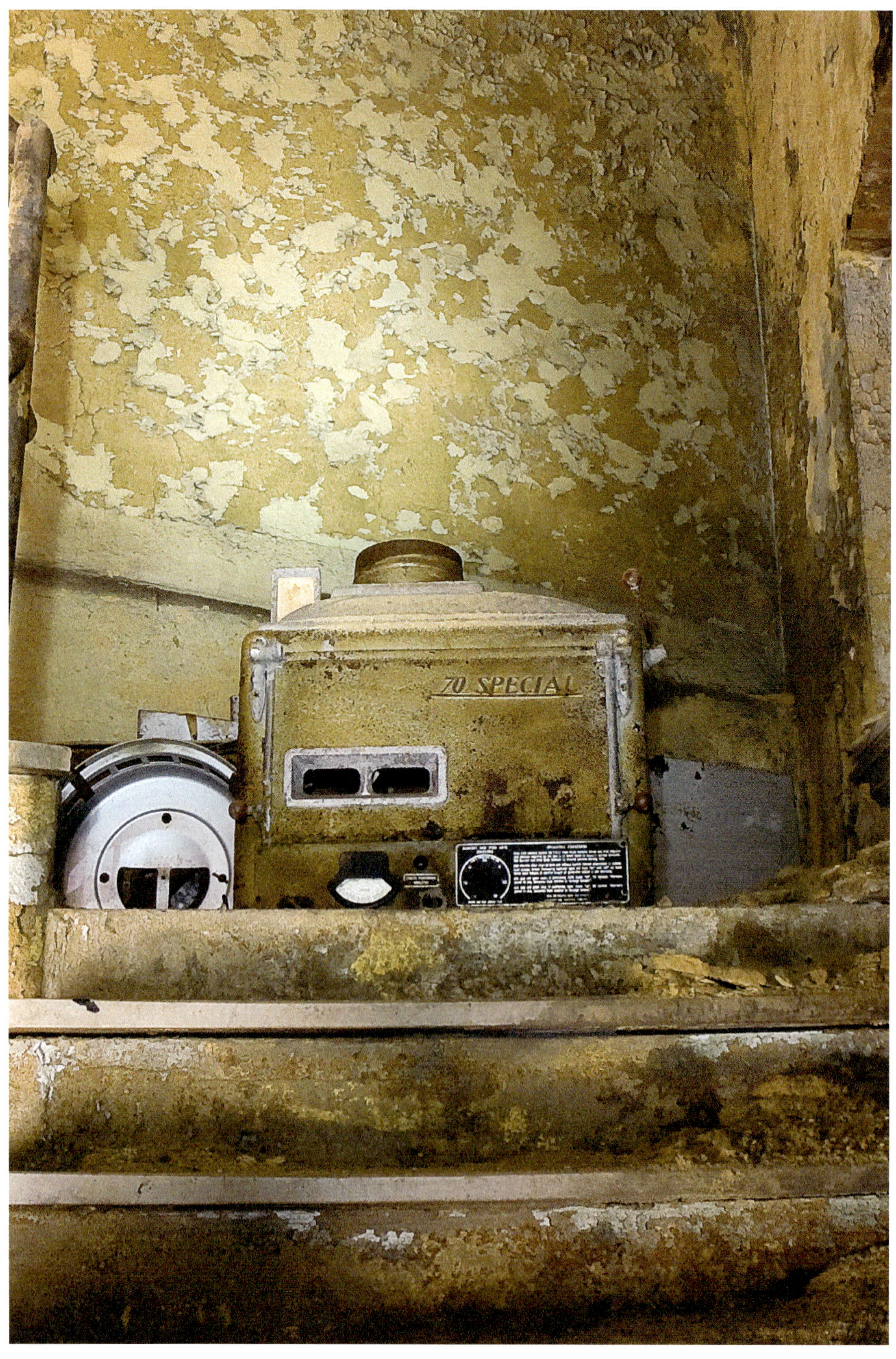

A rusted out lamp house, from an old 35-mm projector, blocks a stairwell.

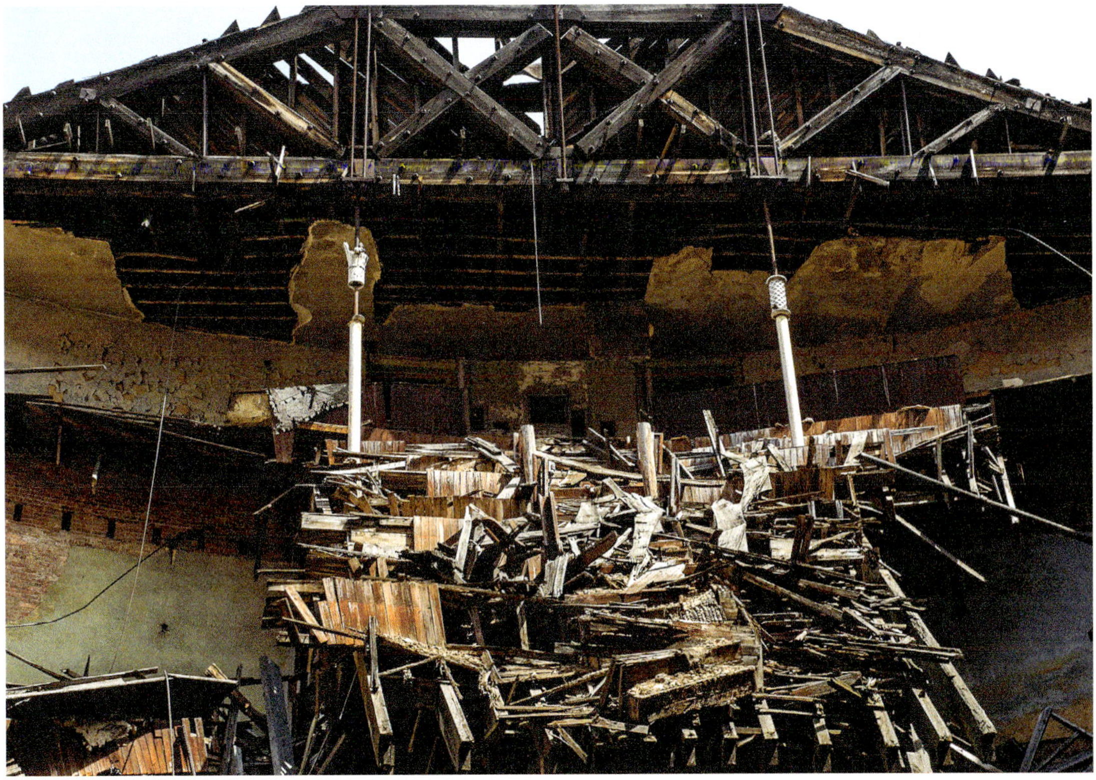

The collapsing balcony hangs on tenuously.

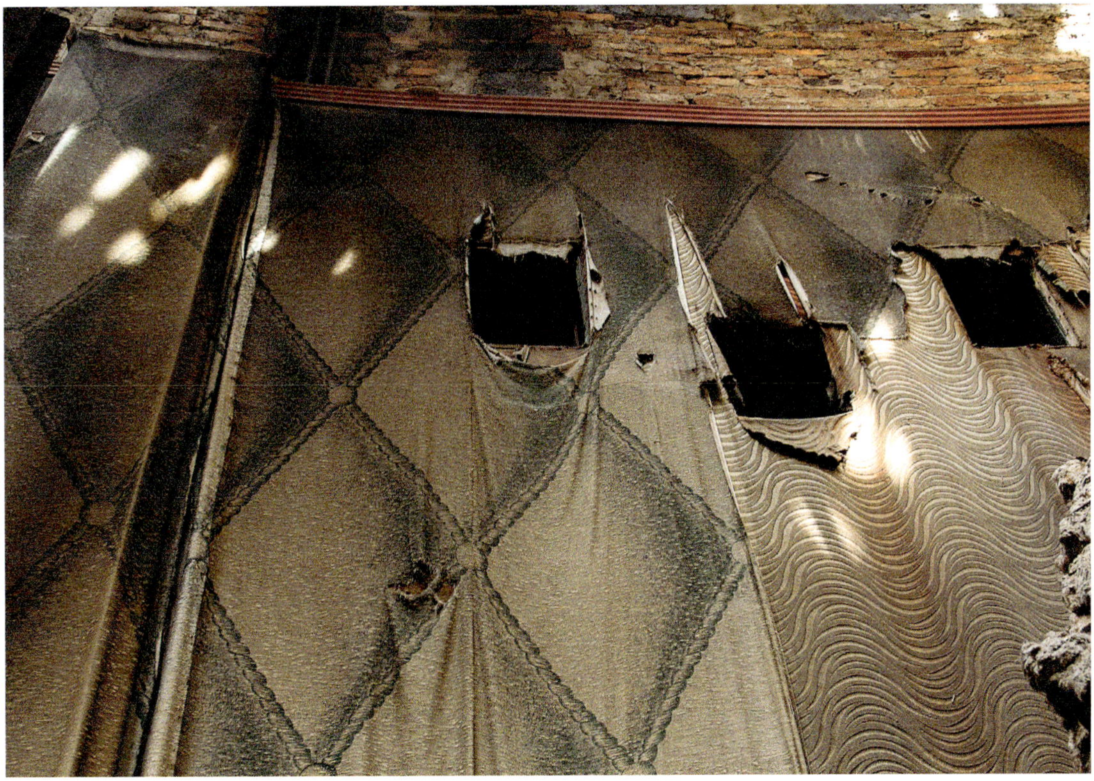

Projectionist room portholes surrounded by richly detailed, woven fabric.

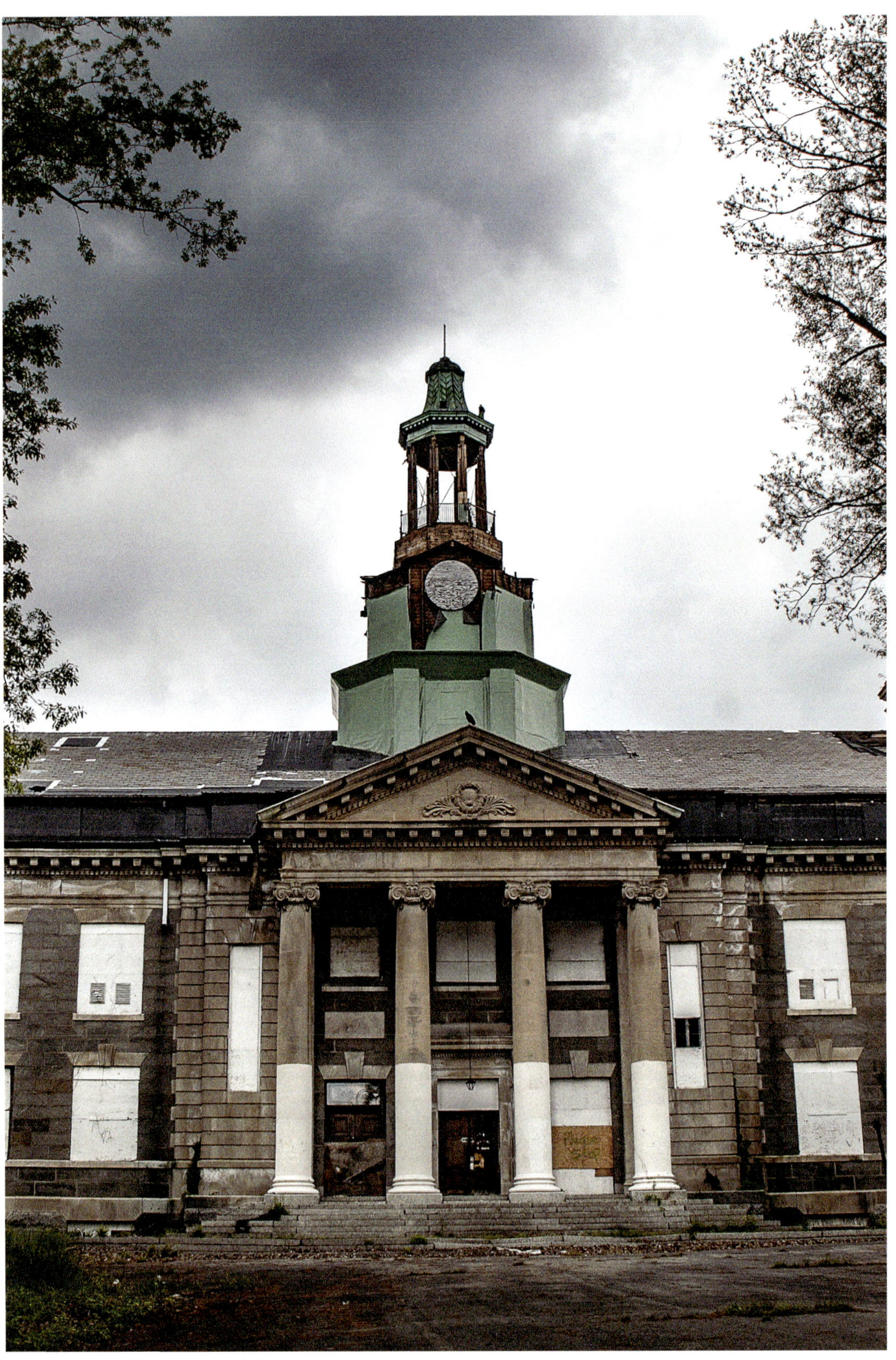

The Jacob Tome School's Memorial Hall. Most of the building and the entire clock tower were destroyed by fire in 2014.

THE JACOB TOME SCHOOL, PORT DEPOSIT

Hundreds of feet above the quaint town of Port Deposit, on the banks of the Susquehanna River, the buildings of the former Tome School for Boys stand in majestic decay.

On May 15, 1903, the Tome School, named after philanthropic founder, Jacob Tome, a Cecil County financier who made his fortune in lumber, formally opened amid great pomp and pageantry. Distinguished guests strolled through ornate Italian gardens. Today unkempt, weed infested grounds greet the curious visitor, giving scant indication of the once manicured richness.

The original single building of the Jacob Tome Institute was located on Main Street, Port Deposit, and opened in September 1894. The completion of the school, hundreds of feet above the original building, in 1903, came five years after the death of Jacob Tome. Tome bequeathed just over $3 million to the school, and his widow Evelyn carried on his legacy, investing $1 million of the endowment to the construction and design of the new school and grounds. The celebration on May 15, 1903, formally inaugurated the school as the wealthiest secondary school in the United States. In the decades that followed, the Great Depression, would negatively impact the school, and the onset of World War II would alter the course of this once illustrious institution forever.

President Franklin D. Roosevelt, who was once a guest speaker at Tome, officially approved the purchase of the land and buildings from the Jacob Tome Institute Board of Directors in early 1942, along with more than seventy farms on adjacent land—and the once wealthy boarding school became the United States Naval Training Center Bainbridge, named in honor of Admiral Bainbridge.

Construction began on May 19, 1942 and by August 14, 500 buildings had been erected. The Bainbridge Center comprised four independent regimental areas, accommodating more than 20,000 recruits. The Naval Academy Preparatory School was housed in the Tome School buildings.

The USNTC Bainbridge closed its doors on March 31, 1976, leaving the Training Center and Tome School buildings abandoned and inaccessible to the public. In 1986, Congress authorized the Navy to dispose of the property. The Navy was required to restore the property to Federal and State EPA standards. This led to the removal 138,000 tons of asbestos contaminated soil and 400,000 cubic yards of demolition rubble.

Residents of Cecil County fought for years to reclaim the land and on February 14, 2000, at a special ceremony outside the main gates of Bainbridge, the Training Center and former Tome School were turned over to the State-operated Bainbridge Development Corporation for redevelopment.

The facades of the grandiose limestone and granite school buildings, although weathered, still echo their proud heritage. Once inside, however, the echo becomes silenced—decay by neglect is heartbreakingly obvious. Water damage, vandals and thieves have eviscerated this once million-dollar school. A devastating fire in 2014 gutted the iconic and unforgettable Memorial Hall. The sweeping marble staircase has become nothing more than a memory. The roof and beloved clock tower, which could be seen by travellers on Interstate 95 crossing the Susquehanna River bridge, succumbed to the flames.

The Bainbridge Development Corporation, still mourning the loss of Memorial Hall and its rightful place as the centerpiece of Jacob Tome's bequeathal, seems unable to alter the course of the former school's future. The $10,000 reward they continue to offer, for the apprehension of those who started the devastating 2014 fire, remains unclaimed. The best they, and property's advocates, can hope for is for the Tome School and its once magnificent buildings to one day inspire architects, planners, and designers to reclaim Jacob Tome's legacy and create something of lasting value, beauty and utility.

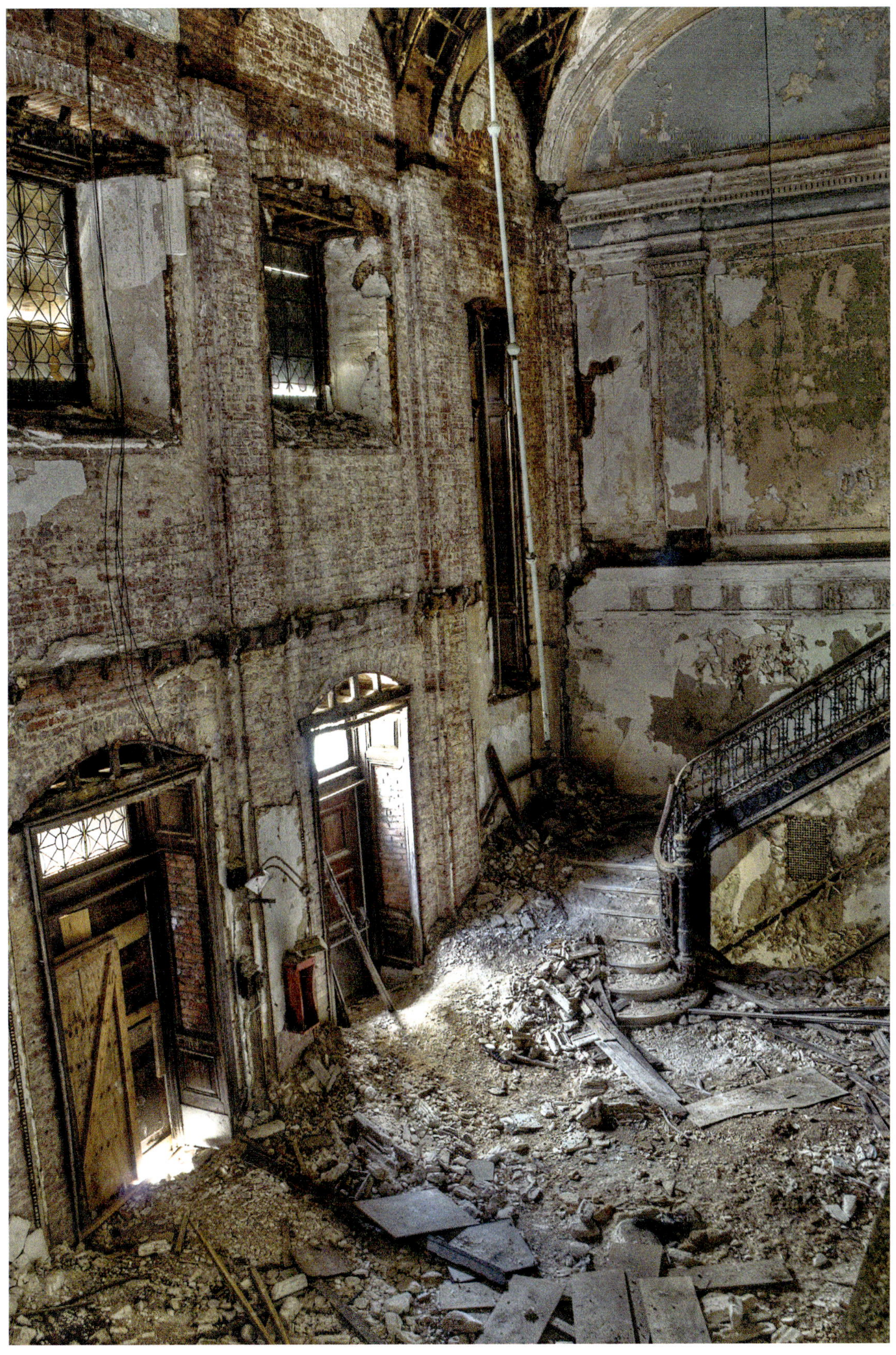

The sweeping marble staircase inside Memorial Hall struggled to withstand water damage and vandals.

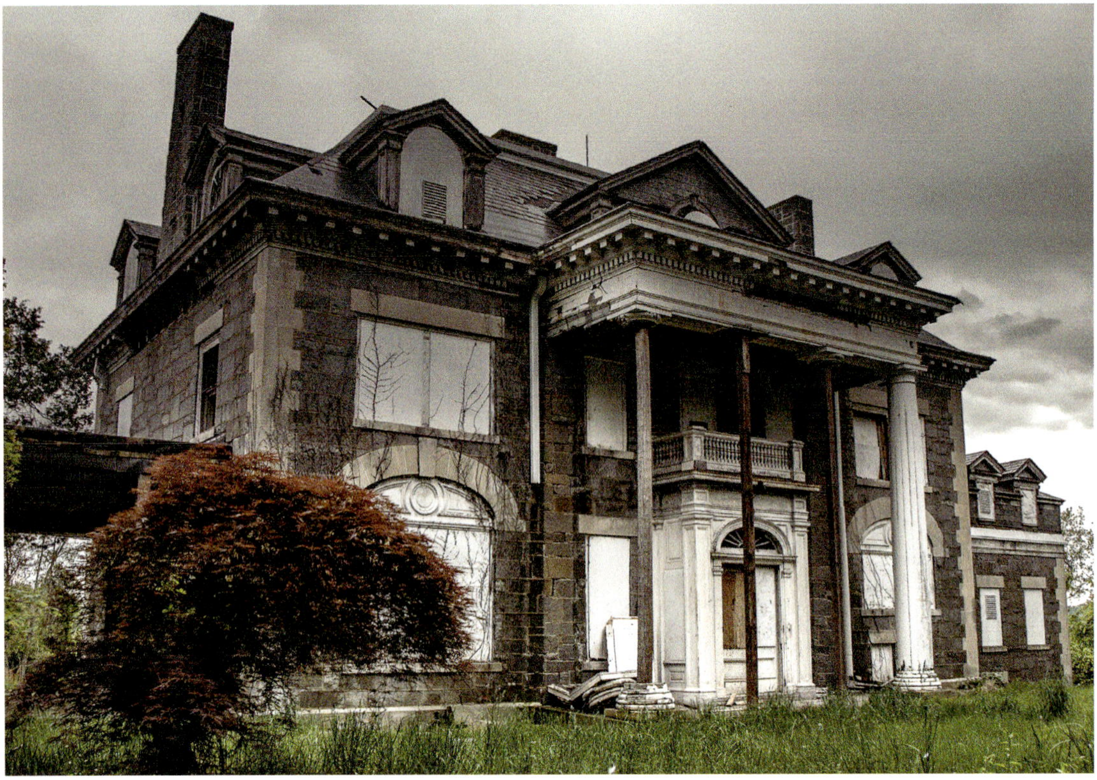

One of many decaying buildings on the property, the former headmaster's home, provides shelter to local birds.

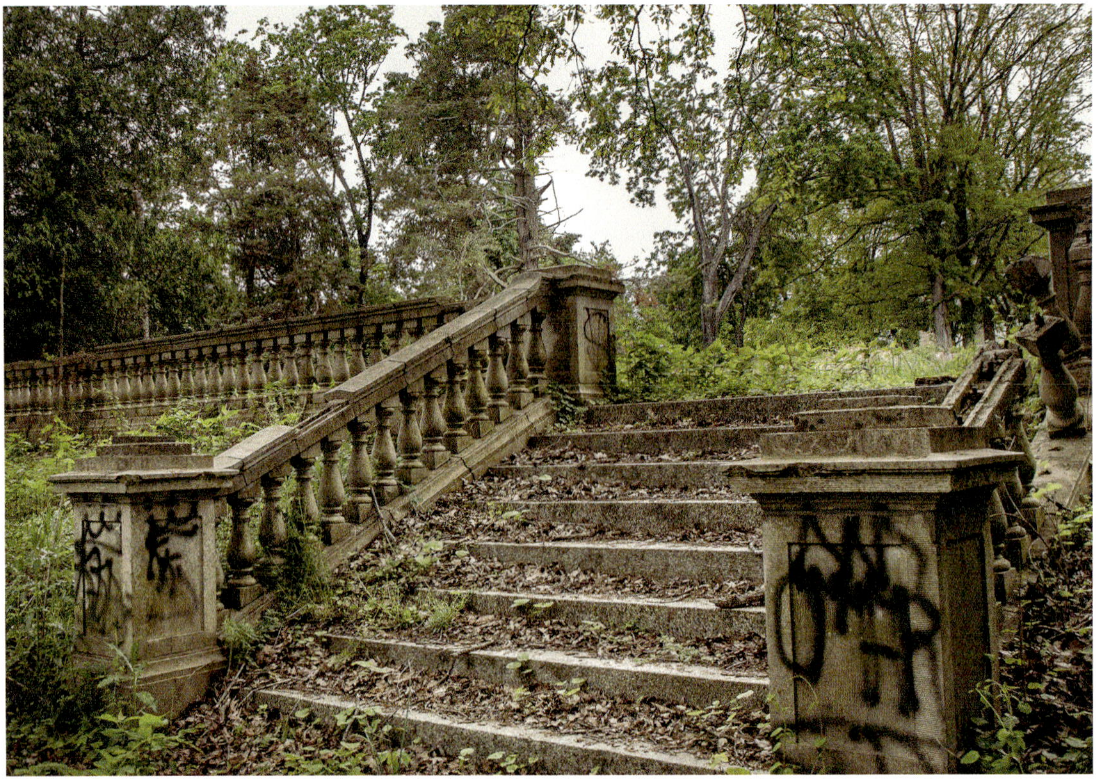

A section of the Italian Gardens, which were designed by famed landscape architect, Frederick Law Olmsted.

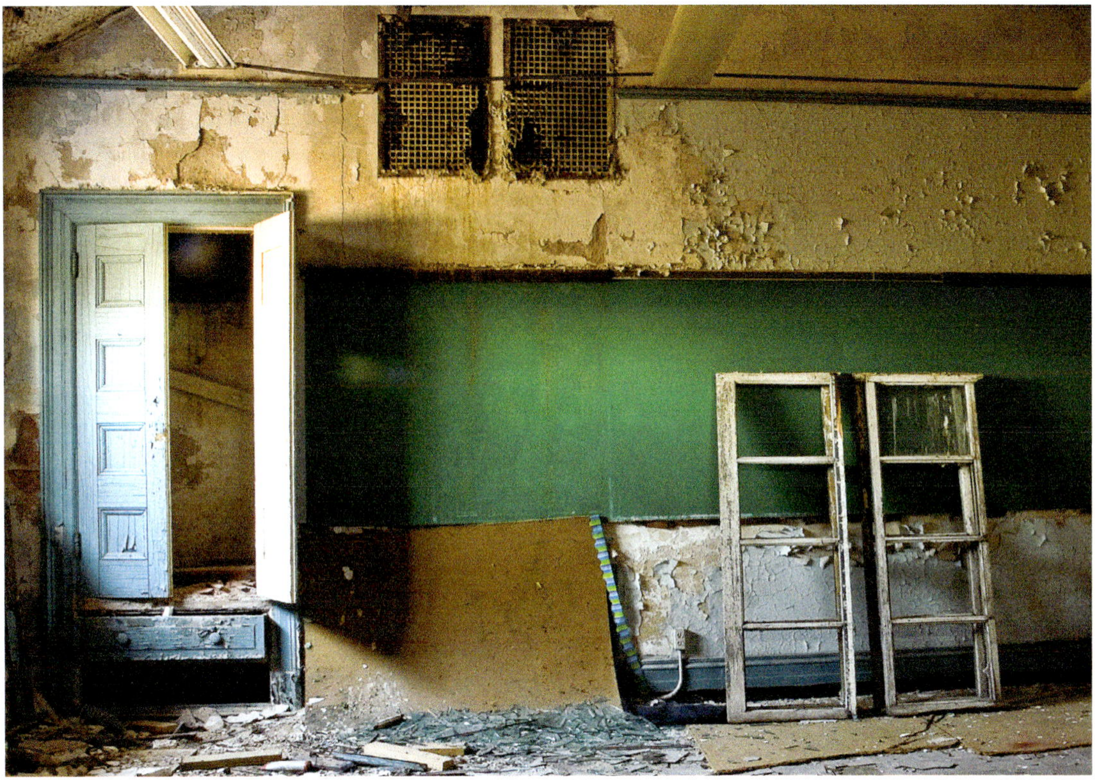

Bright colors of a chalkboard and storage cupboard, draped in light, give vibrancy to an otherwise desolate classroom.

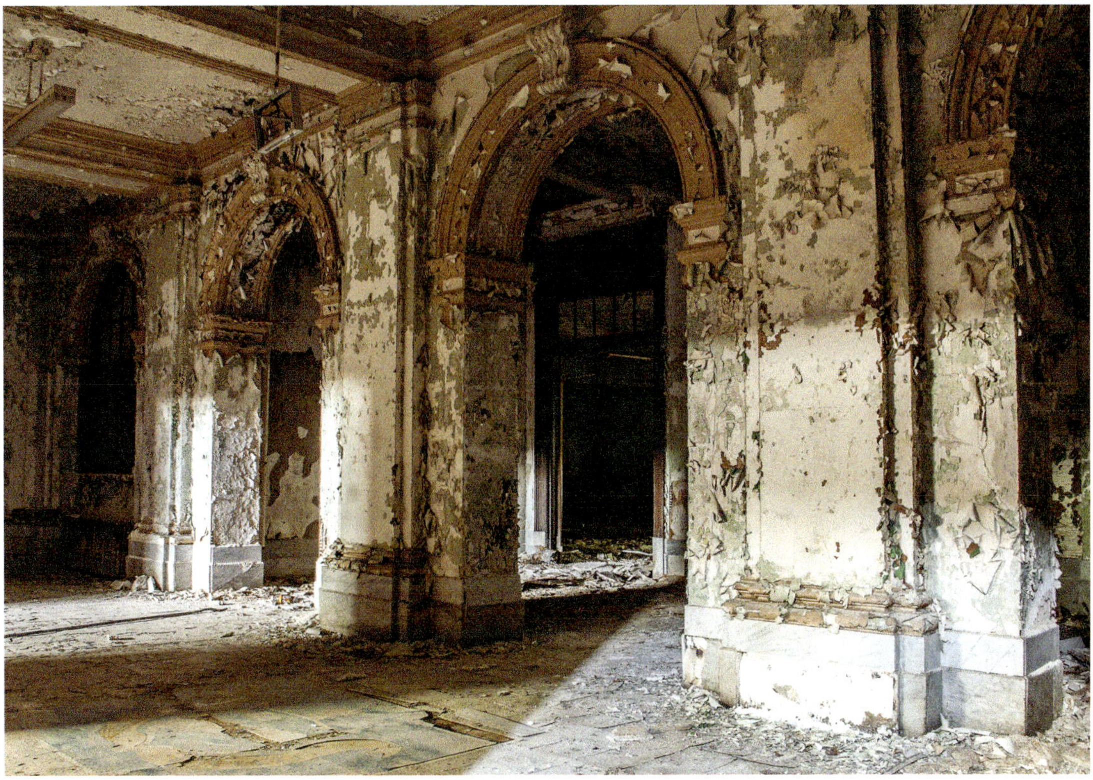

Shadows, cast by broken windows, add drama to layer upon layer of peeling paint in Memorial Hall's first floor hallway.

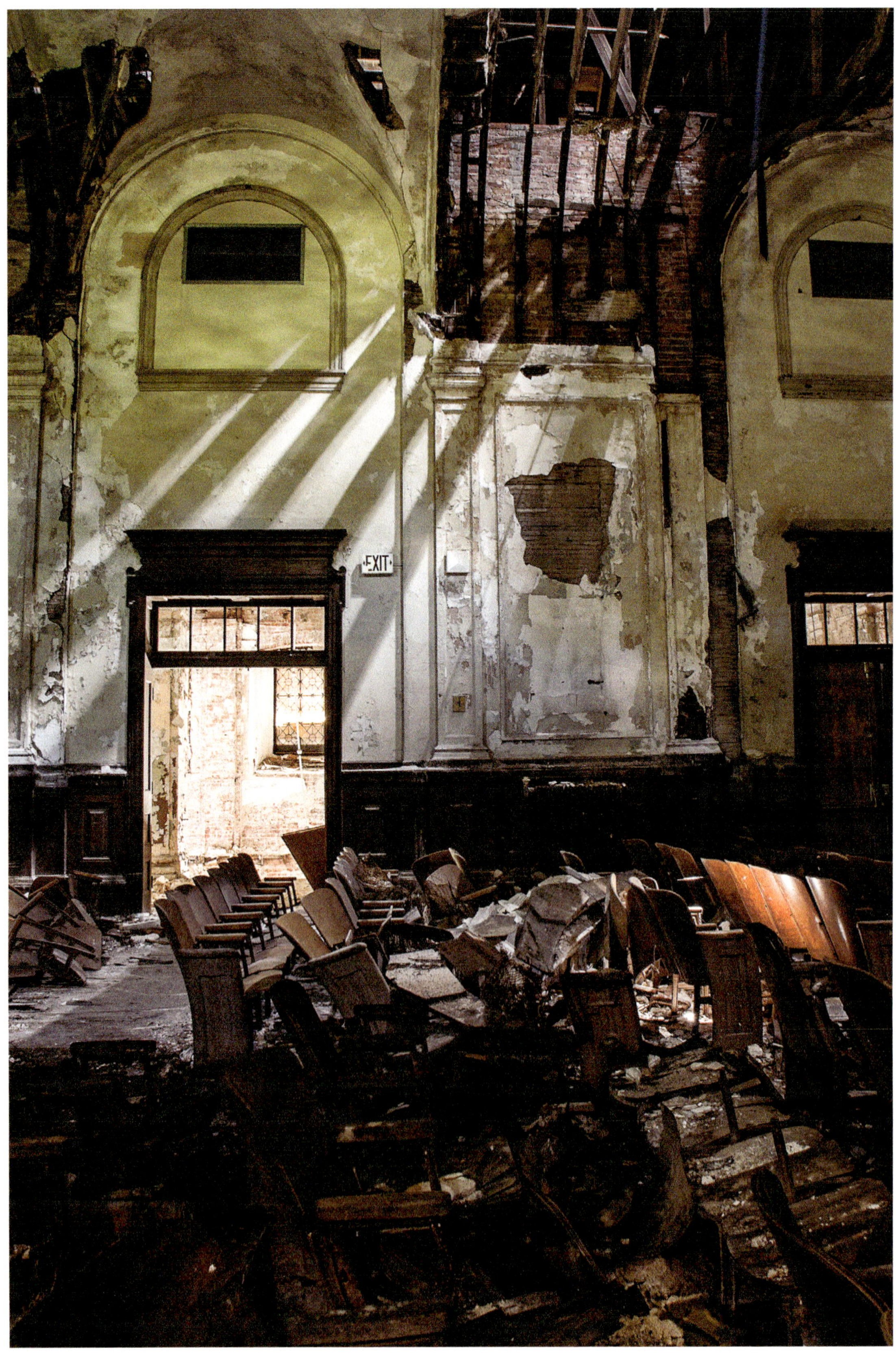

Collapsed chairs have succumbed to fire and water damage in Memorial Hall's auditorium.

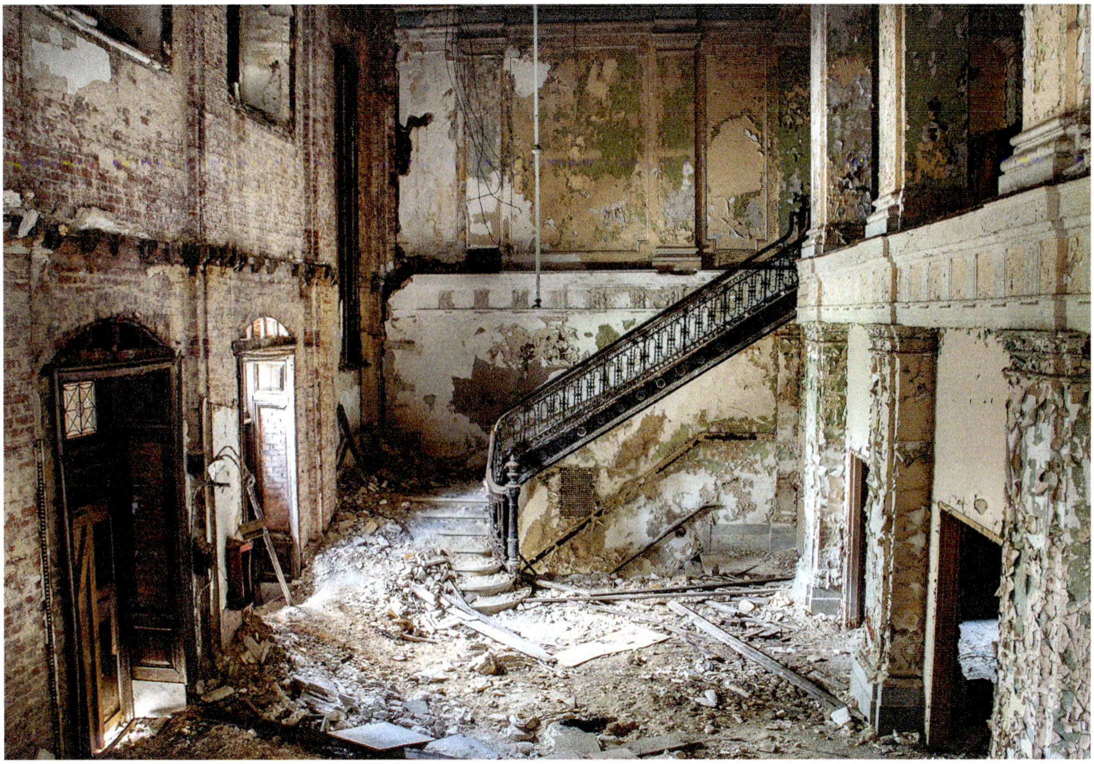

Only one of two sweeping ornate wrought iron balustrades remained before the devastating 2014 fire.

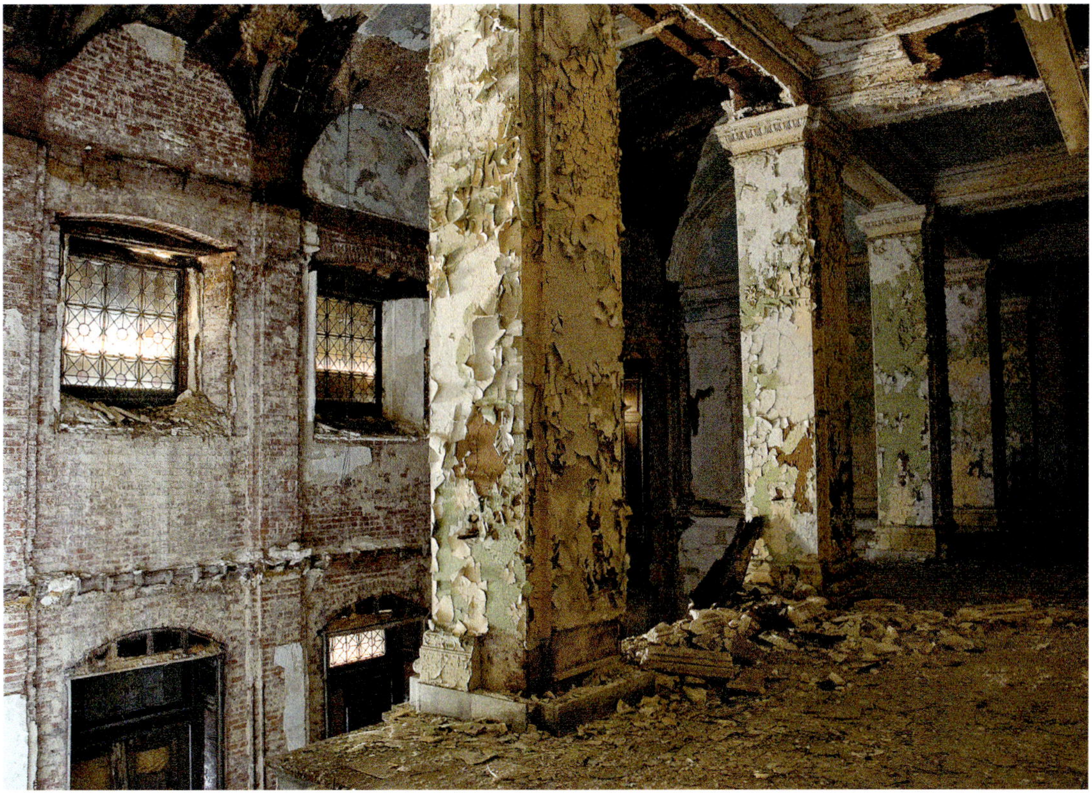

Pillars line Memorial Hall's first floor balcony, standing resolutely amongst the rubble.

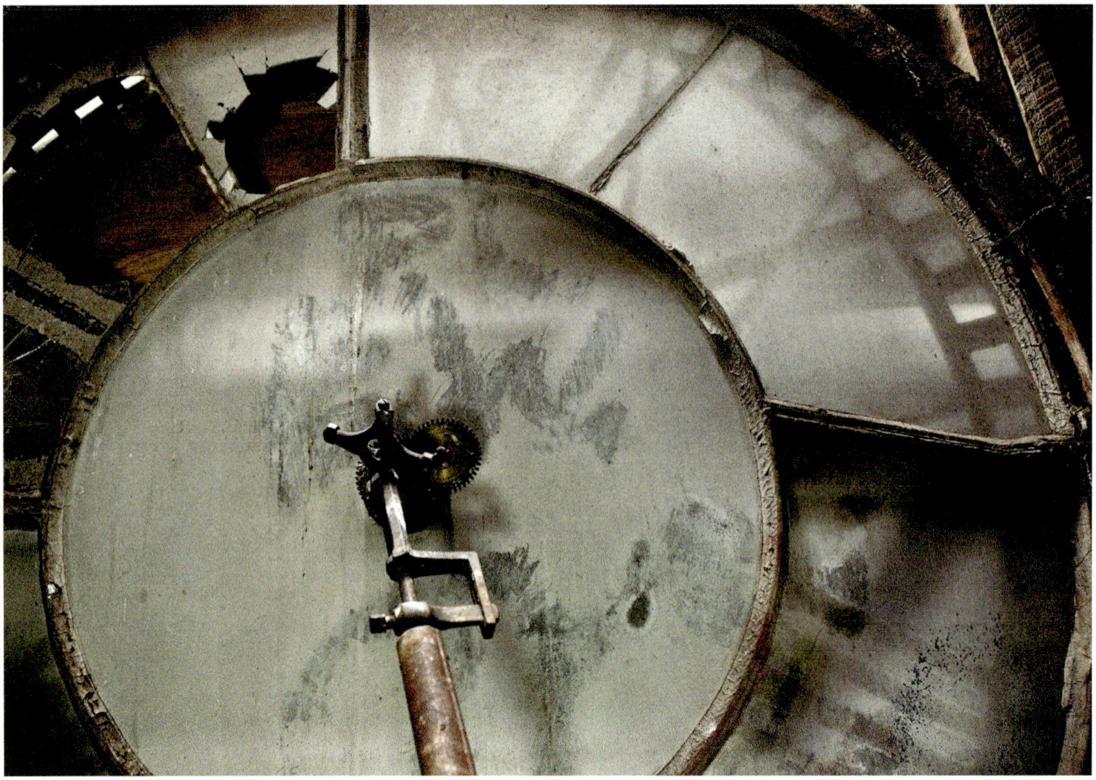

Inside Memorial Hall's clock tower, cog wheels and a copper arm form part of the clock's mechanism.

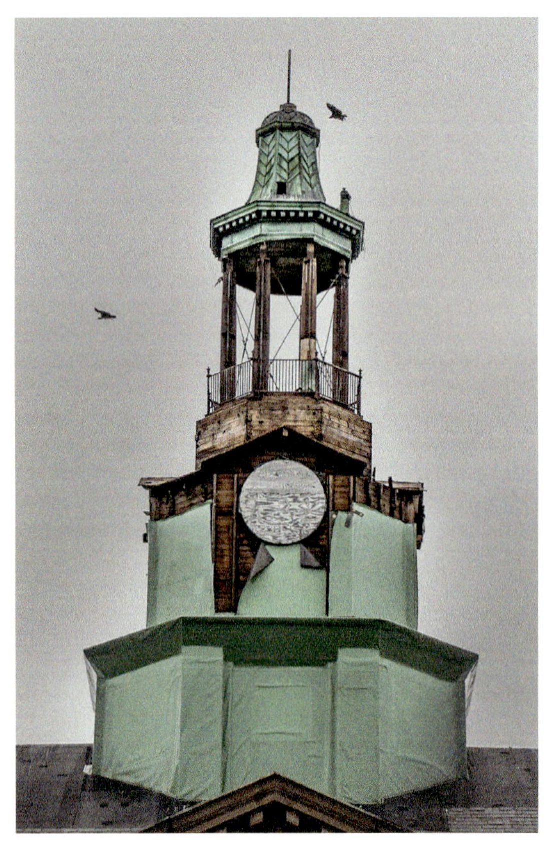

Turkey vultures circle the clock tower.

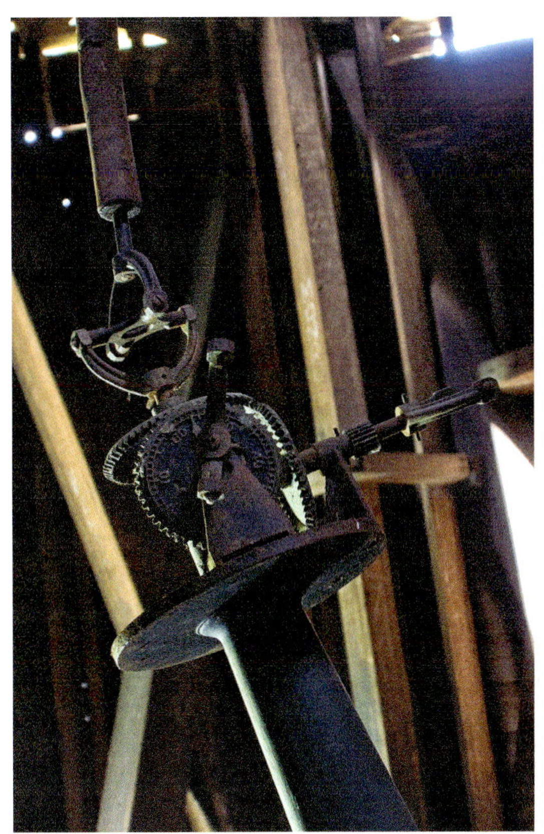

Internal drive mechanism of the Tome School clock tower.

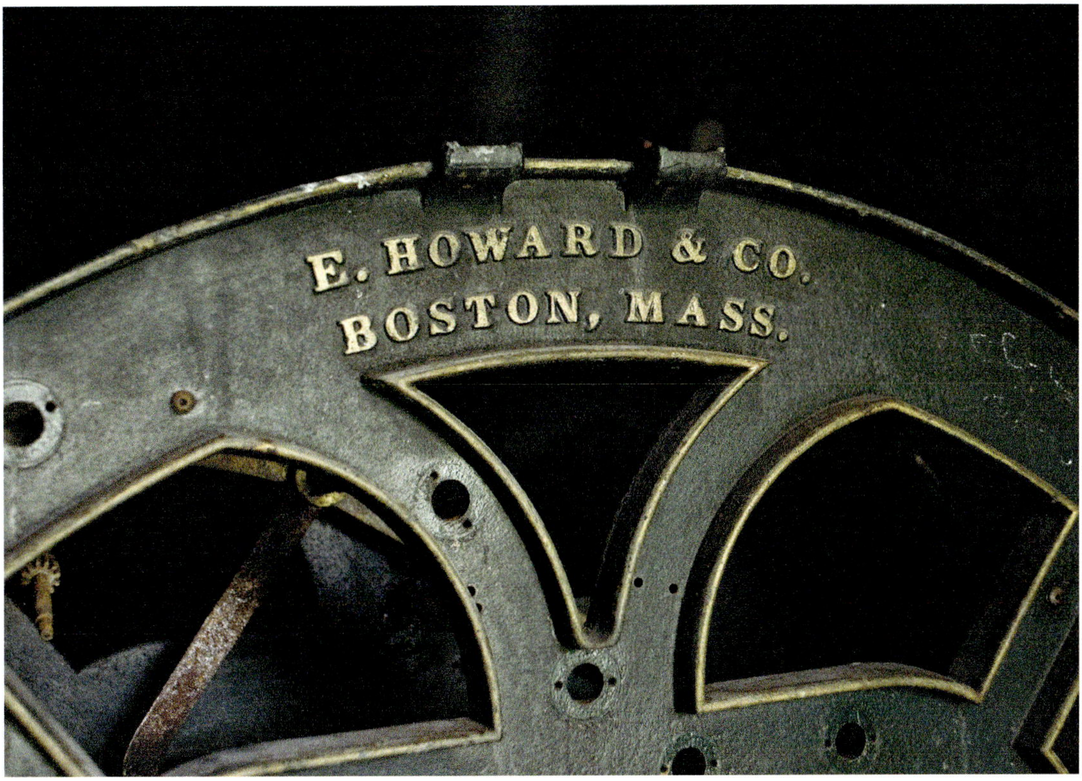

The Tome School clock was manufactured by E. Howard and Co., a company established in Boston in 1858.

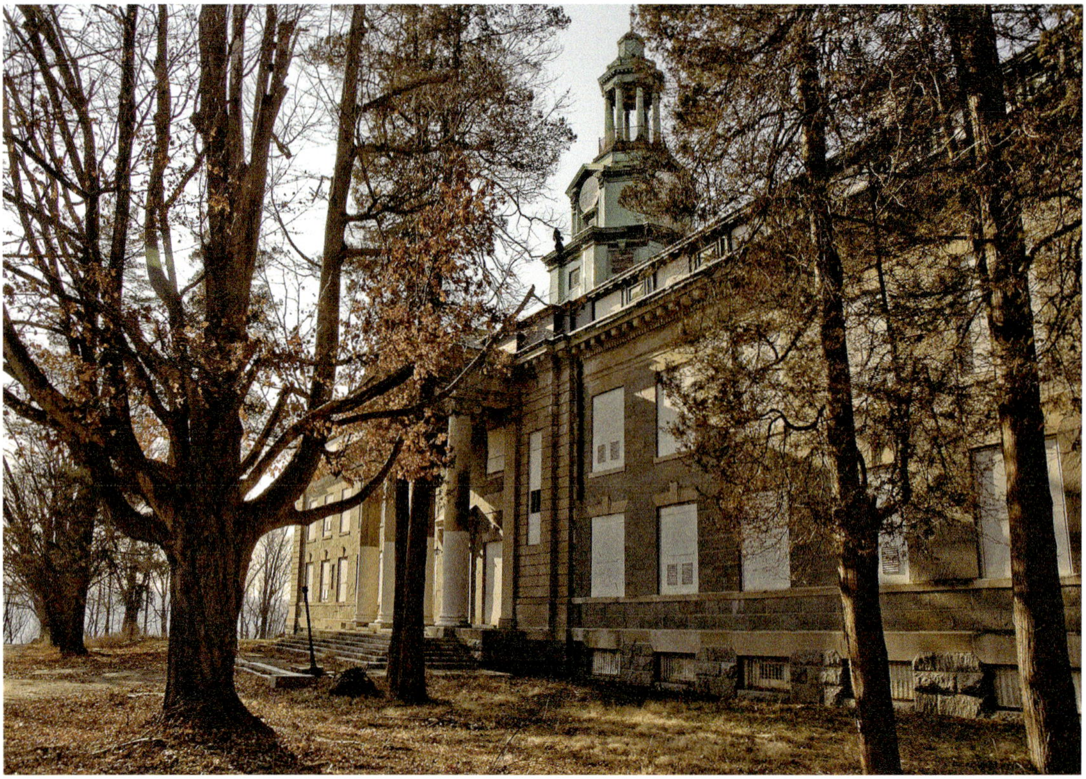

Memorial Hall's shuttered facade hides the toll that years of neglect and vandalism have inflicted on the interior.

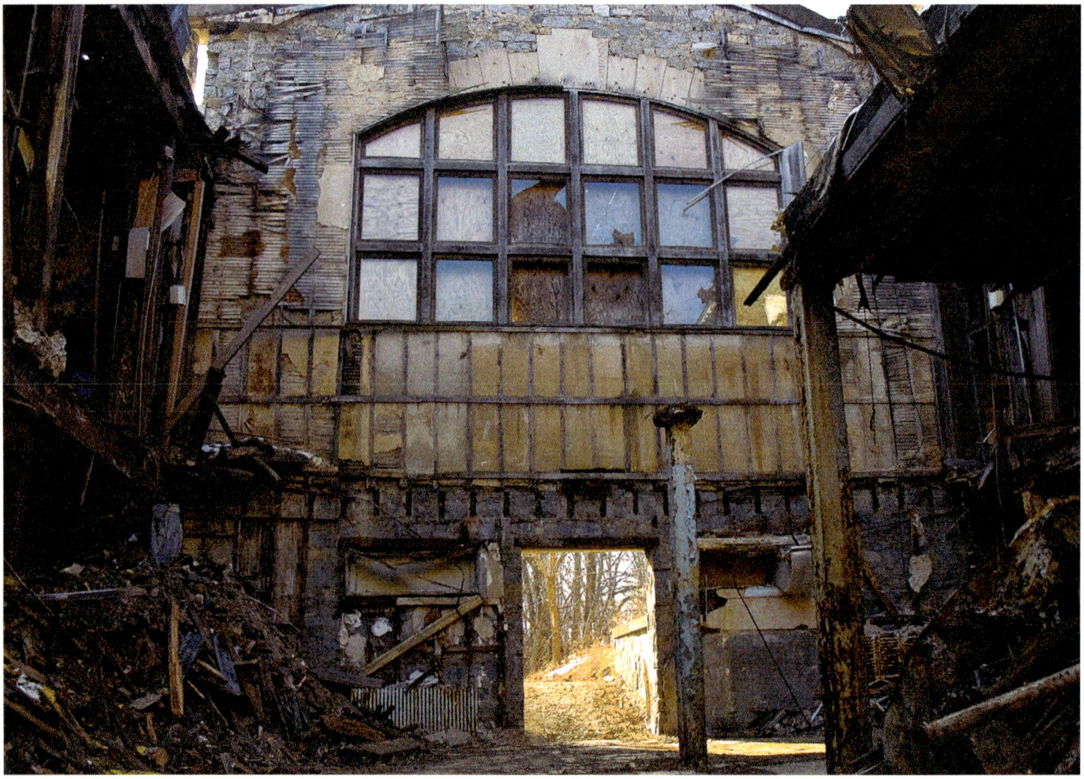

The roofless gymnasium, reduced to rubble by a fire.

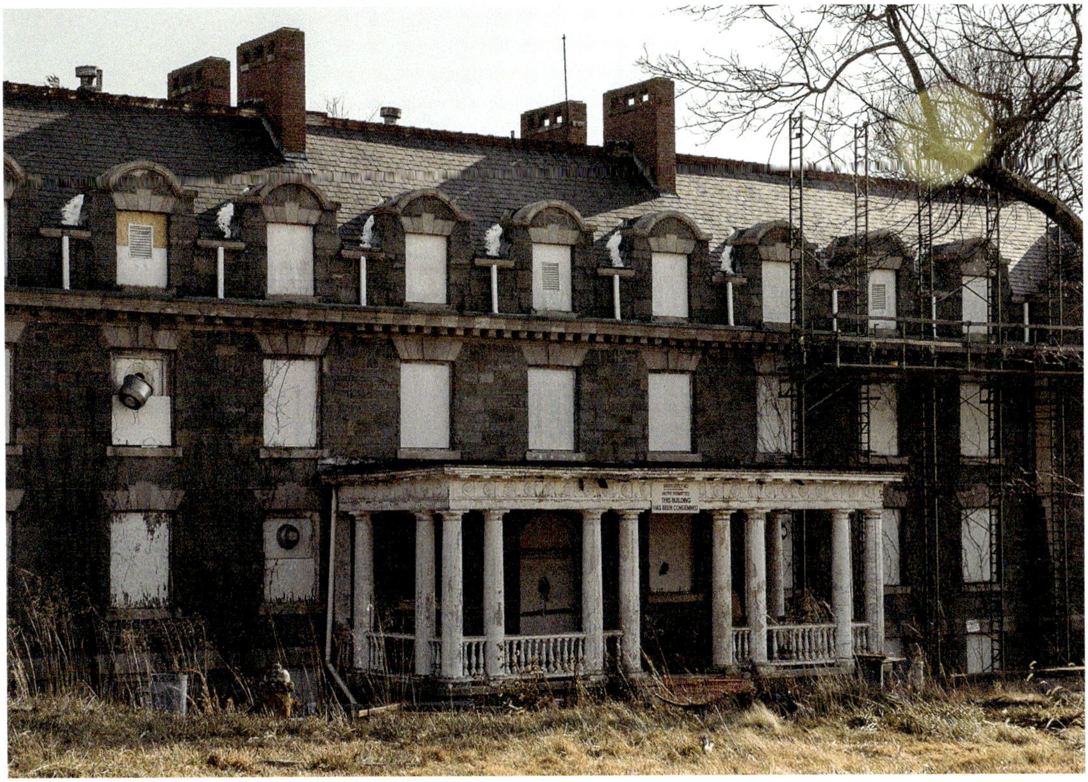

Harrison Hall, one of three dormitories on the property, is in danger of collapsing.

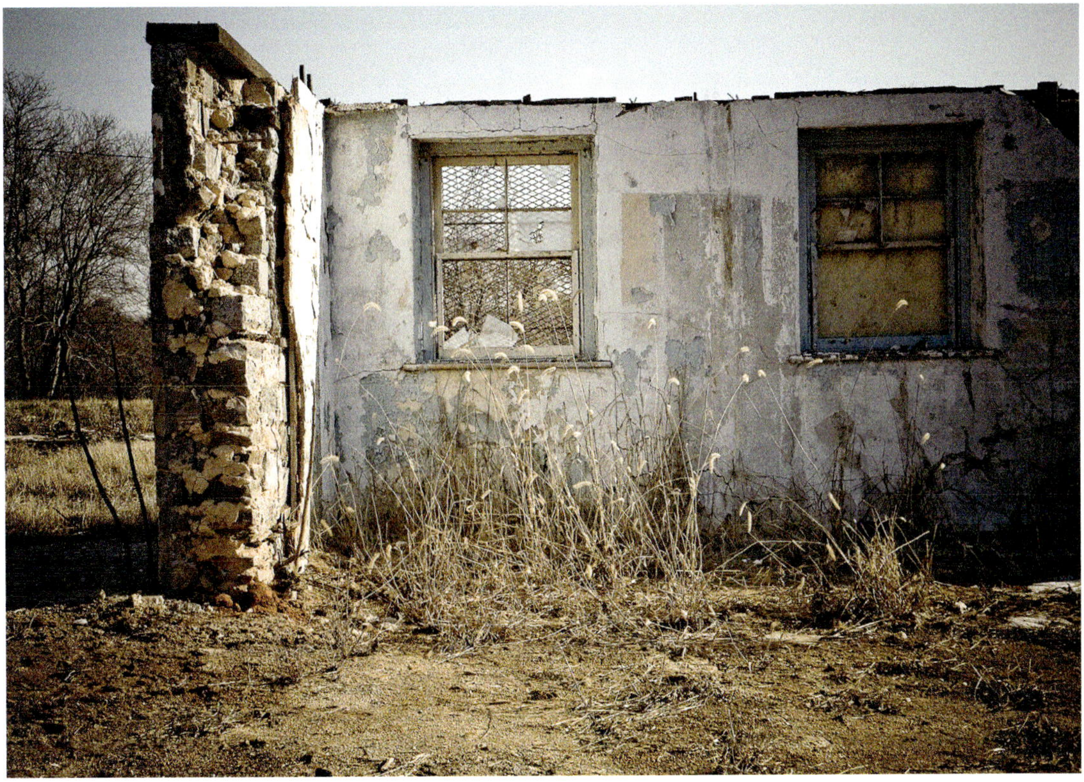

Little remains but the shell of a former maintenance building.

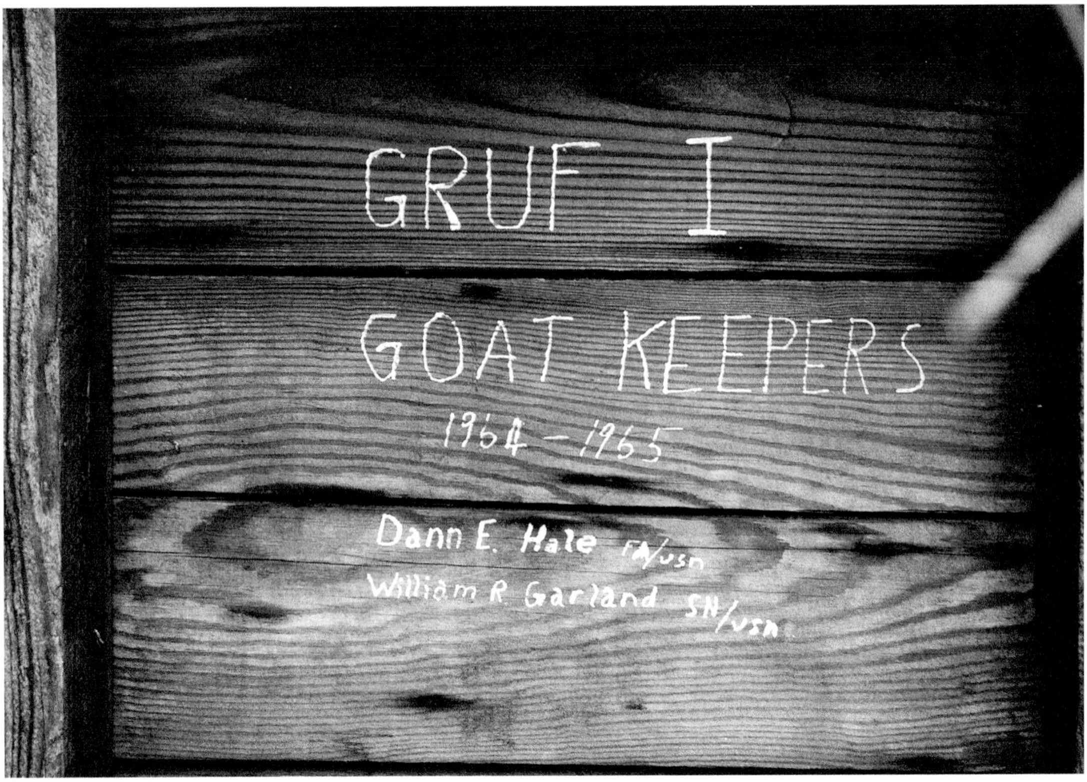

Dan E. Hale and William R. Garland, members of the United States Navy, left their mark on an outer building.

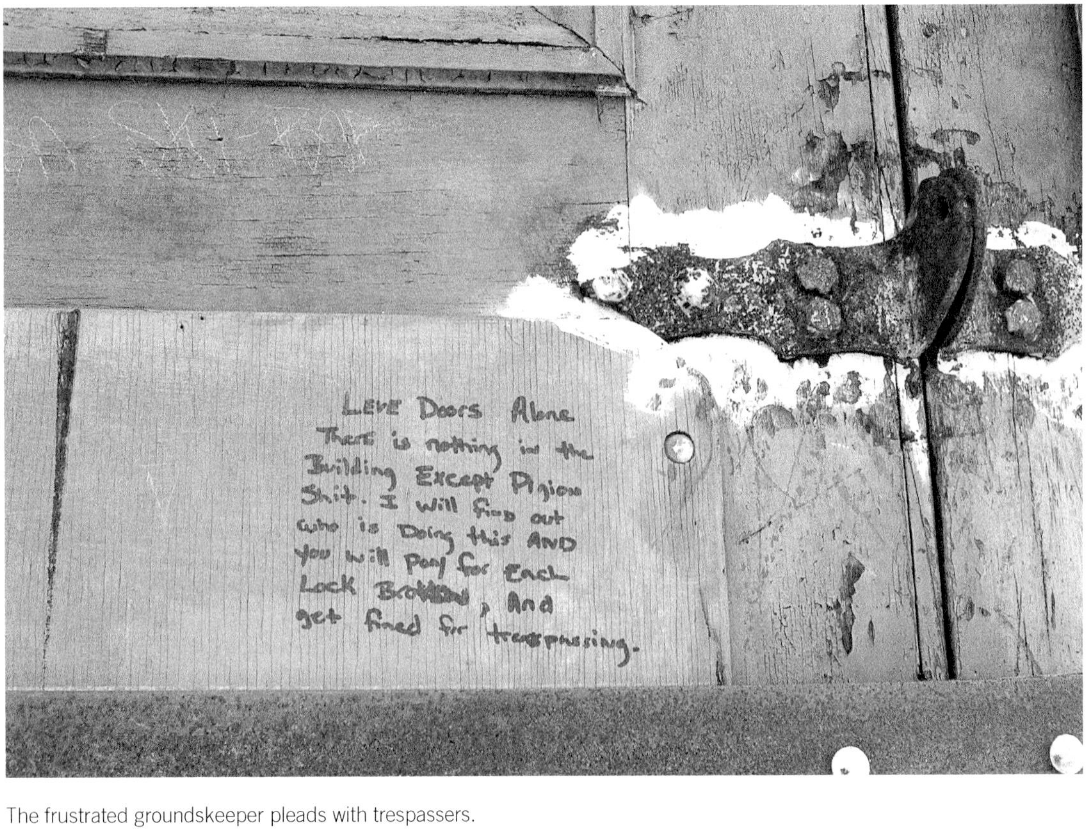

The frustrated groundskeeper pleads with trespassers.

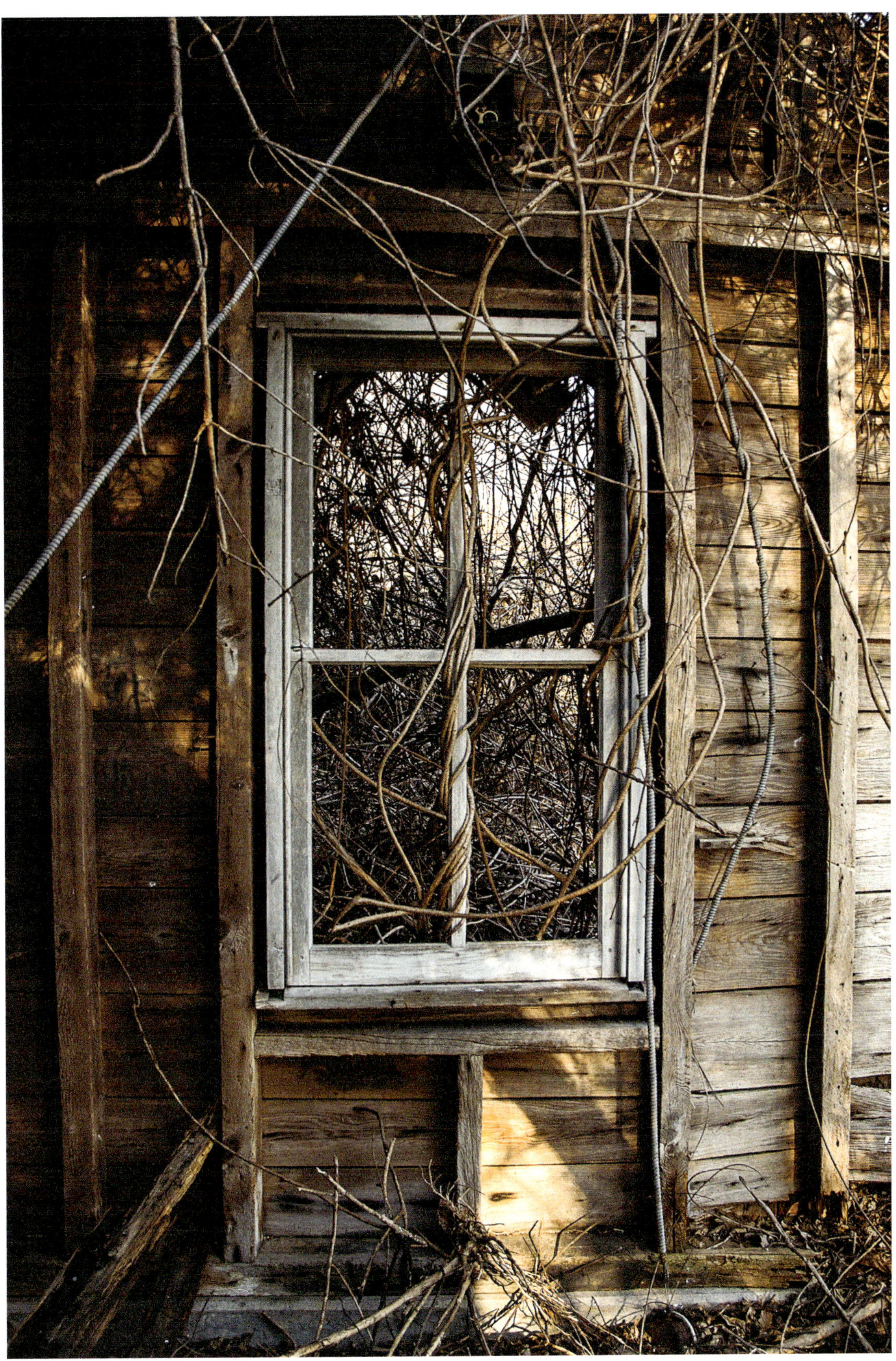

Mother Nature reclaims a window frame and supports the structure with a one-half-inch thick vine.

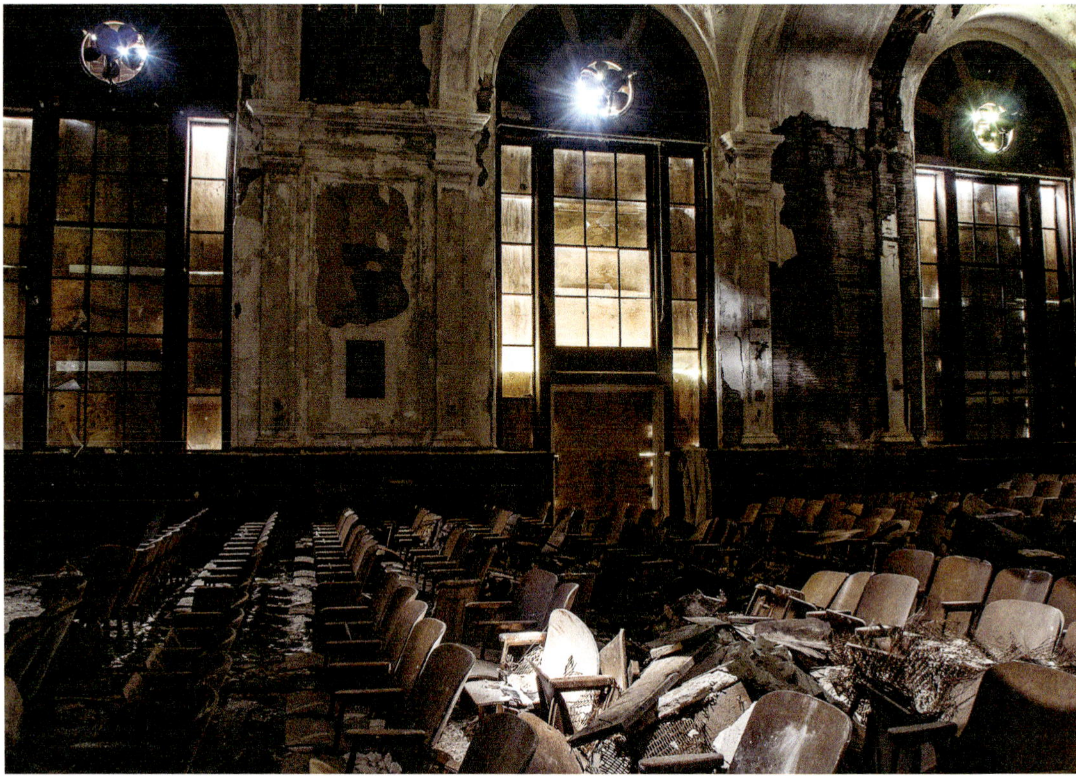

Sunlight streams through exhaust fans and illuminates seats in the auditorium.

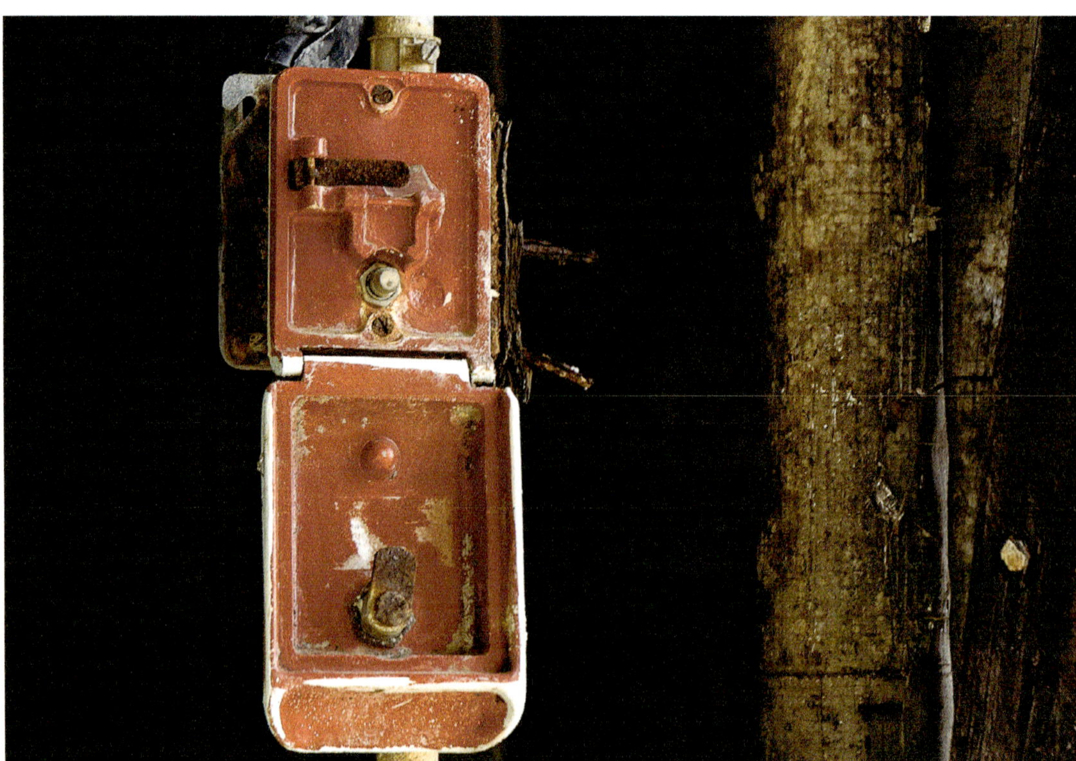

An emergency power switch has long been disconnected.

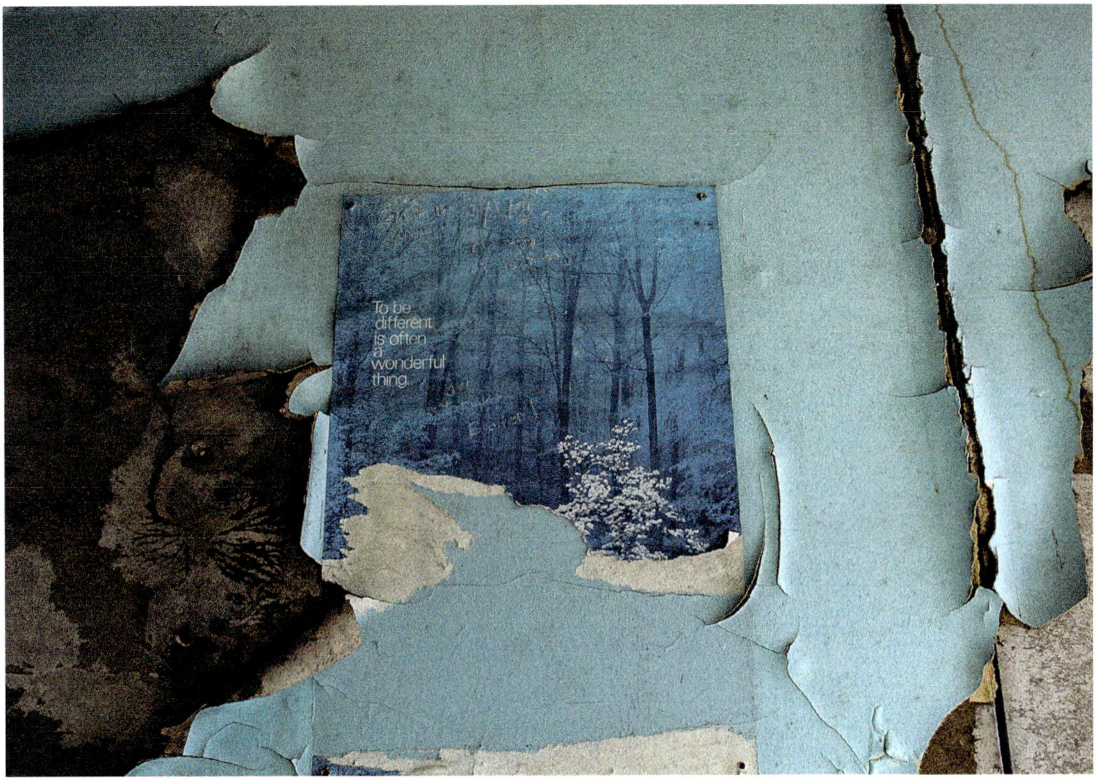

A Harrison Hall dorm room displays what remains of a poster, probably pinned by a naval academy member.

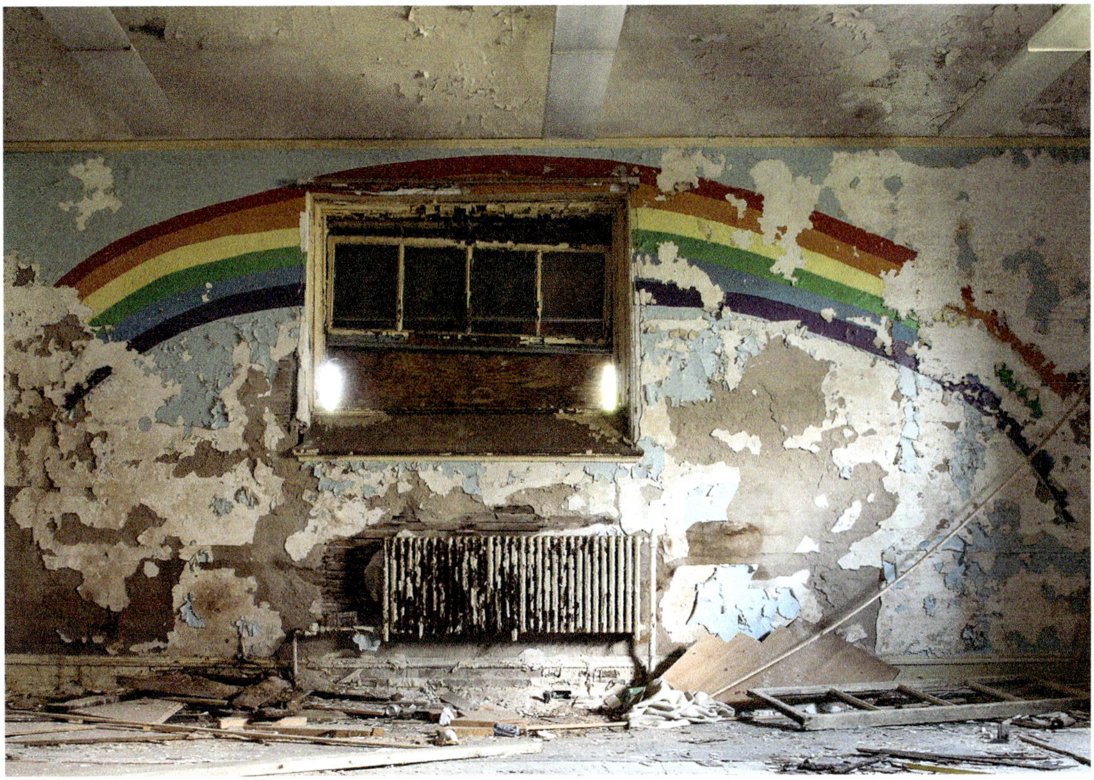

A deteriorating room in Harrison Hall with a rainbow as its primary feature.

GLENN DALE HOSPITAL, GLENN DALE

Glenn Dale Hospital's twenty-three asbestos-ridden buildings occupy 210 acres of serene parkland in Maryland's Prince George's County. The hospital, built in 1933–34, and officially established in 1937, treated children suffering tuberculosis, and then later expanded to treat adults.

Surrounded by as much folklore as fact, Glenn Dale's closed doors, boarded up windows and live-in police inspire a full spectrum of imaginary tales: medical conspiracies, packs of ghost dogs, that are said to terrorize trespassers, and other scary and dubious legends haunt the hospital. One rumor suggests bodies were removed from Glenn Dale's two morgues and taken to the large incinerator building on the grounds. In fact, the incinerator was used exclusively for hospital waste. Another story claims the buildings' walls are full of disease and will infect anyone who enters. The story is not true, of course, but it serves as a very effective "no trespassing" sign.

Glenn Dale hospital closed in 1982, and has been caught in a perpetual bureaucratic limbo between the State of Maryland, the District of Columbia, and the Maryland National Capital Park and Planning Commission (M-NCPCC). No one wants to pay the $3 to $4 million to remove the asbestos and hazardous waste from the buildings. And so the ghost hunters and thrill seekers continue to risk arrest and ghost hunt and thrill seek. And the bureaucrats continue to be bureaucrats and 210 acres of precious parkland are off limits and going to waste.

The hospital has suffered atrociously at the hands of vandals and scrappers, and barely resembles the institution it once was. At present, Glenn Dale Hospital has no future—there are no plans—and so it waits in a twilight zone. It will take imagination, bureaucratic resolve, and money to find a creative re-use for Glenn Dale Hospital and its grounds. Until those forces come together, Glenn Dale Hospital will remain a haunted derelict.

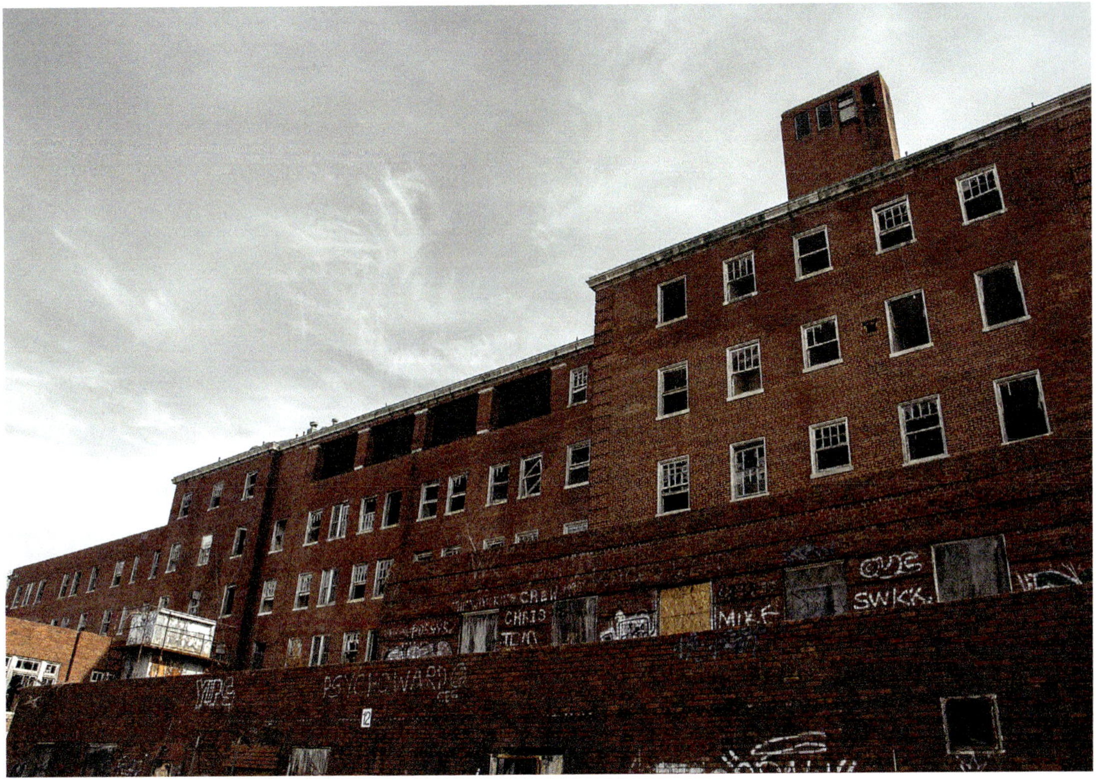

The rear of the adult hospital building at Glenn Dale has been extensively vandalized.

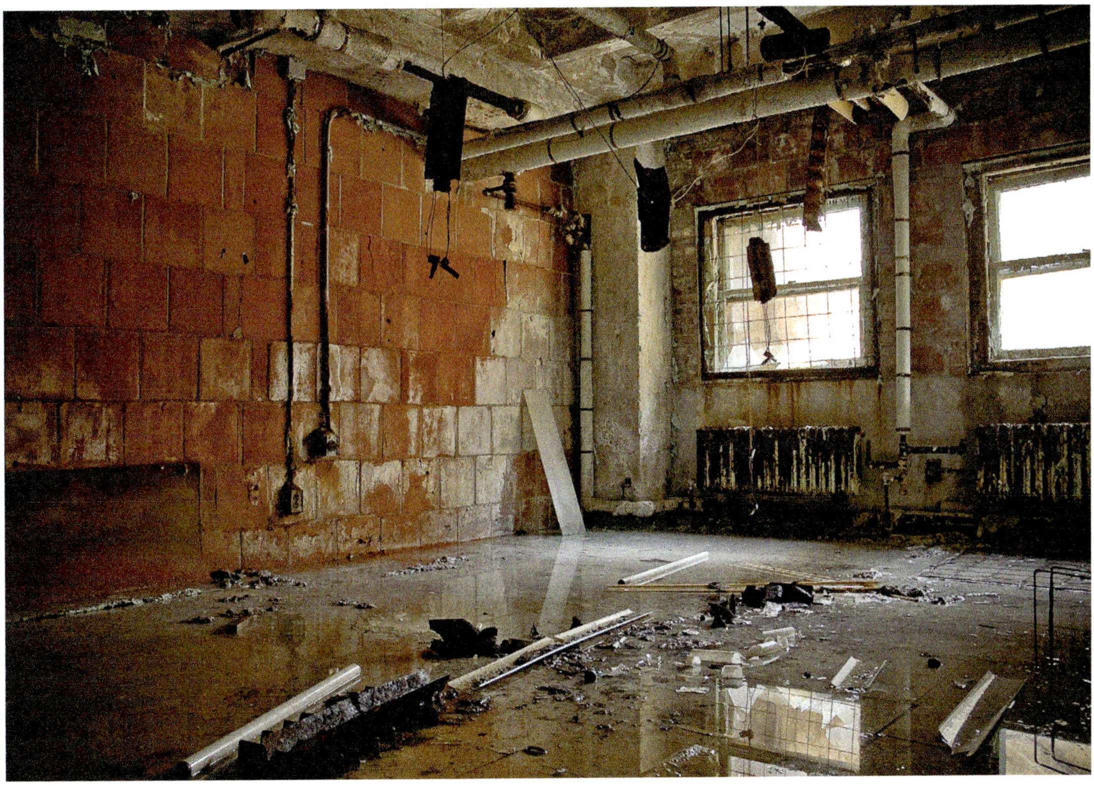

A flooded room in the hospital basement reflects the damage caused by years of neglect.

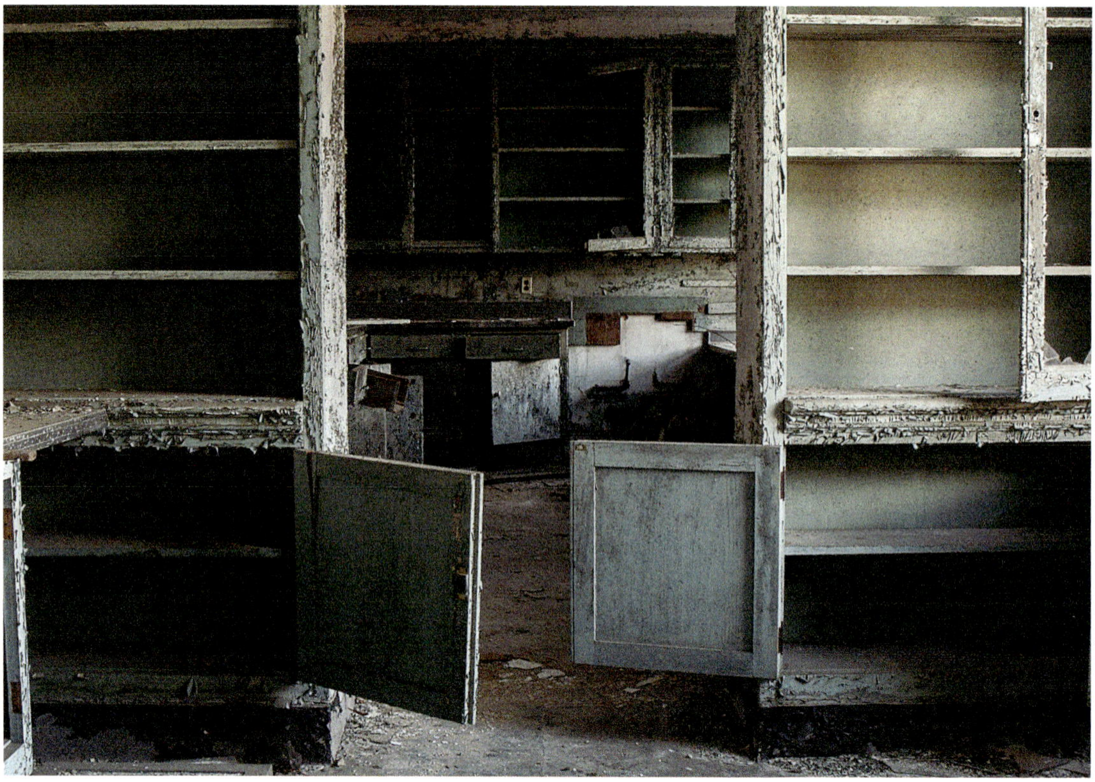

Swinging doors form the entrance to a preparation area.

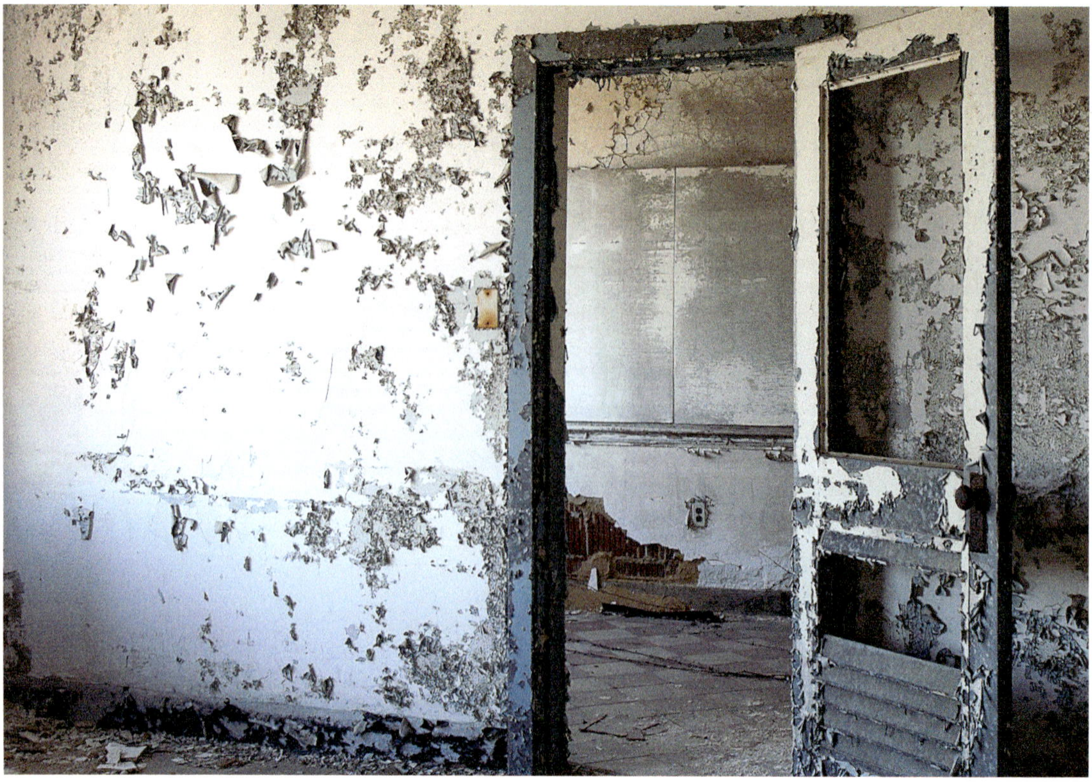

A glassless door opens into a decaying administration room.

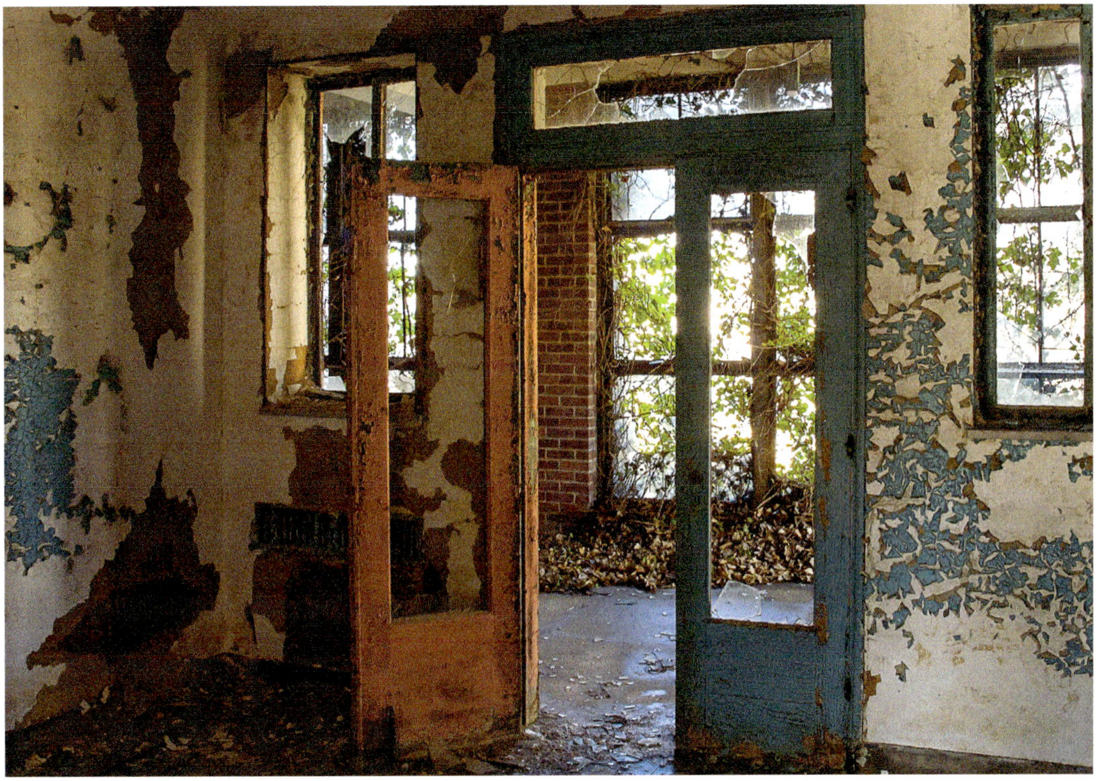

Throughout the main building brightly painted walls and door frames lead to wide airy balconies.

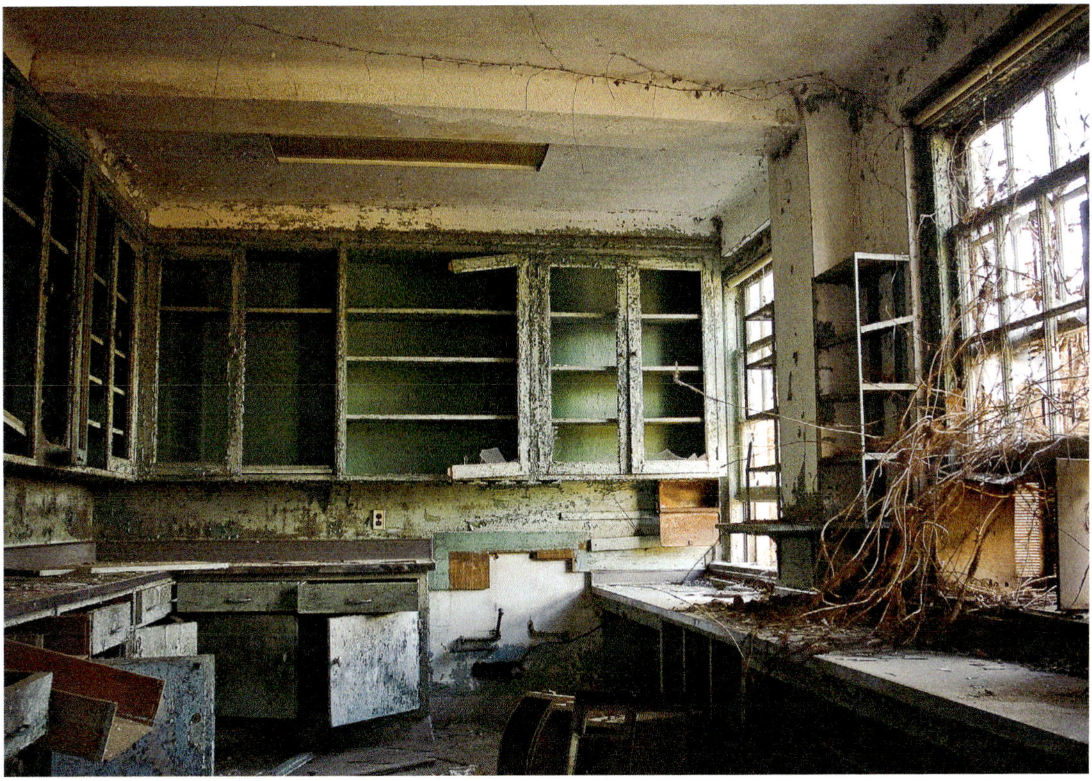

Thick vines have found their way through smashed window panes to invade the preparation area.

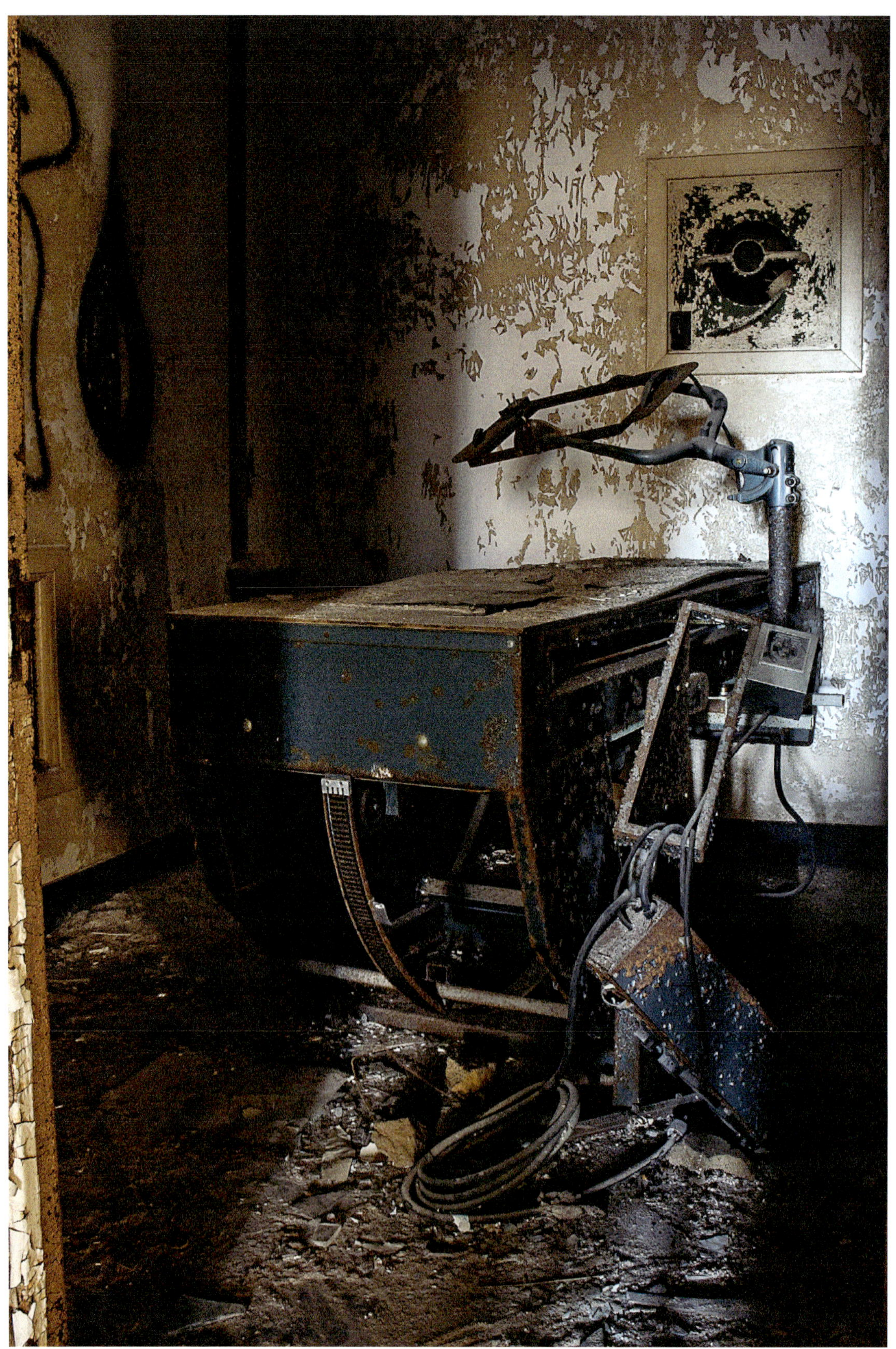

An examination table waiting for patients who will never return.

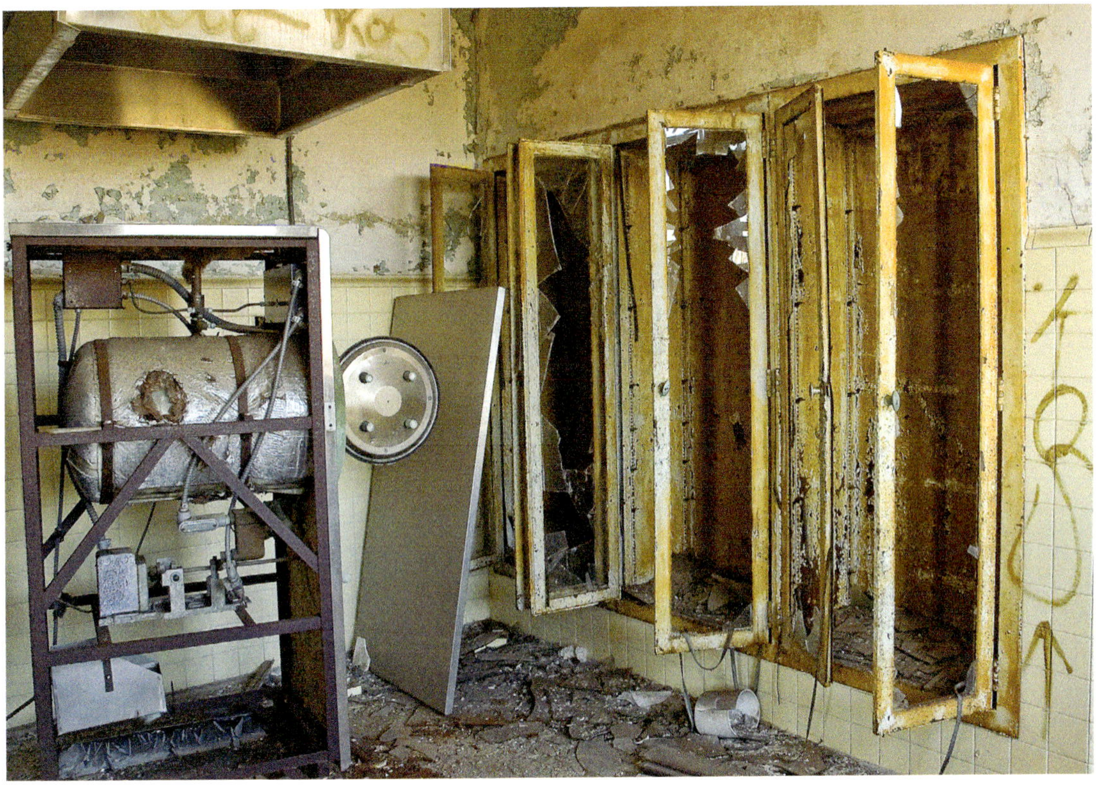

The previously glass fronted cabinets once stored sterilized instruments.

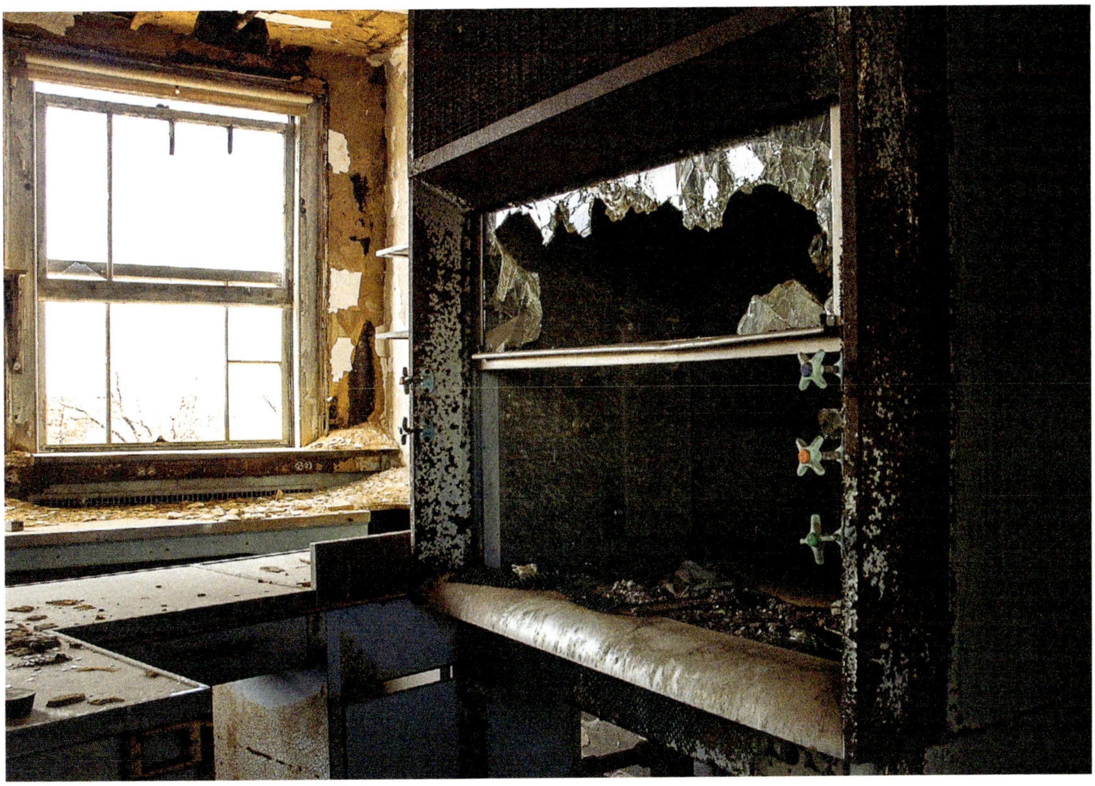

A laboratory hood used to maintain a sterile environment during testing procedures.

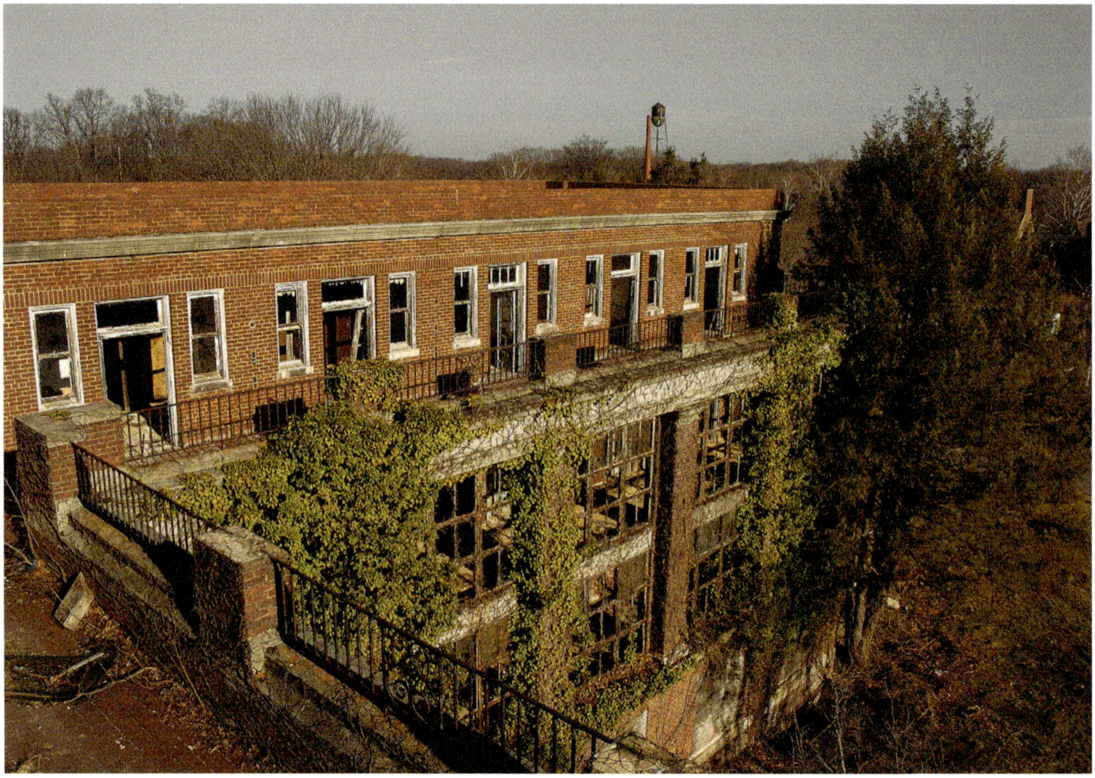

The view from the roof shows thick ivy covering the exterior. All windows have been smashed.

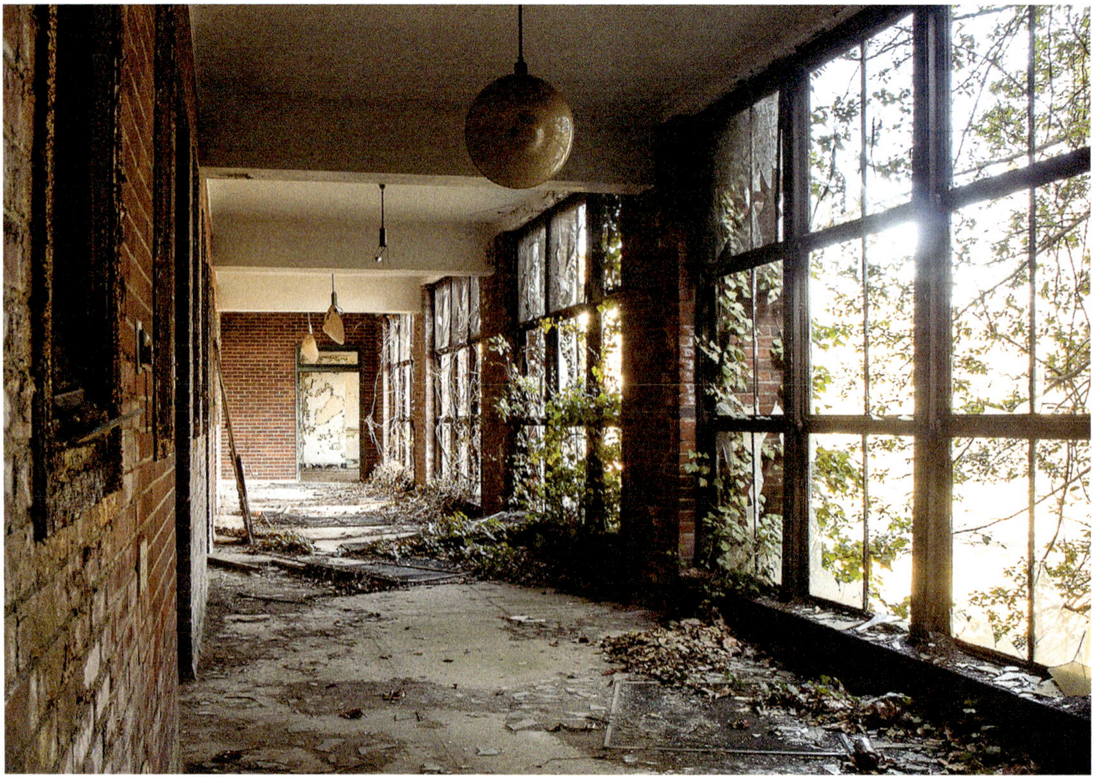

Light streams through the ivy covered broken window panes. Shards of glass cover the floor.

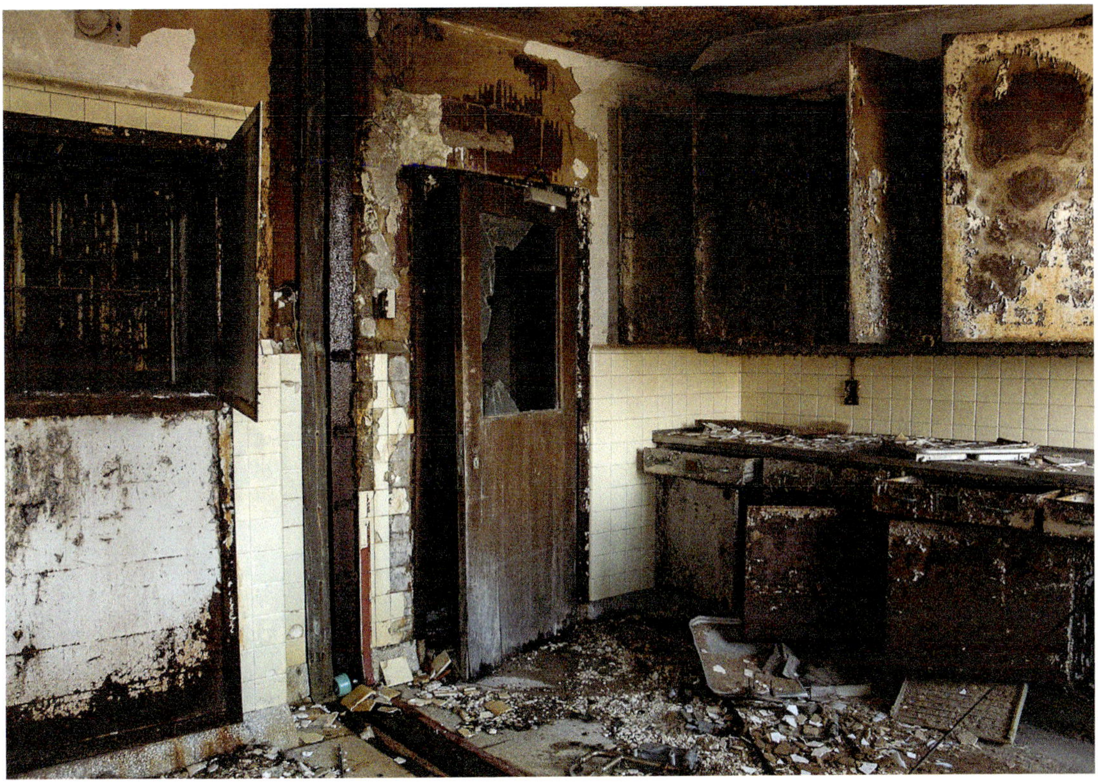

A sterile testing room has been decimated by fire.

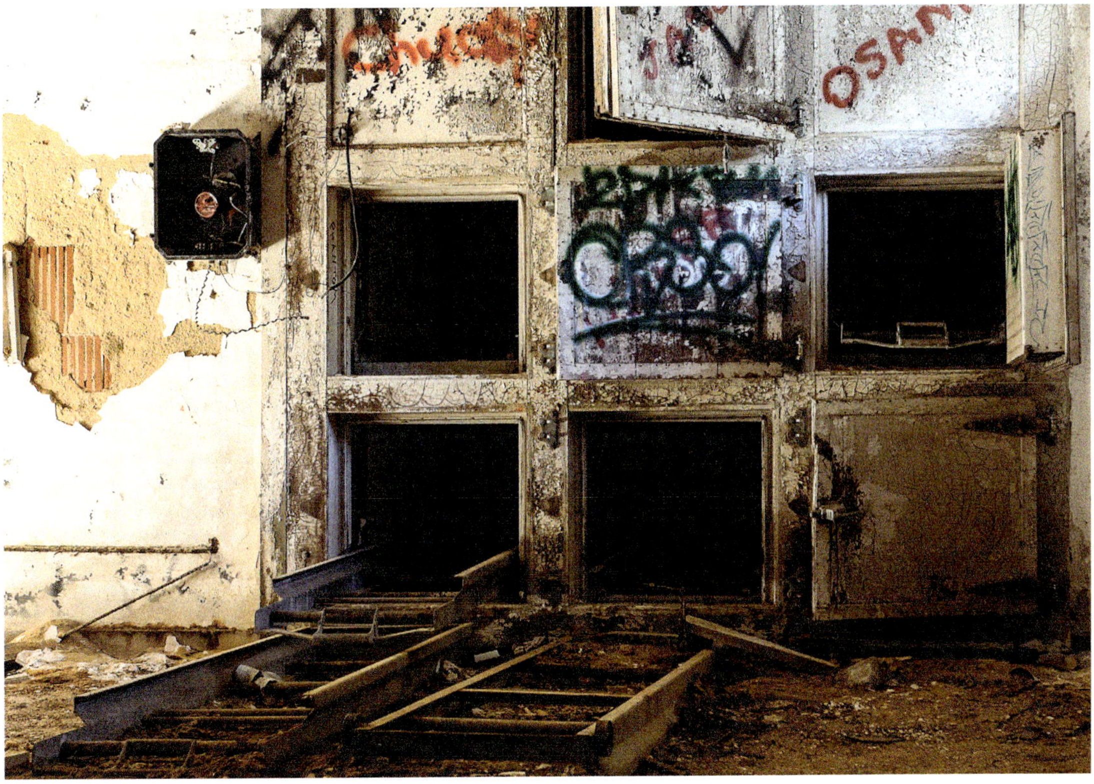

The adult building's morgue refrigerator reveals empty body trays.

THISTLE MILL, ELLICOTT CITY

A history of devastating floods and destructive fires surrounds historic Thistle Mill. For almost 200 years, the mill stood on the banks of the Patapsco River, 2 miles downstream from Ellicott City. Built in 1824 by Alexander Fridge and two Scottish merchants, George and William Morris, the mill, though extensively damaged by fire and vandalism, stood steadfastly to its place in history until 2013.

Thistle Mill adapted to many different phases of industrial development. Originally built on almost 100 acres, purchased from John Ellicott in 1821, the founding partners proceeded to build a dam, millrace and a 50 by 100-foot, granite, five-story mill to produce cotton. Alexander Fridge soon sold his share to the Morris brothers, who then built a village of thirty to forty granite mill houses—several of which still stand, although only their shells remain.

In its heyday, the mill had as many as 500 employees, and a 1850 tax record lists the value of the mill at $80,000. The mill housed 100 power looms and over 1,000 spindles used in the production of cotton duct for ship sails. The prosperity, however, did not last. Just as the free-flowing Patapsco could give power, it could just as easily take it away—in 1866, floods crippled the dam, slowing production, and then, in 1868, flood waters entered the lower portions of the mill. In the early 1920s, the mill was refurbished and converted by the Bargis brothers to a paper-making facility.

In June 1972, Hurricane Agnes all but destroyed what had become a thriving paper recycling plant owned by Simkins Industries. In November of the same year, just as the mill was recovering, another of nature's forces chose to intervene—a four-alarm fire ripped through the building. As in the past, the mill recovered, and thrived. But just over thirty years later, on June 23, 2003, flames engulfed the mill again—this time there would be no recovery.

For a decade, the Thistle Mill/Simkins Industries Recycling Plant stood as a gutted-out reminder of our industrial past. Guarded by twenty-four-hour security, the historic granite building contained hazardous waste, while the thick concrete floors, which once contained giant vats used to make pulp, lay cratered and crumbling. The power plant on the opposite bank of the river, which escaped the 2003 fire, stood alone, stripped of valuable copper and other reusable materials.

Another fire in 2011, and a Voluntary Cleanup Program incentive, offered by the Maryland Department of the Environment, sealed the fate of the historic Thistle Mill and its power plant. In June 2013, Simkins Industries contracted a local demolition company to raze the property. Today, the land, scarred by the massive footprint the mill left as a reminder of its existence, remains owned by Simkins. Many state and local advocates are optimistic the land will be absorbed into the Patapsco Valley State Park system.

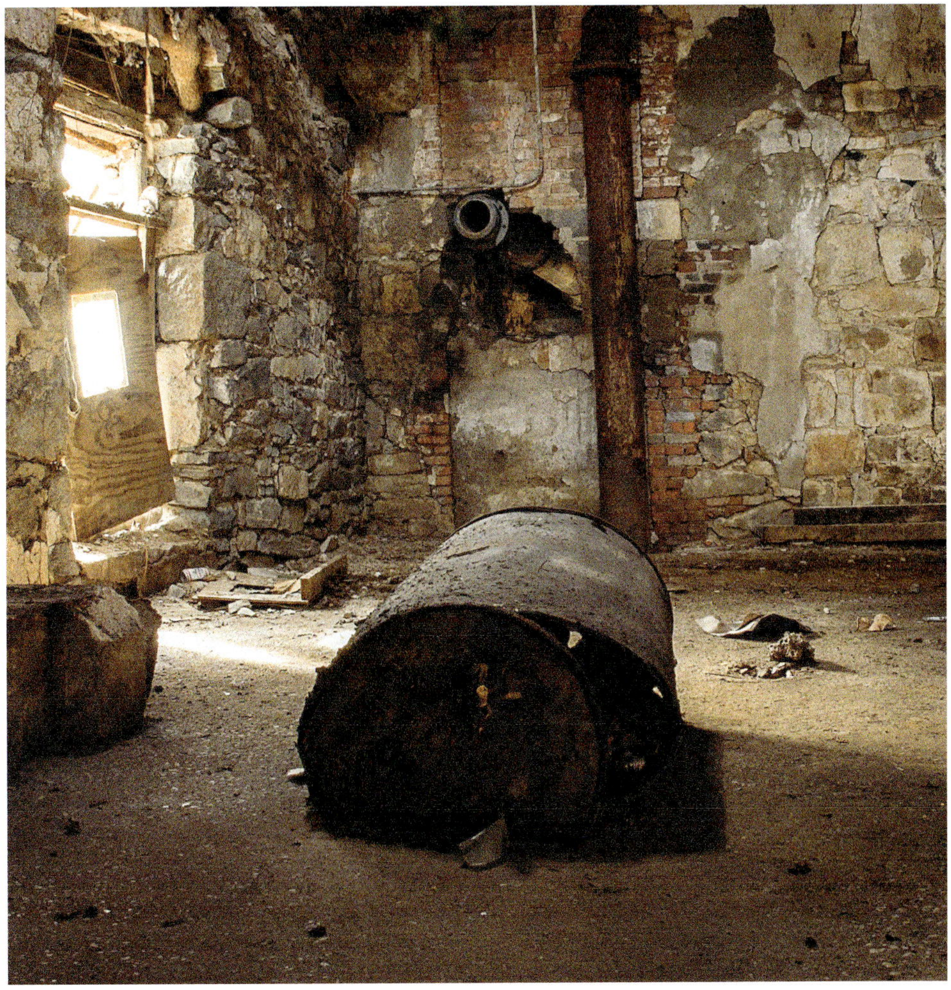

The tales of time: eighteenth-century granite, nineteenth-century brickwork, and twentieth-century concrete inside the mill.

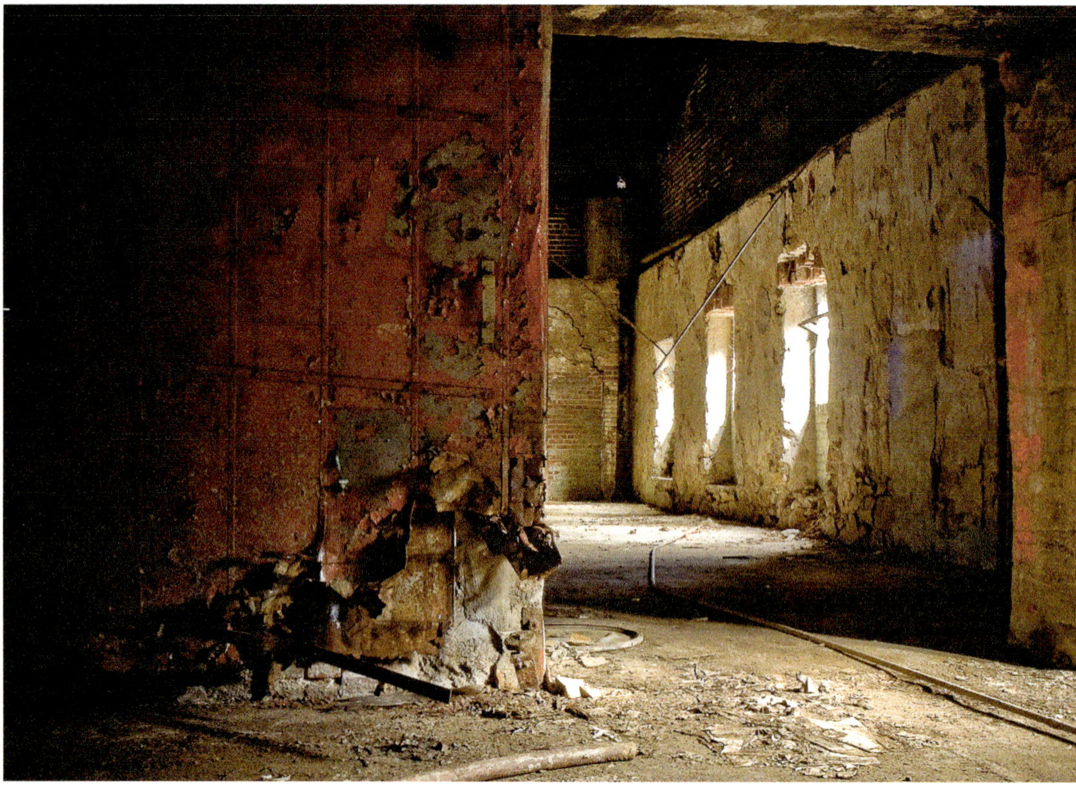

A nineteenth-century steel fire door used to separate storage areas.

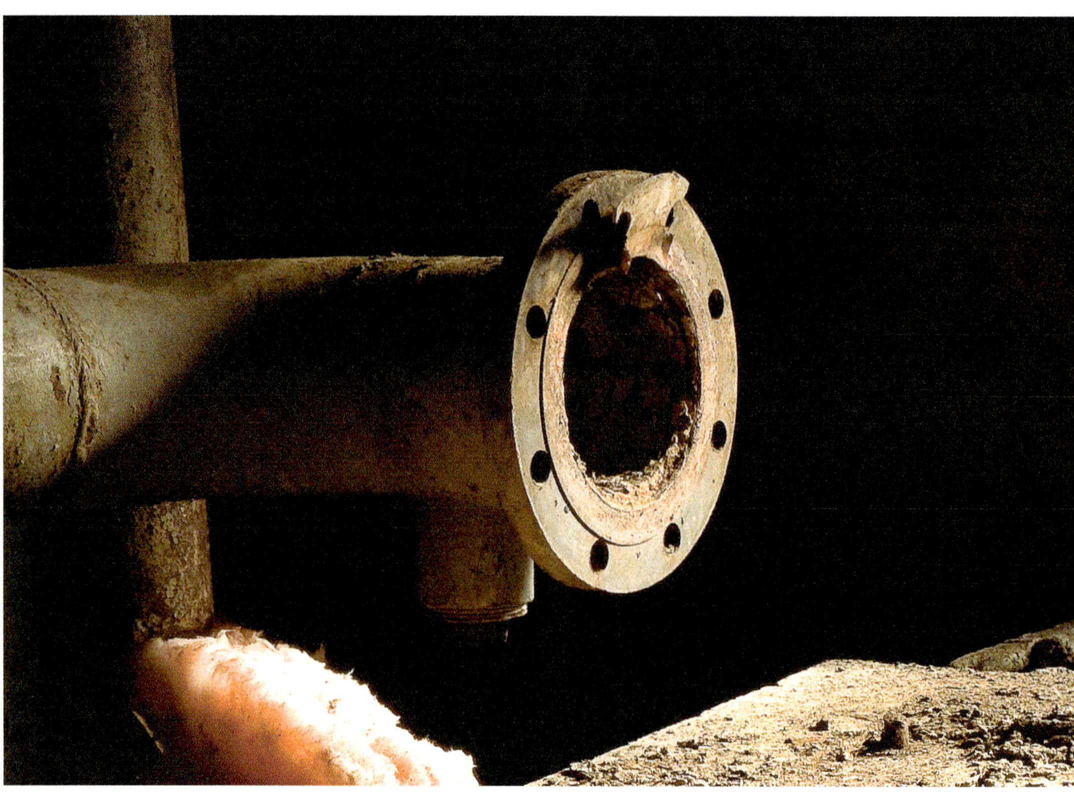

Severed pipes protrude from crumbling walls.

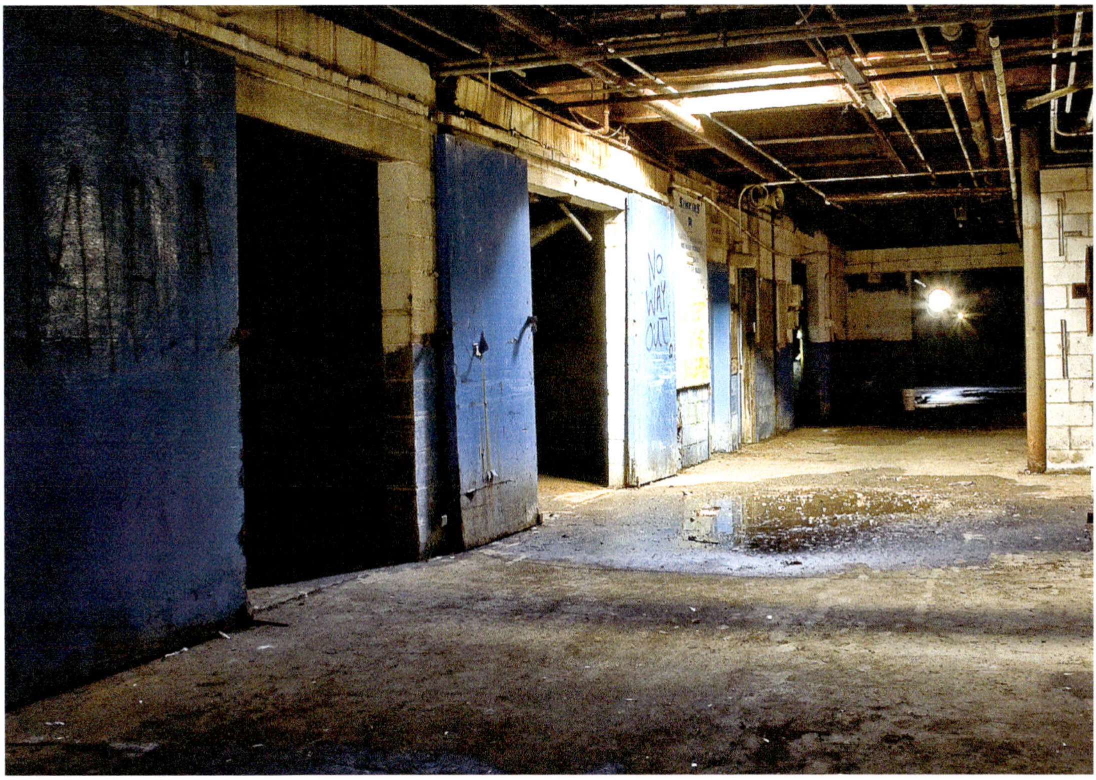

A corridor lined with blue steel doors leads to a loading dock area.

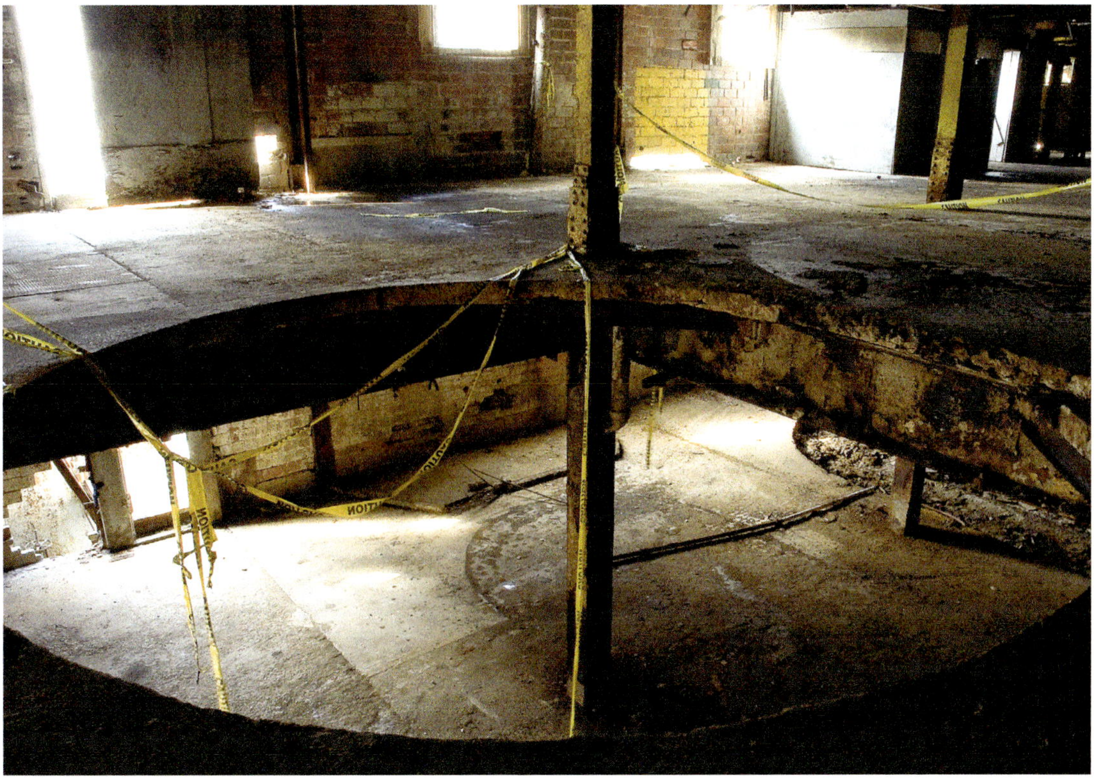

Gaping holes in the thick concrete floors, where the vats once stored the pulp slurry, are spread throughout the mill.

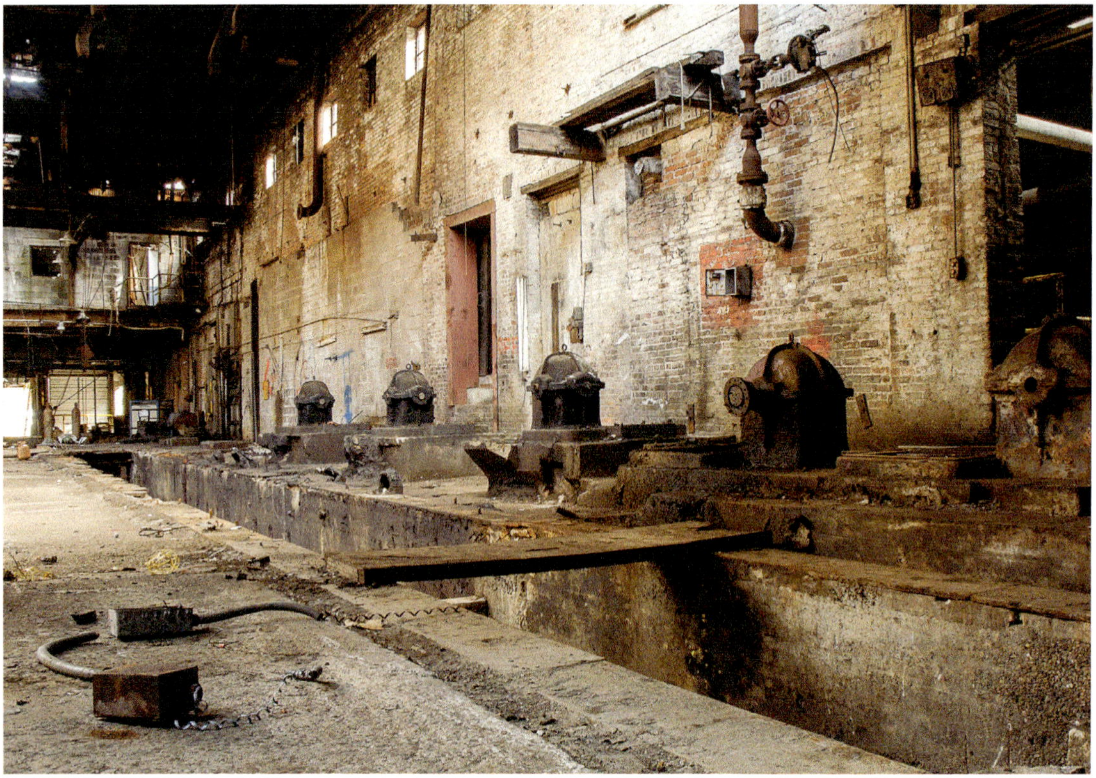

Axle hubs once held the rollers, which rolled out the wet paper and now stand like silent sentries, guarding the paper room floor

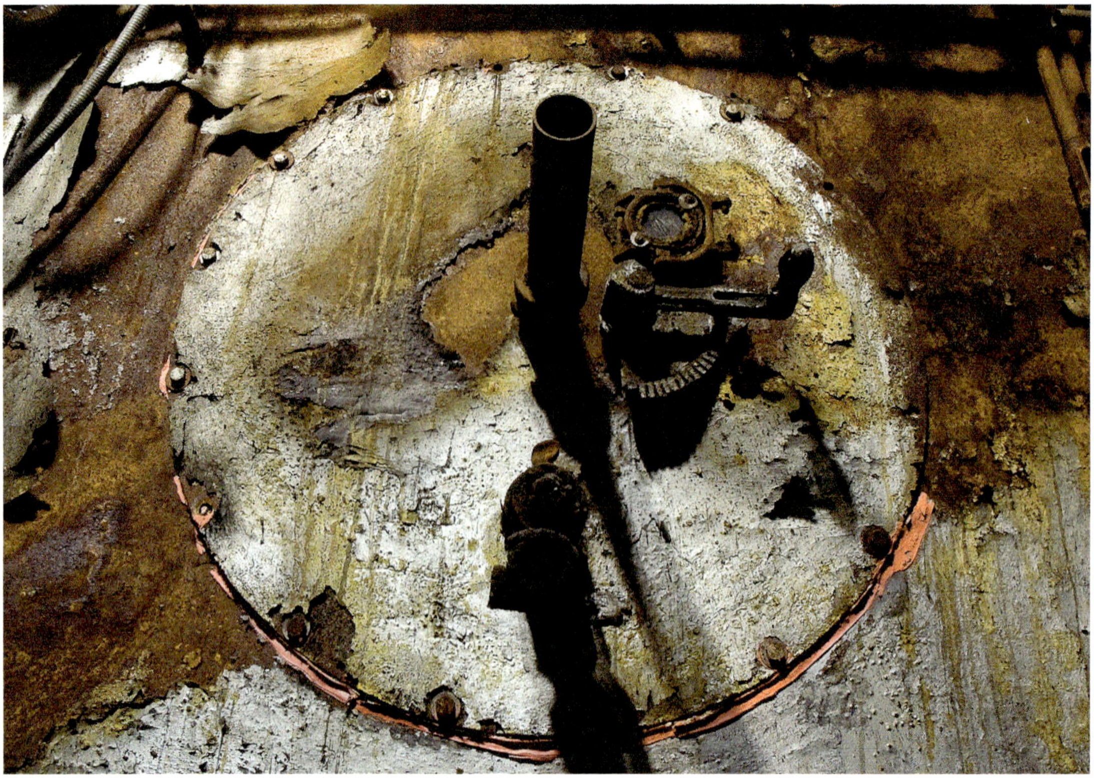

The internal mechanism is all that remains of this mill equipment.

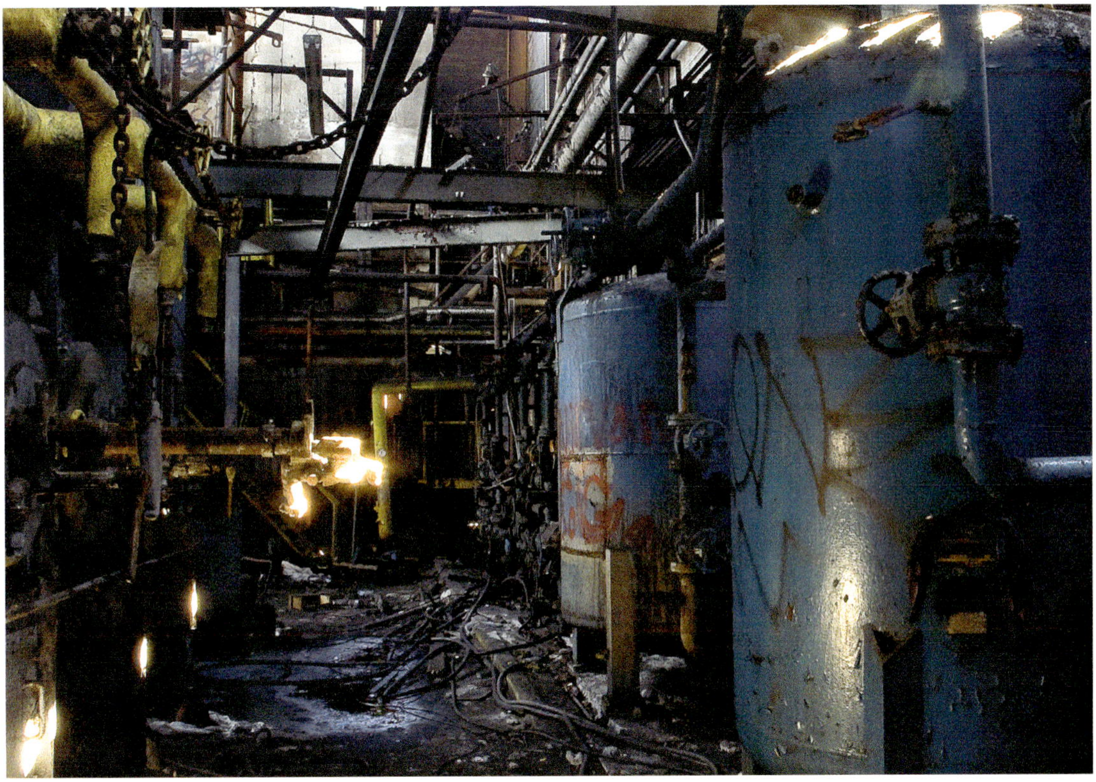

Boiler and steam tanks on the main floor of the mill's power plant.

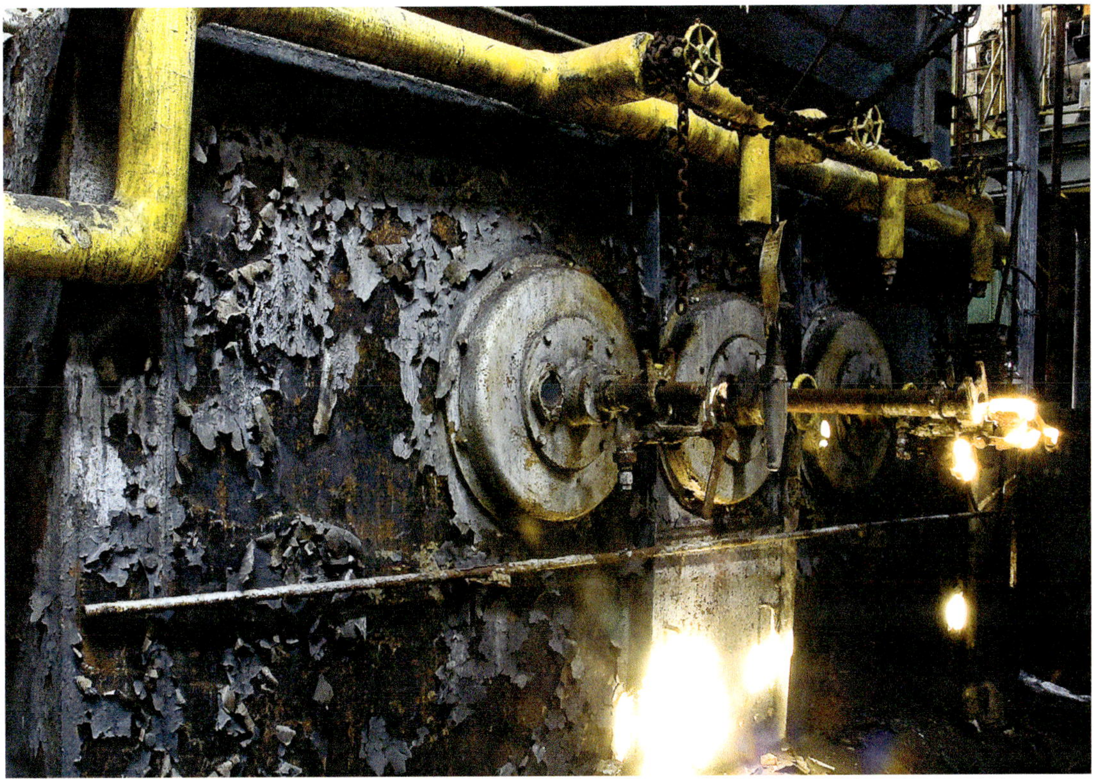

Rays of afternoon sunlight ignite the boiler tank control arms, giving them an other-worldly glow.

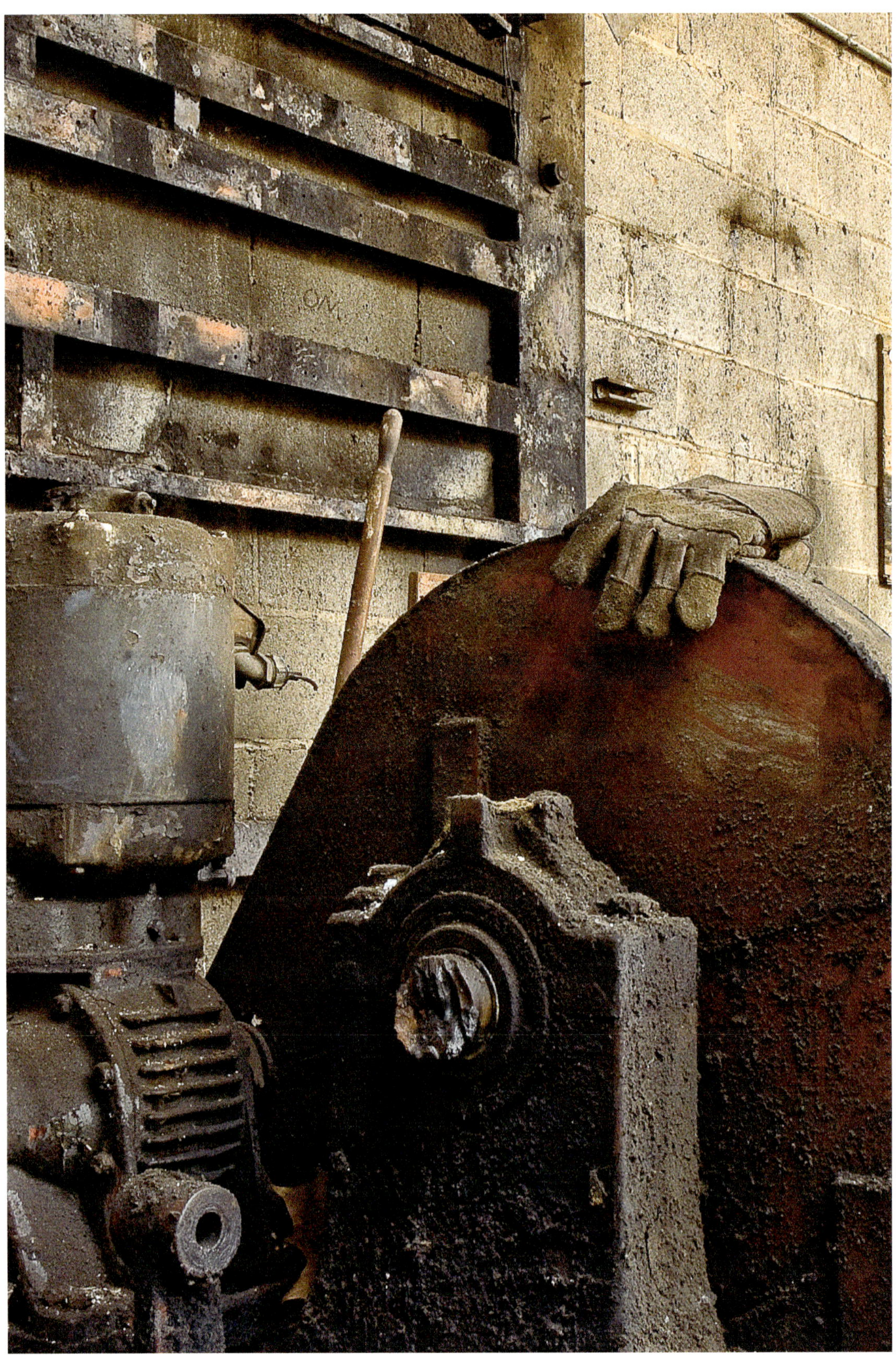

A worker's glove lies discarded atop aging machinery.

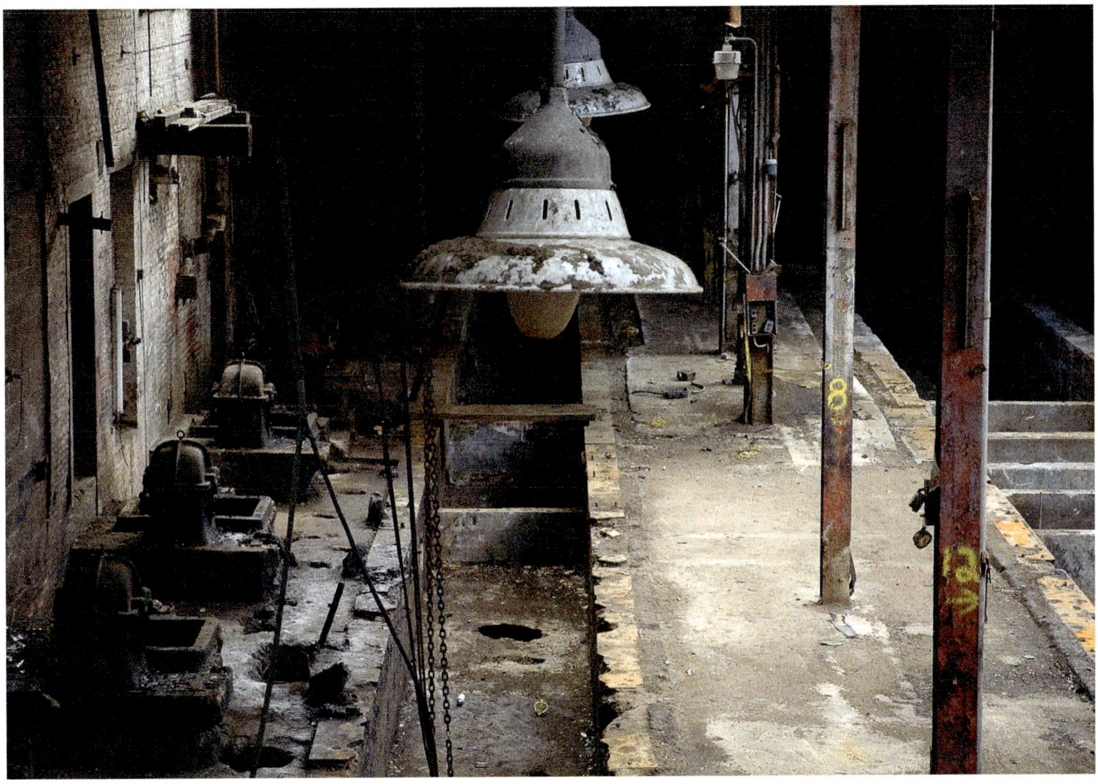

Factory shop lights hanging above the paper room floor.

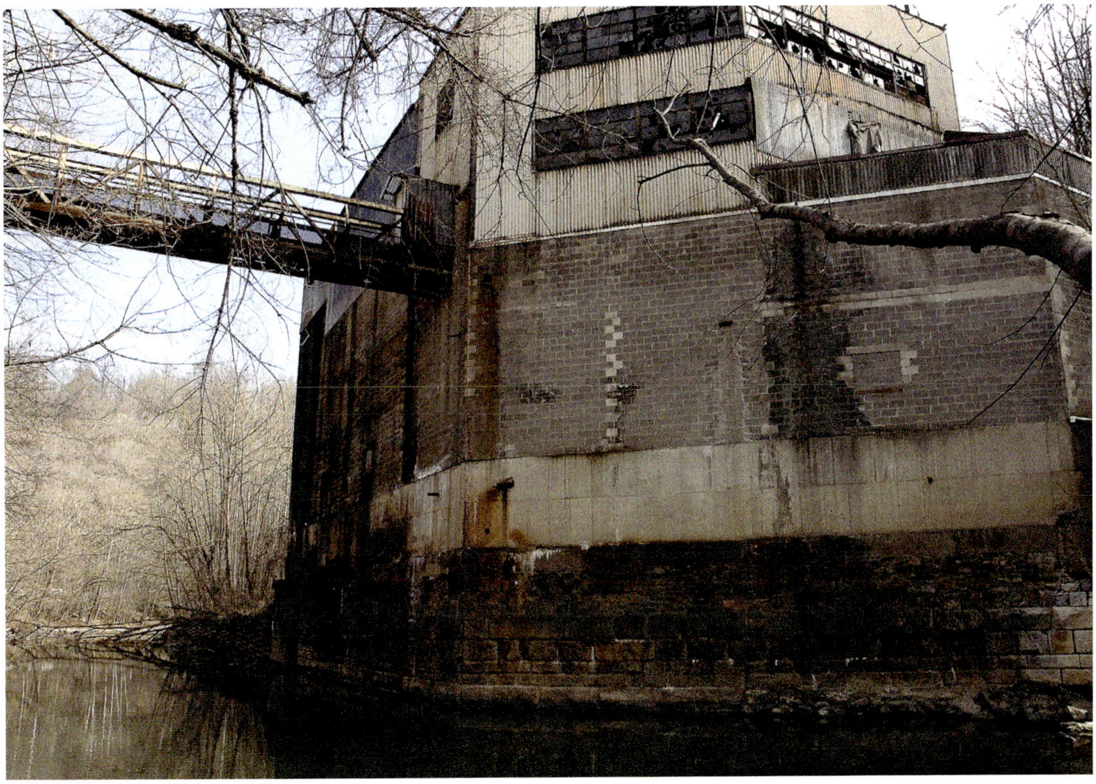

This catwalk replaced the one destroyed by Hurricane Agnes in 1972, where a body was found in the wreckage.

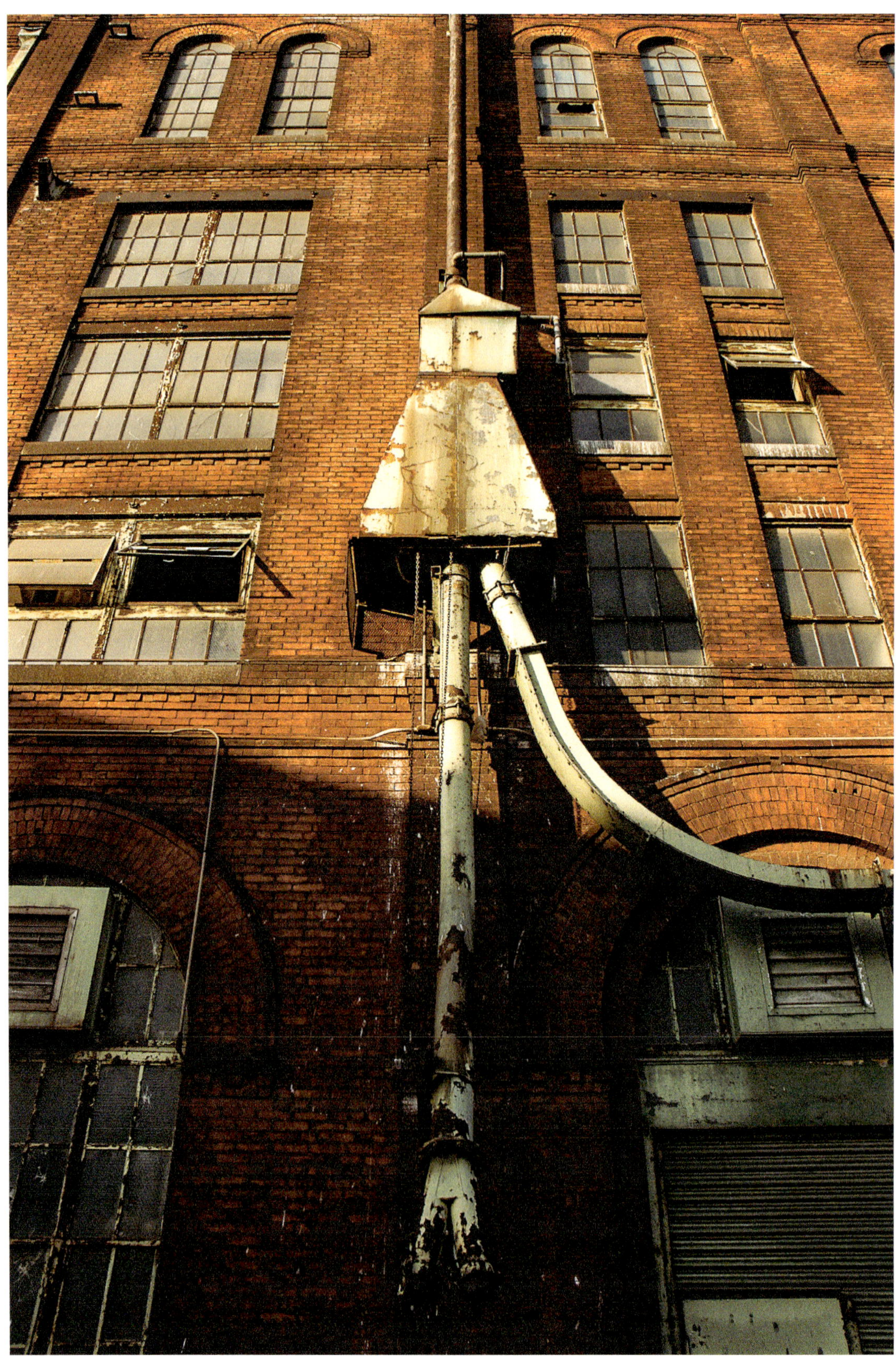

Rusted pipes, attached to the exterior, once sucked grains into the brewery from rail cars.

GUNTHER BREWERY, BALTIMORE

Situated in the heart of Baltimore's Brewer's Hill district, the Gunther Brewery began operations in 1881. Founded by Bavarian immigrant George Gunther, the brewery was one of the area's leading breweries throughout much of its ninety-seven-year history.

Friendly rivalry existed between Gunther and neighboring brewery, the iconic, National Brewery, located just a stone's throw away on the opposite corner of O'Donnell Street. National produced the much-loved National Bohemian label with its signature Natty Boh symbol. Both breweries are long since closed, but former workers are happy to reminisce—according to a local story every Friday afternoon workers from each of the rival breweries engaged in a neighborhood softball match with the loser having to drink the other's beer.

In 1959, the Theo Hamm Brewing Company purchased the Gunther Brewery. Hamm immediately ceased marketing the Gunther brand and lost favor with locals. Hamm sold out, only four years later, to the F. & M. Schaefer Brewing Company, a large Brooklyn-based firm. The Schaefer Company continued operations until 1978. The National Brewery had moved out three years earlier to a larger more modern facility—and so with Gunther's closure the once bustling brewery district fell silent.

Once considered a blight on the Brewer's Hill skyline, the Gunther Brewing buildings have undergone a remarkable transformation. Retaining many of its original features, including tile and brickwork, the main brewery building opened in 2014 as a 300,000-square-foot, 160 apartment complex.

Forty years after losing its major industry, Brewer's Hill has become a bustling mixed-use urban community. Under the guidance of Obrecht Properties LLC, redevelopment of the National Brewery and the Gunther Brewery buildings is now complete.

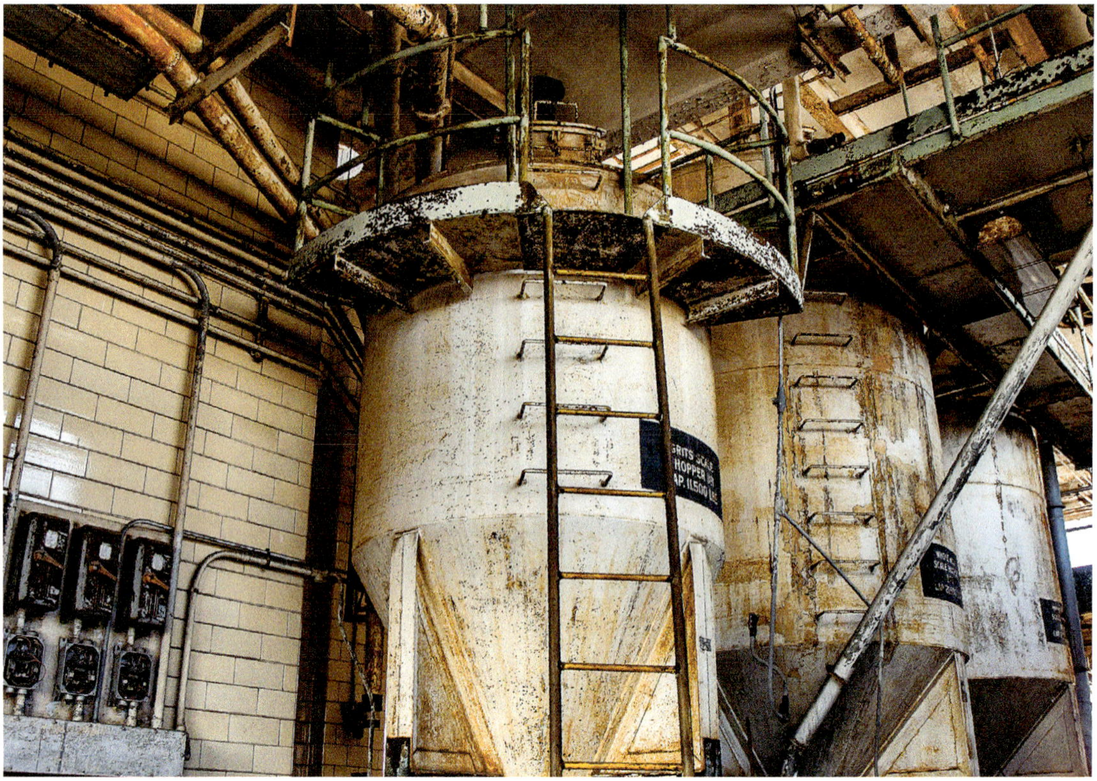

Rusting hoppers.

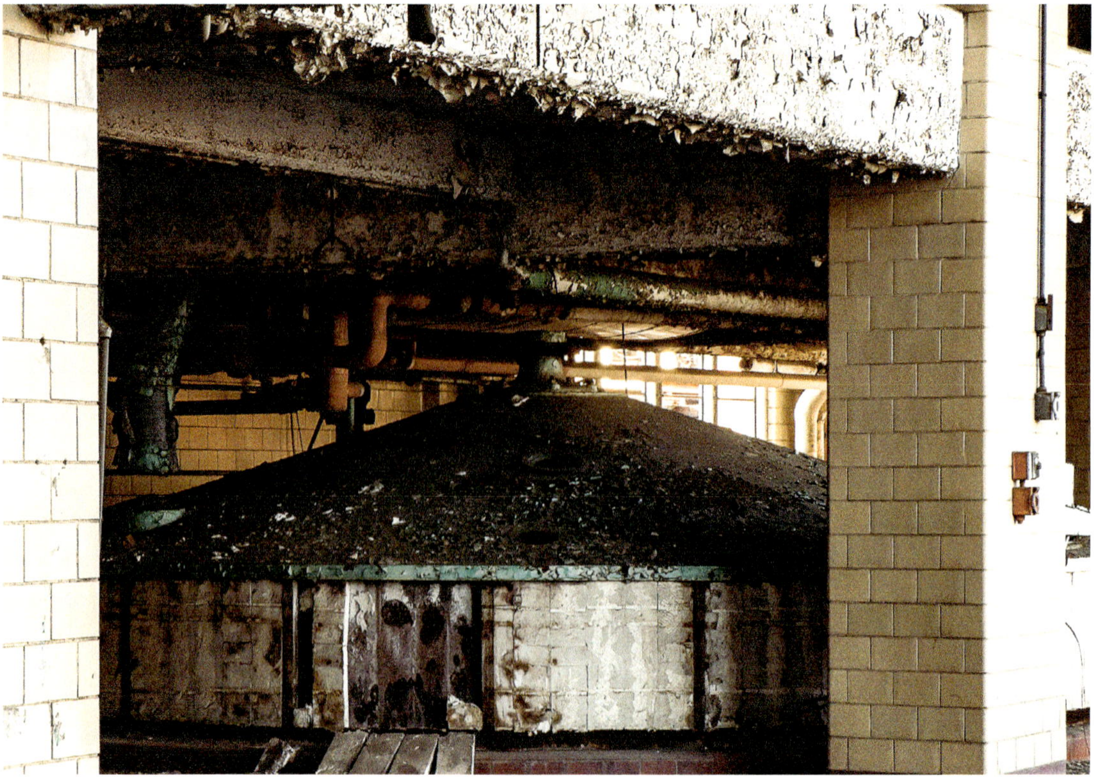

A decaying mash tun.

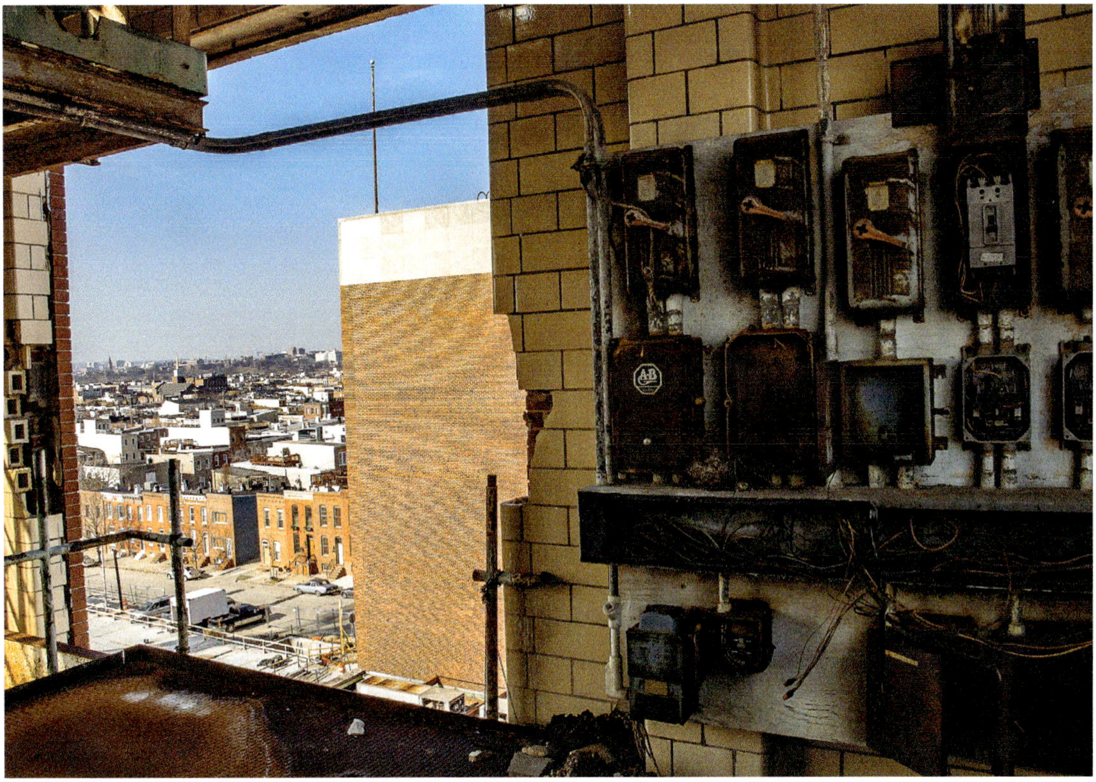

Part of the north-east facing wall was demolished to remove the silos.

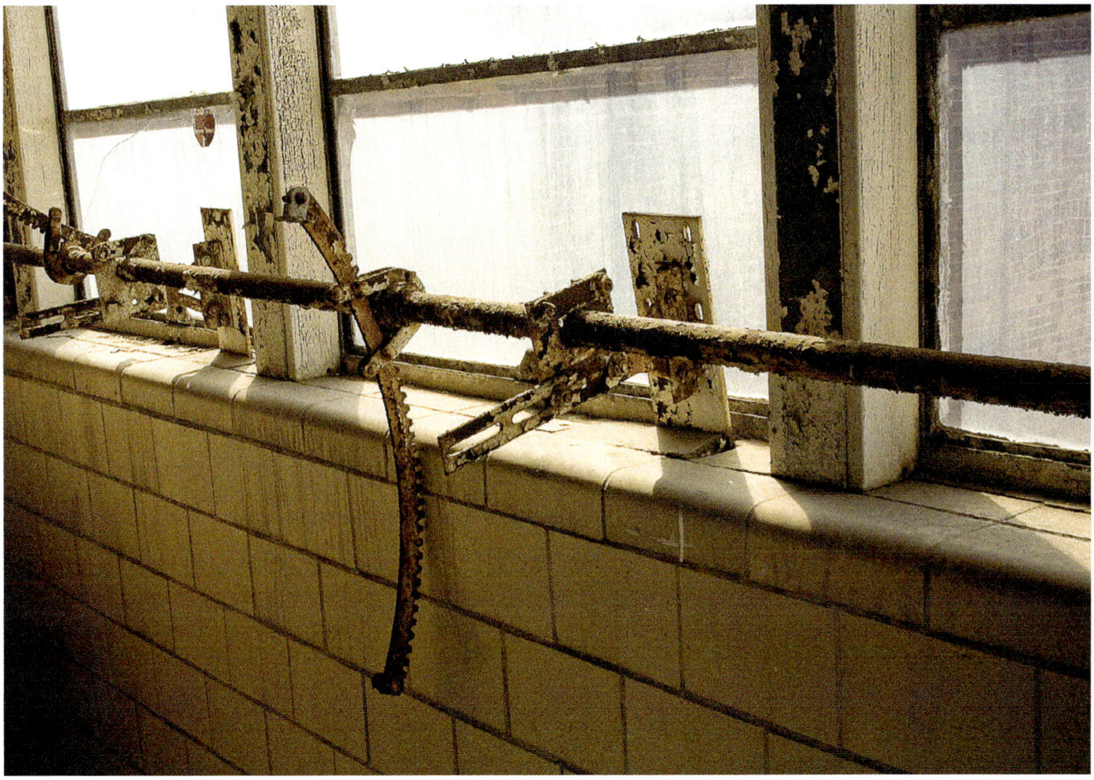

A mechanism for measuring grain quantities from the silos.

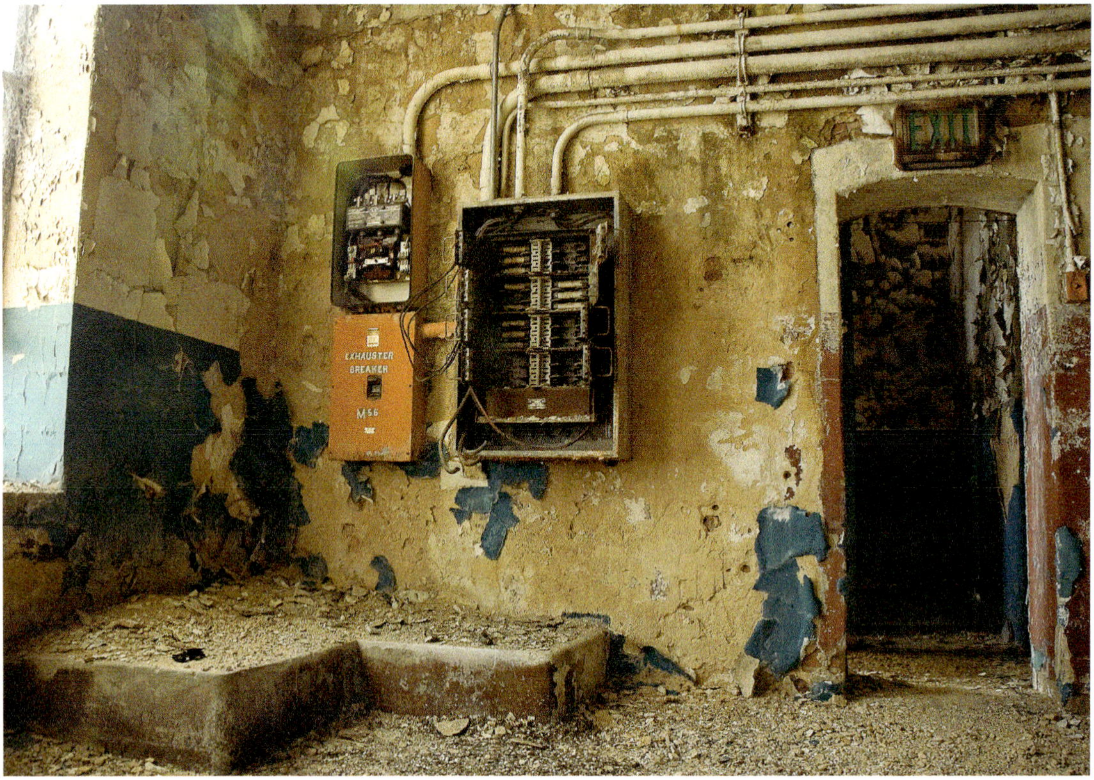

An exit door leads to a narrow hall and even narrower maintenance elevator.

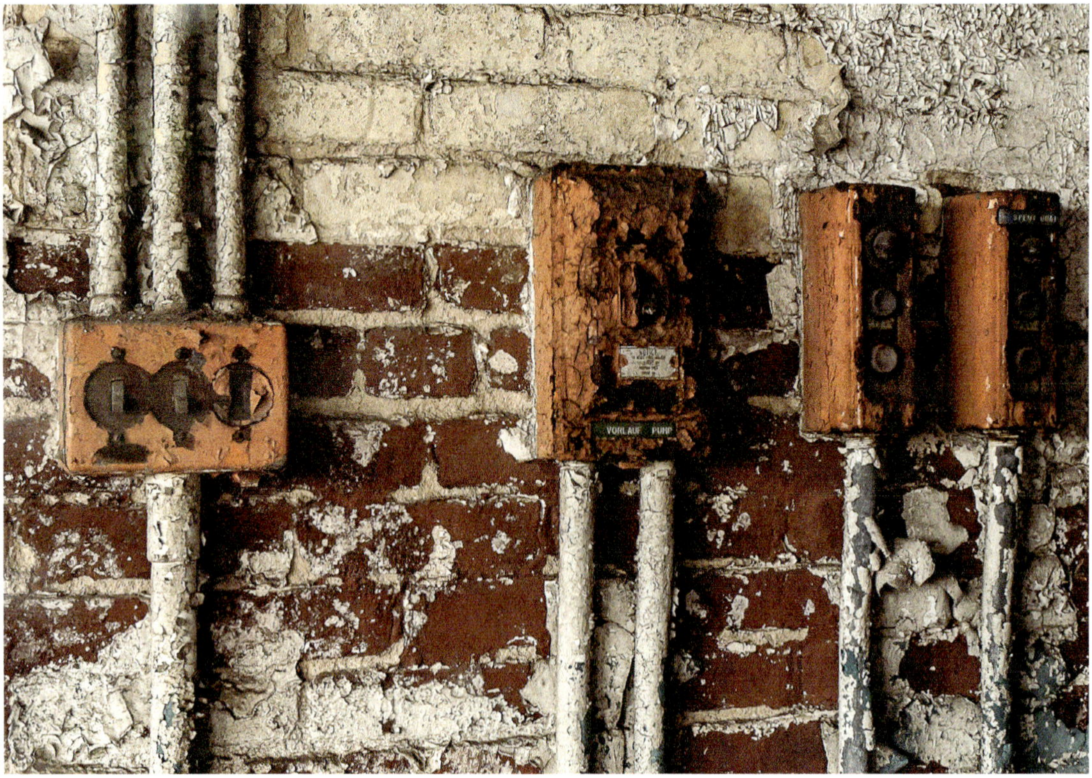

Peeling paint covered pump switches.

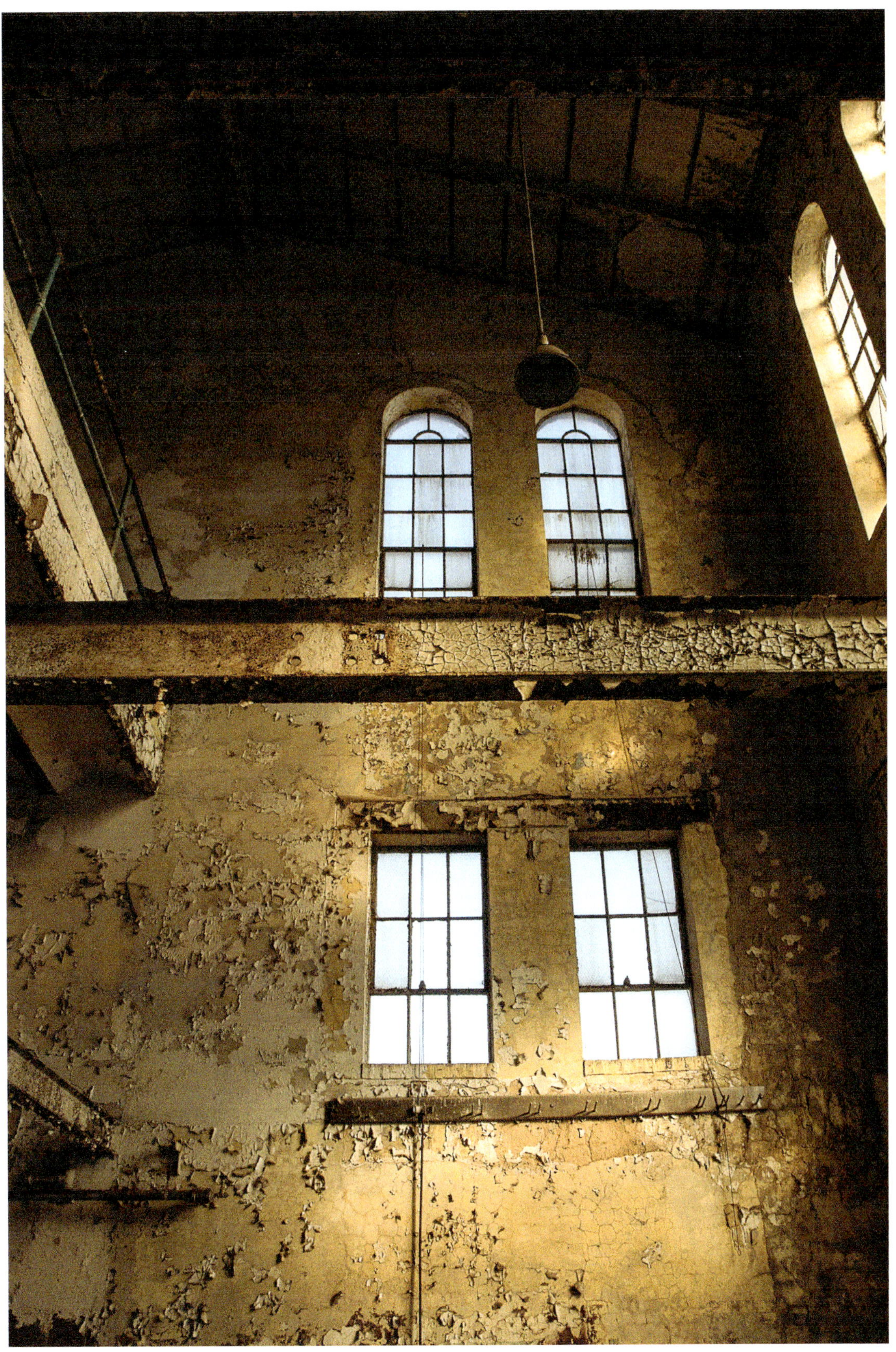

When more vertical space was required during remodeling of the brewery, areas of the floor were removed.

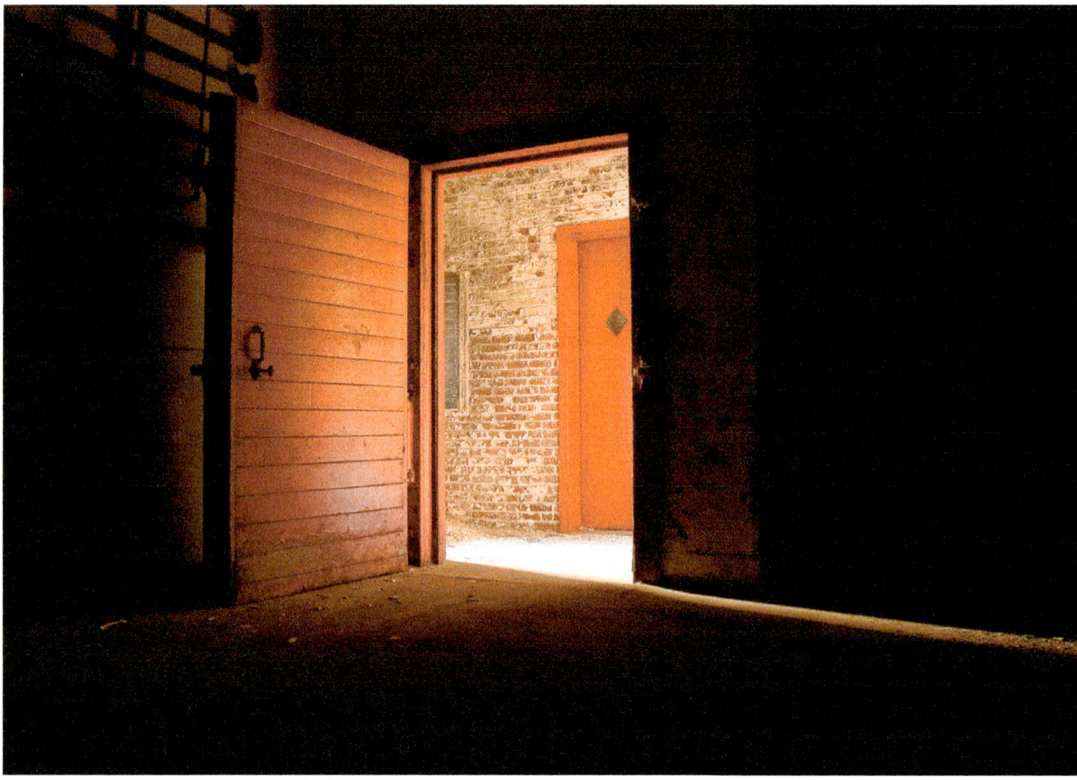

The bright red fire door leading out of the refrigeration room to the elevator.

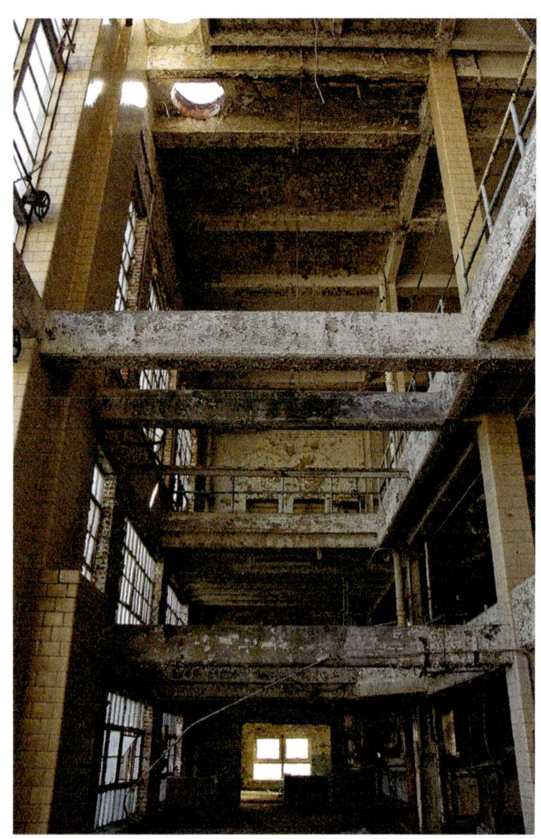

Areas where the floor was removed. The tiled wall on the left is a feature in the restoration.

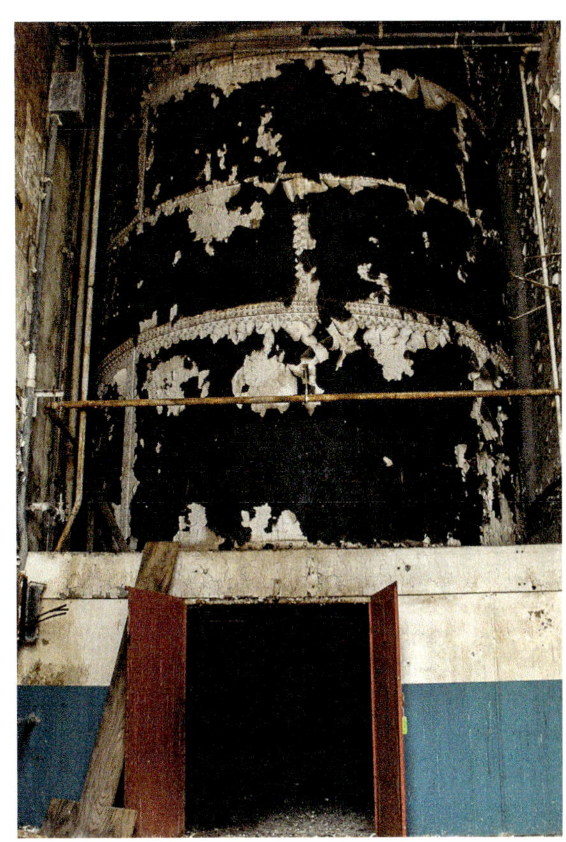

Very little paint remains on a fermentation tank.

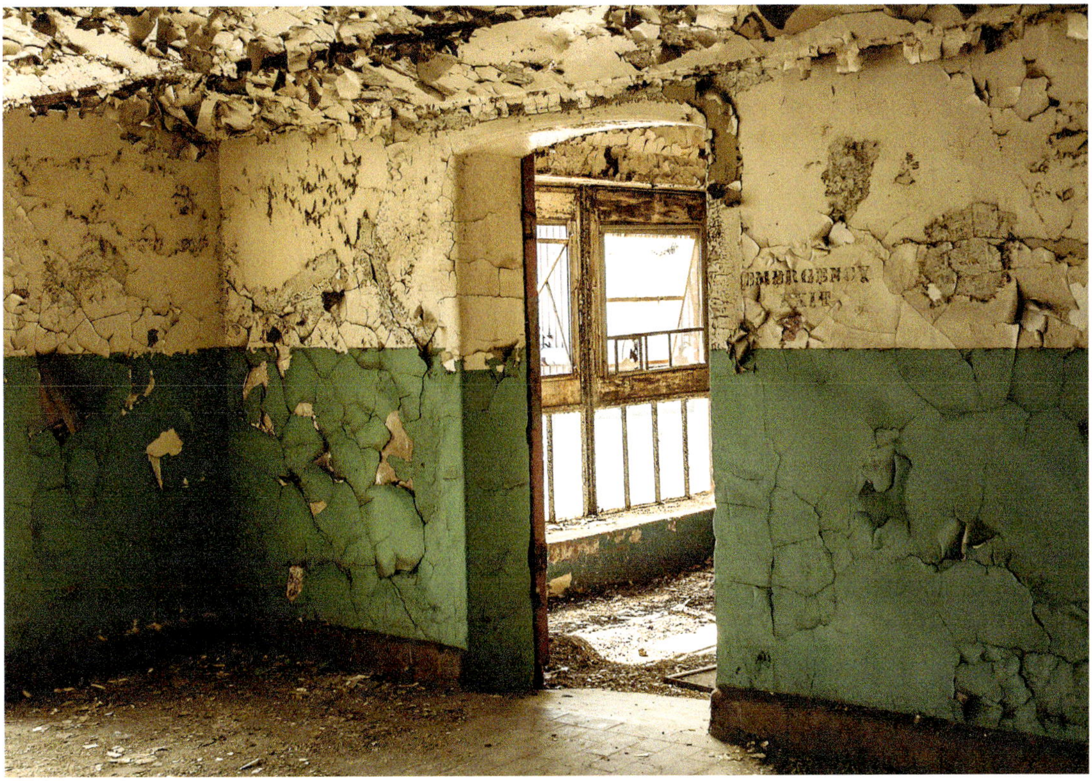

Afternoon sunlight streams through the Toone Street windows, highlighting a former emergency exit.

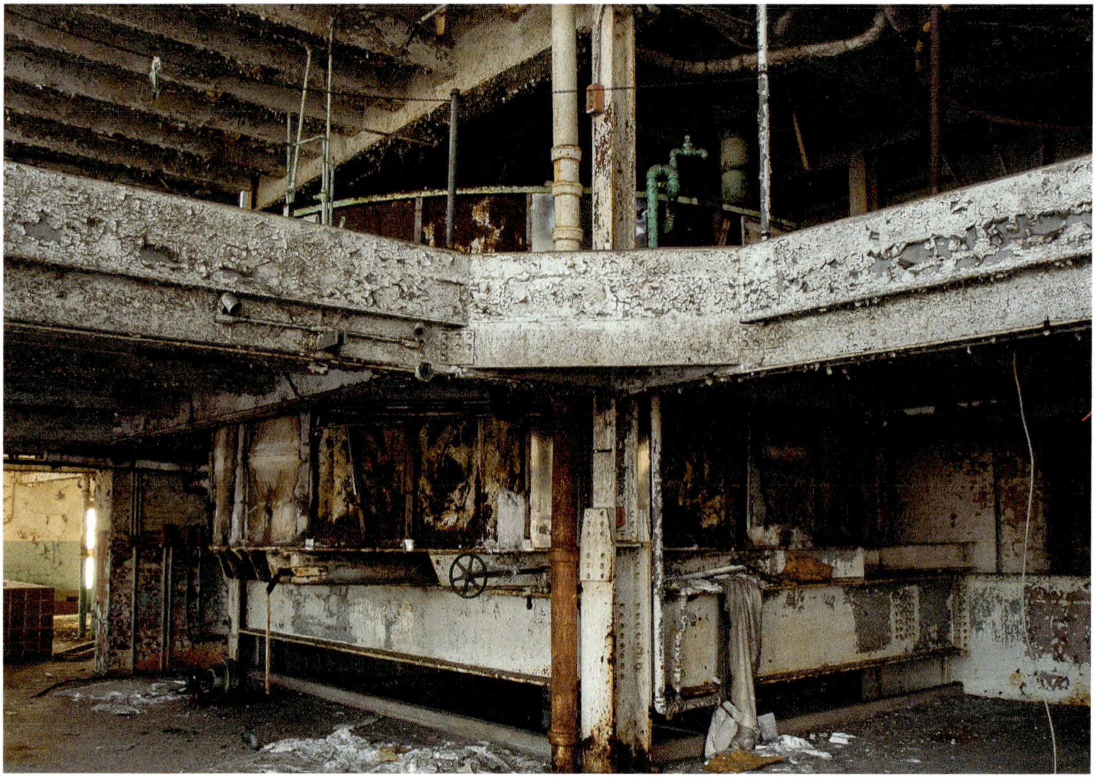

Mash tanks, surrounded by debris and discarded equipment.

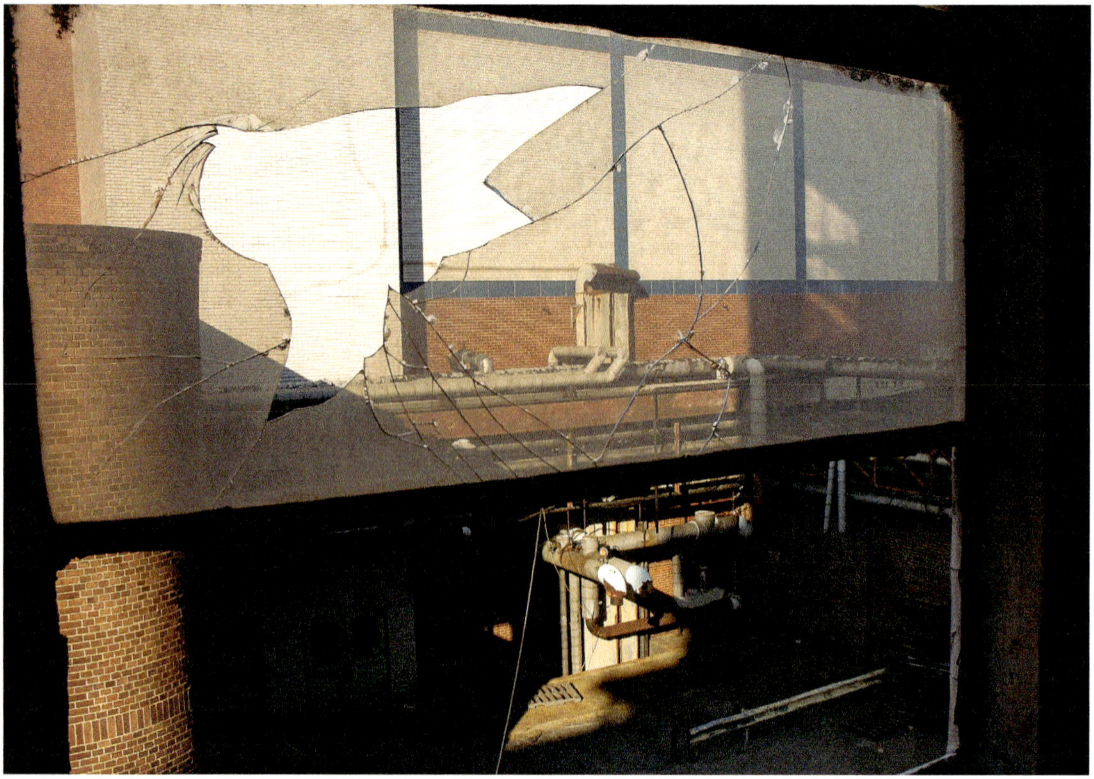

A broken window, frames exterior water pipes.

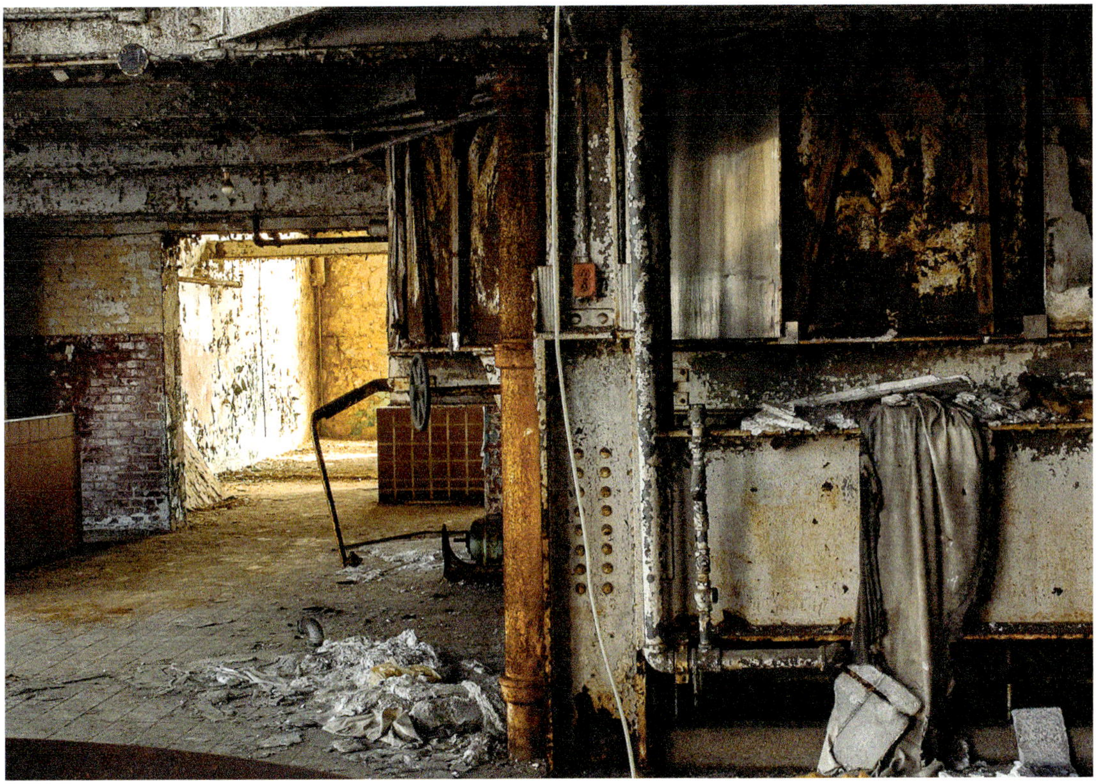

Sunlight creates an other-worldly glow in the decaying room adjacent to the mash tanks.

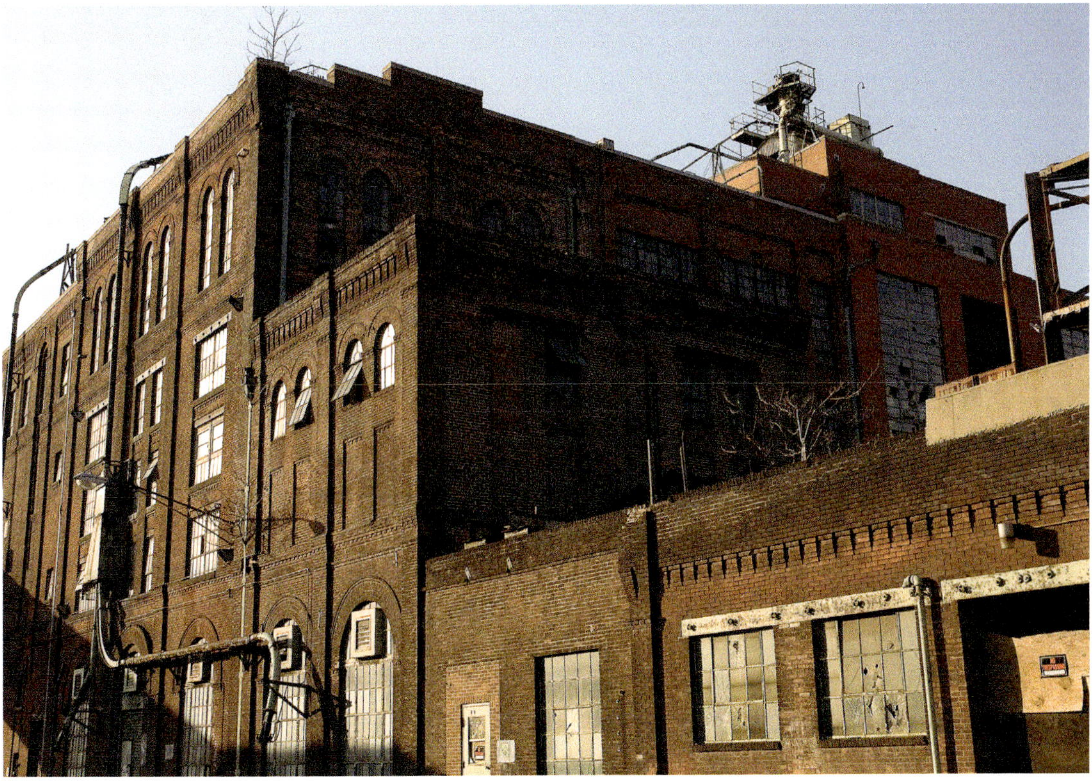

The Toone Street entrance to the brewing house.

PARKWAY THEATRE, BALTIMORE

The doppelgänger myth fits Baltimore's Parkway Theatre well. Some 3,600 miles away from the Parkway's location on North Avenue, in London's West End, on Coventry Street, sits the Parkway's almost exact replica, the Rialto Theatre. The Parkway opened on October 23, 1915 with seating for 1,100 patrons. The first film to grace the screen was the silent romantic drama, *Zaza*, starring Pauline Frederick.

The Parkway was designed by local architect, Oliver Birkhead Wight for the Henry W. Webb Northern Amusement Company. Built by the J. Henry Miller Company, the front of the building was completed in the style of the Italian Renaissance: light gray terra cotta with a combination of light and dark brick. The building was a stately example of the architecture of the time.

The twin theatres shared much, including the auditorium's egg shape and opulent interior. Designed after the fashion of the Louis XIV period, intricate plaster work surrounded the upper level balcony, stage and murals adorning the walls. The ceiling, was the true centerpiece of the auditorium, and a spectacle to behold; the large ornamental dome with a suspended sunburst, surrounded by an oval of recessed lights,was and still is, wondrous.

Like many theatres of the time, the Parkway would undergo significant changes throughout the coming decades before its closure in 1978. Sold to the Whitehurst corporation in the early 1920s, it was purchased by Loew's Theatres Incorporated in 1927. Loew's hired architect John Eberson to remodel, and in 1928, they installed the Movietone and Vitaphone. In 1939, the theatre was once again remodeled at a cost of $30,000. Successful business man and theatre owner Morris Mechanic purchased the Parkway in 1952 and, as he had done with several theatres in the region, he shuttered it.

Mechanic leased the Parkway to a local theatre organization, but they were never truly successful and struggled to run for two seasons before closing in 1953. By 1956, the Parkway was in slow decline, but it would undergo another renovation and become

5 West. Classic and foreign films played at 5 West, often for extraordinarily long runs, until the 1970s, but by 1978, patron numbers were in decline, as was the North Avenue neighborhood, and the Parkway's role as a theatre officially ended.

A succession of owners had no vision for the theatre and at one time a group of Korean businessmen used it as a corporate headquarters. The building was shuttered in 1998 and remained that way until 2012. The Parkway waited almost twenty years for its chance at restoration. When its rescuers arrived, in the form of the Maryland Film Festival, Maryland Institute College of Art, Johns Hopkins University and the Stavros Niarchos Foundation, it was ready to take on the role of the showpiece of North Avenue once again.

In May 2017, more than 100 years after its initial grand opening, the Parkway welcomed Baltimore's movie-going public once again, this time as the Stavros Niarchos Foundation Parkway. The foundation donated five million dollars to the restoration and local architects at Ziger/Snead remained true to the theatre's proud history and kept much of the aging facade and exquisite interior. Given a second chance at the role of a beacon of contemporary theatre, in Baltimore City, the former Parkway looks certain to shine.

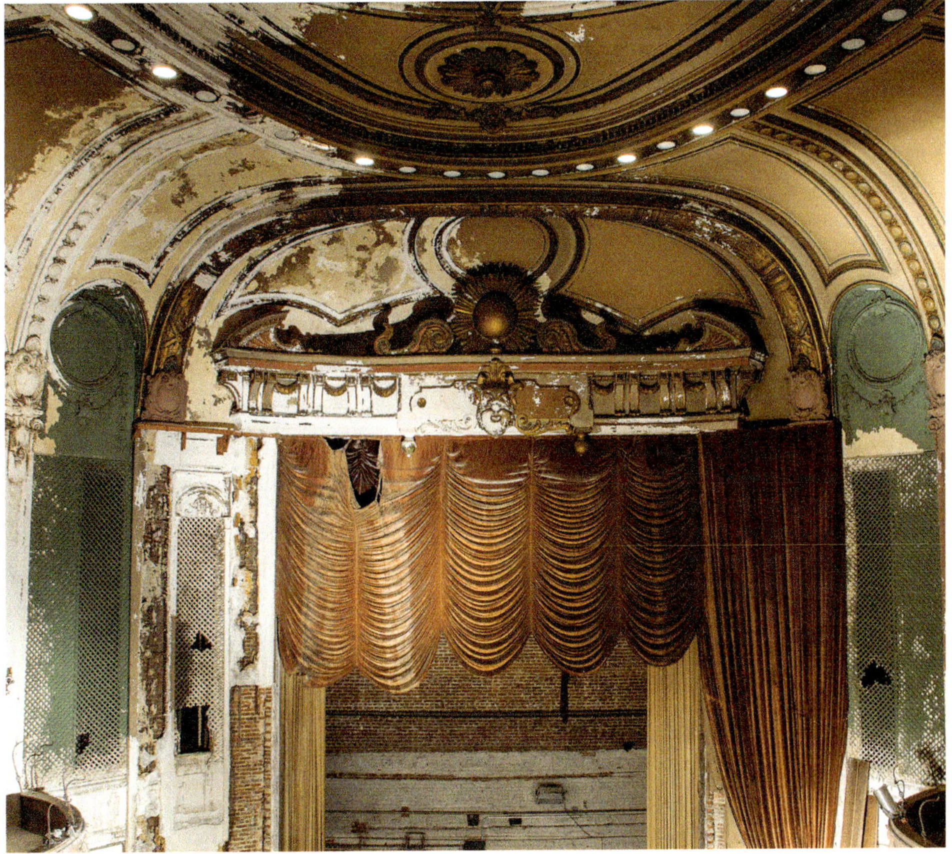

Part of the stage, showing the fading stage curtain and the intricate detail of the ceiling and walls.

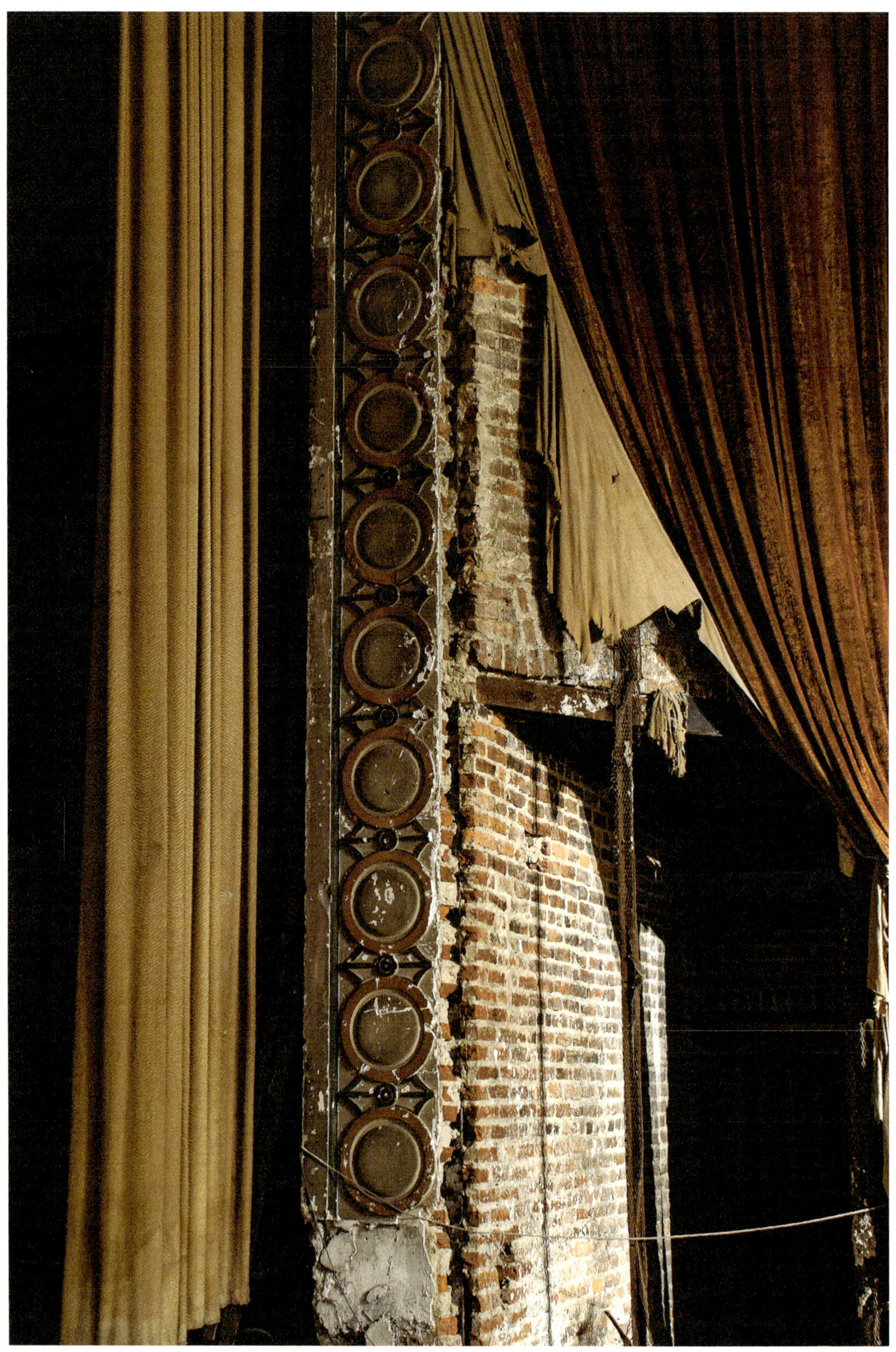

Disintegrating curtains surround the edge of the stage, exposing the original brick and plaster work.

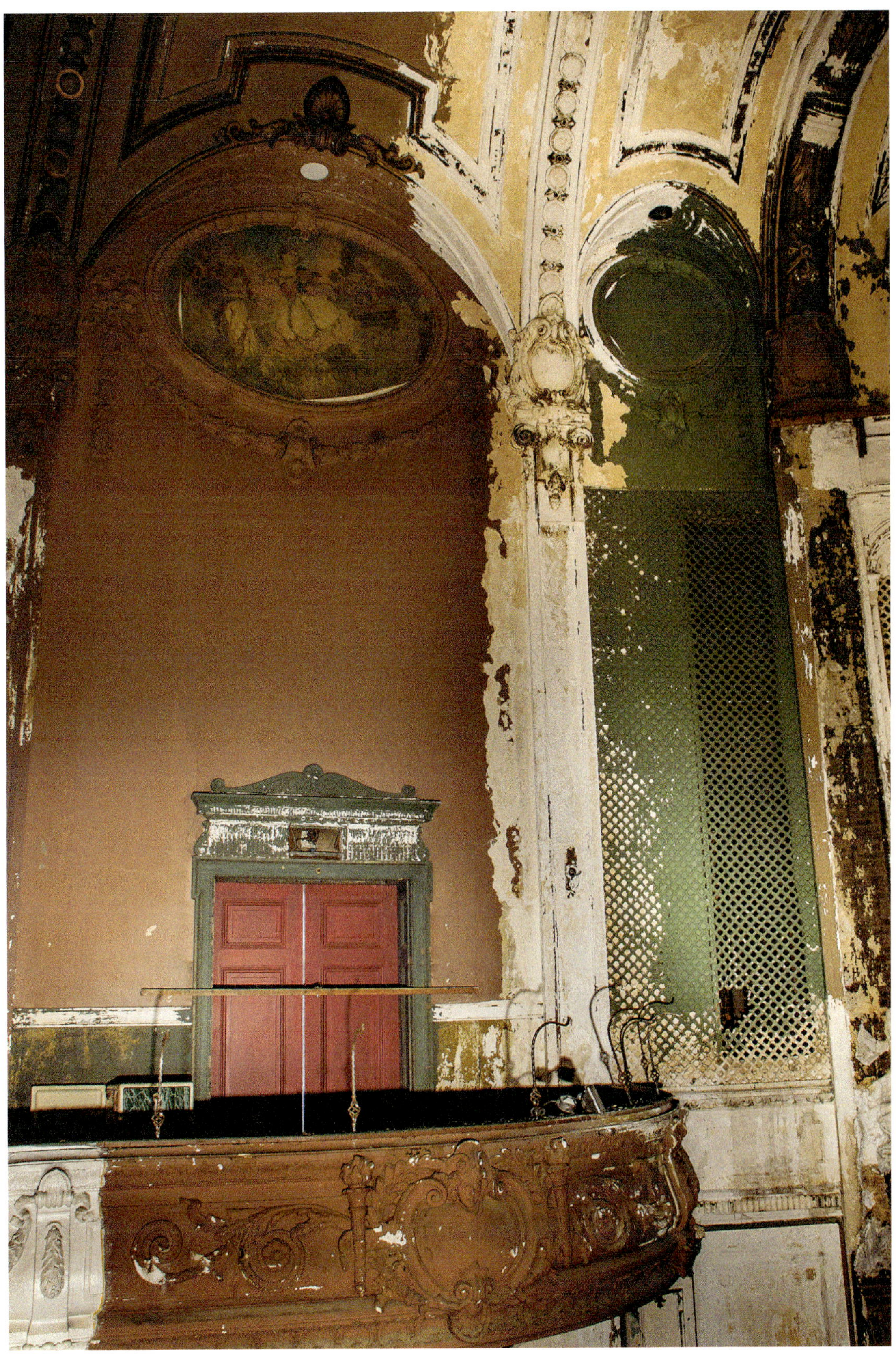

A balcony showing the elaborate ornamental plasterwork.

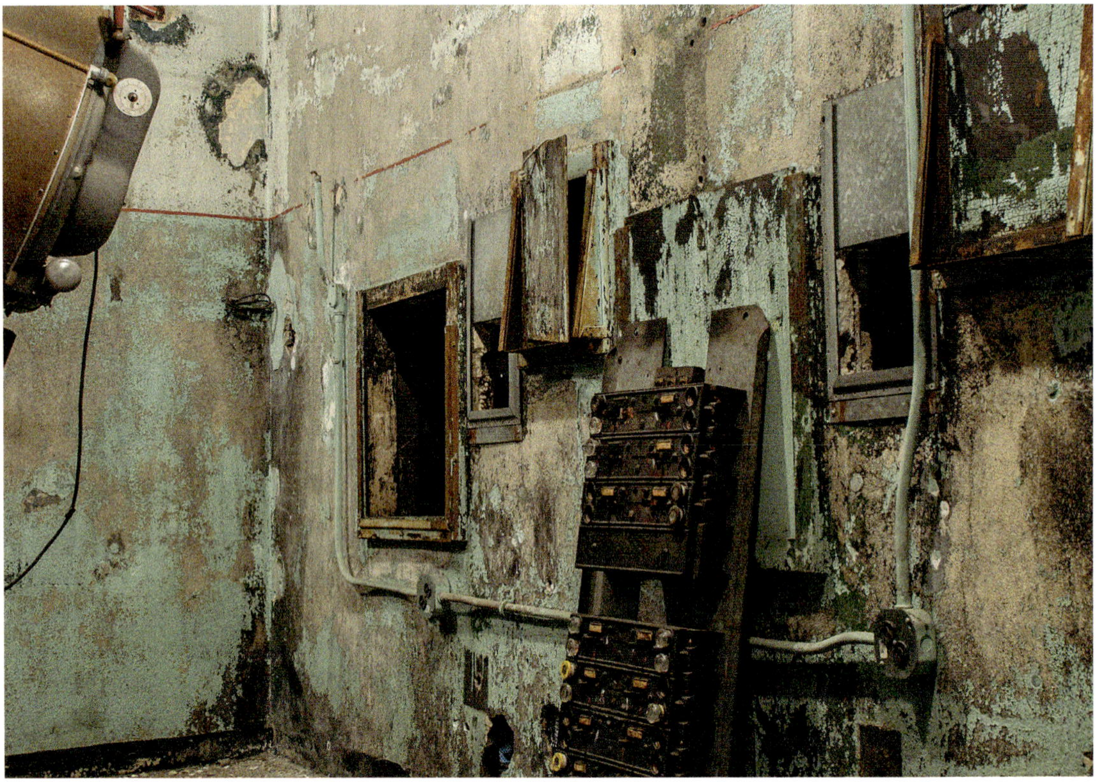

A discarded switch panel in the projection room.

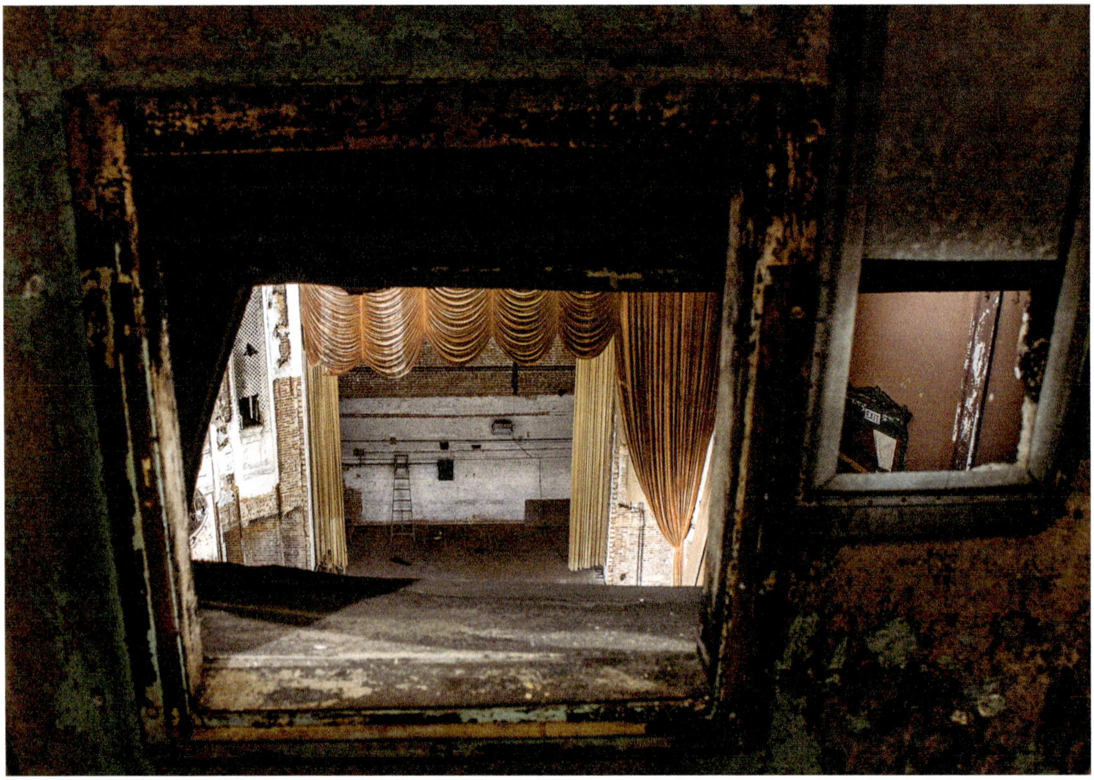

The view of the stage through the projection room portholes.

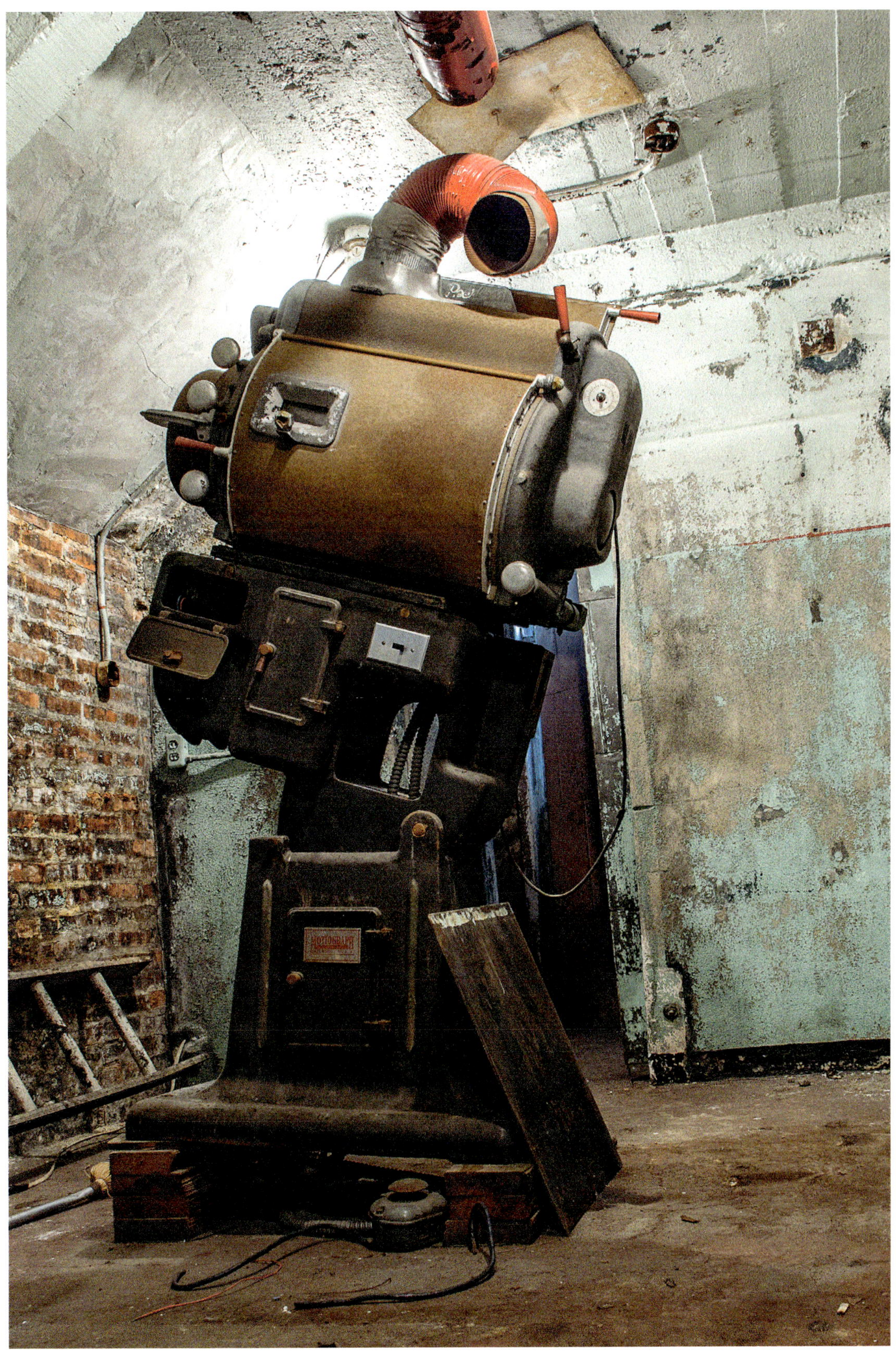

A Motiograph projector standing idle in the projection room.

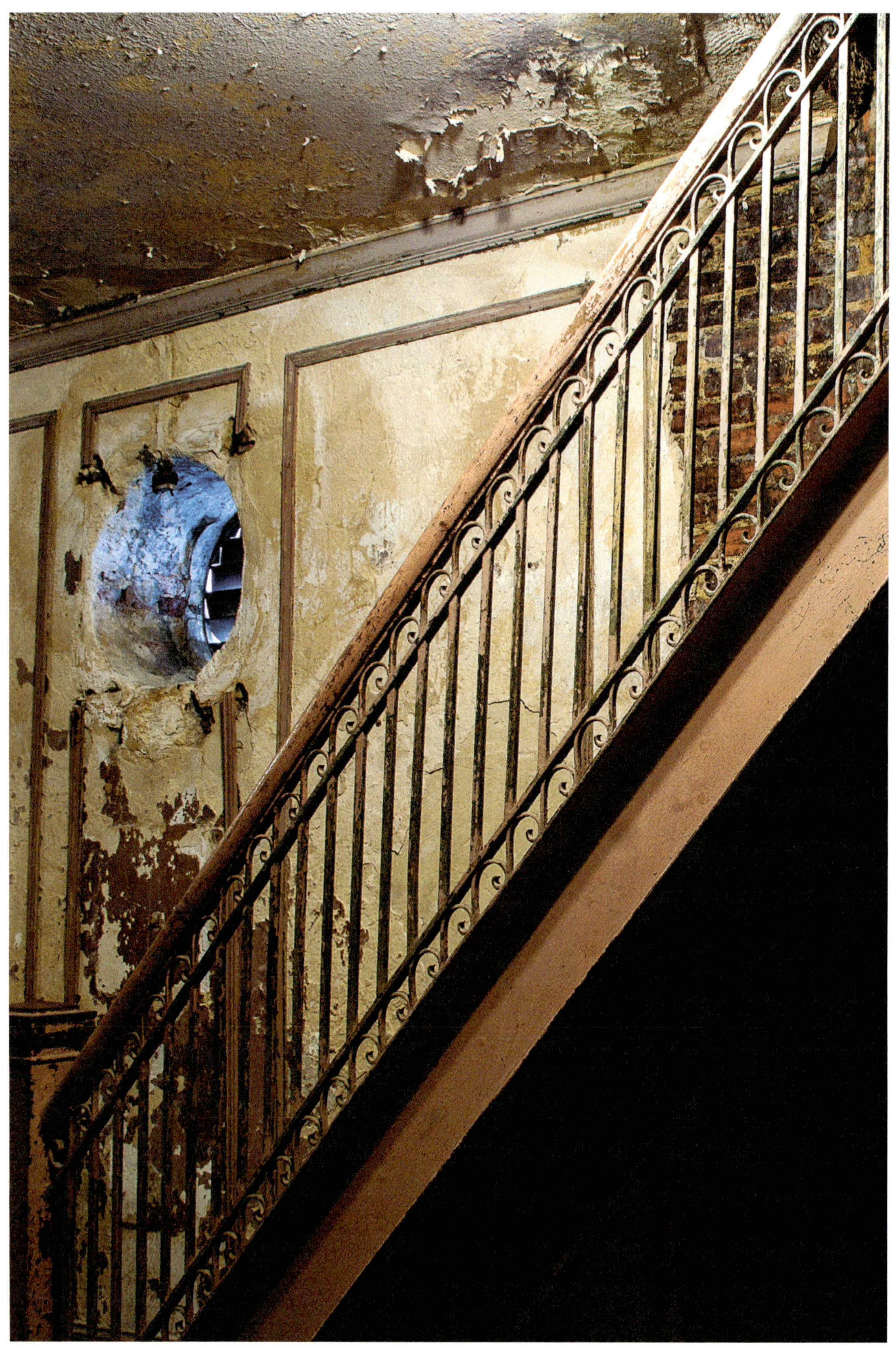

The stairway leading to the projection room.

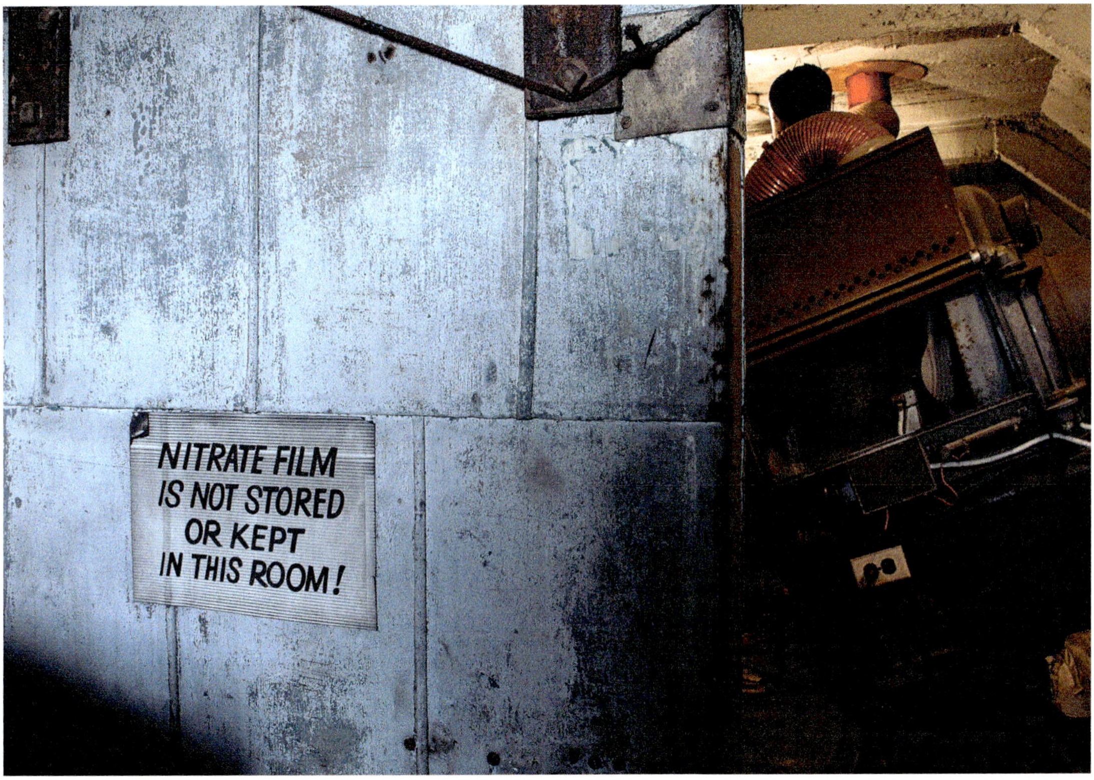

The heavy sliding steel door to the projection room.

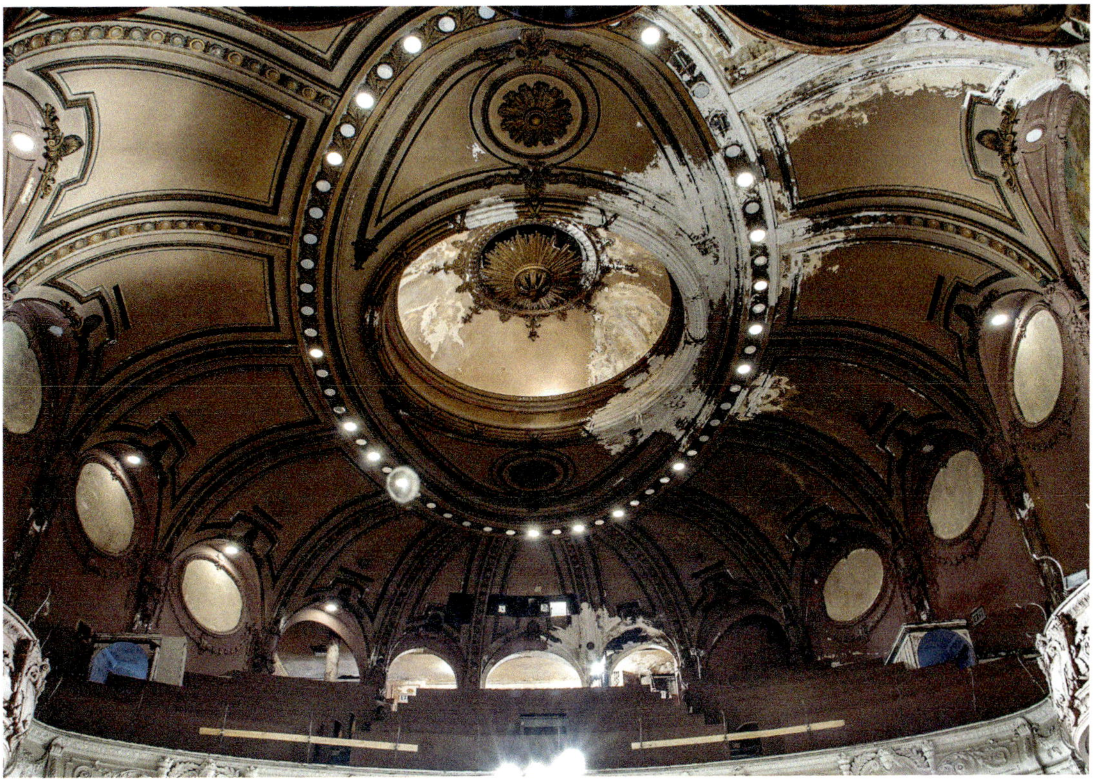

The exquisitely detailed ceiling's sunburst centerpiece has witnessed much of motion picture history.

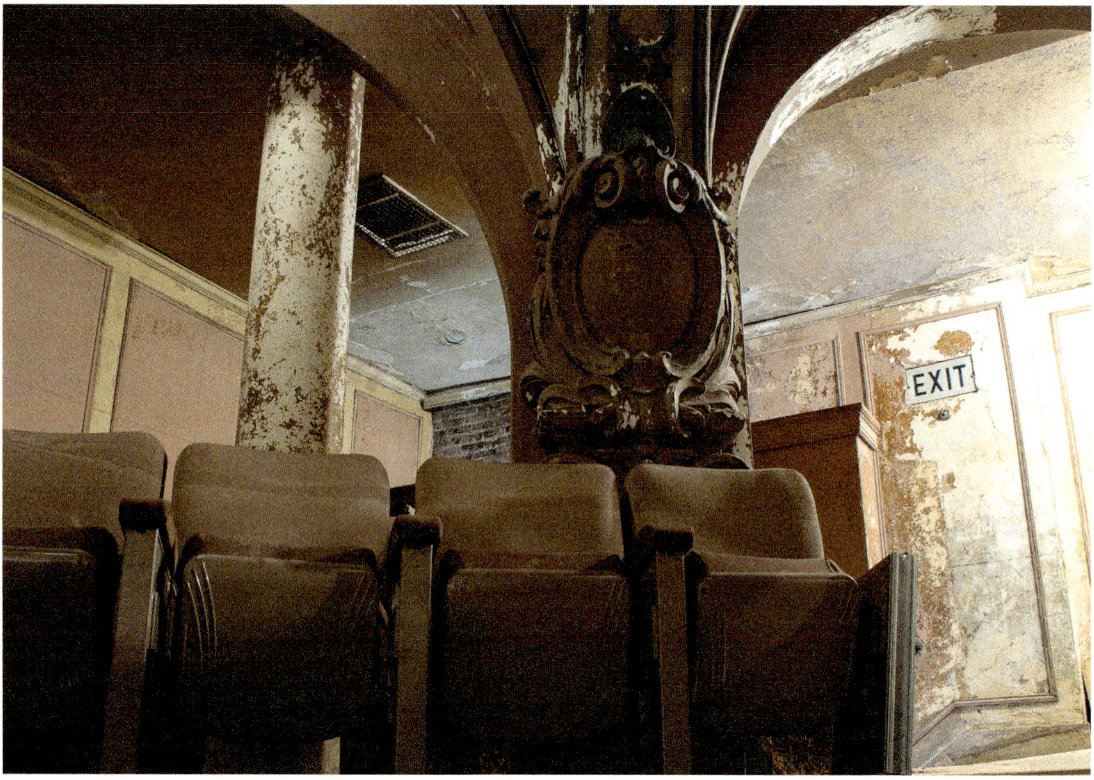

Upper level seating gathering dust.

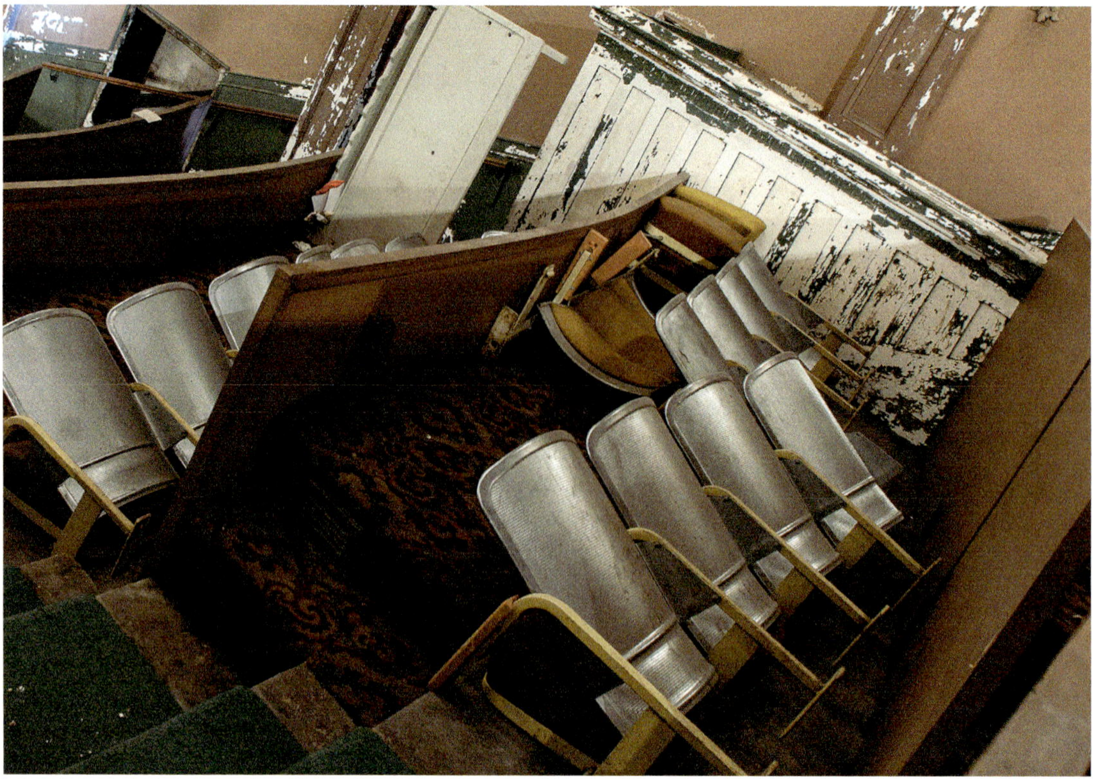

Row after row of overturned seating, waiting to be replaced, filled the theatre during renovation.

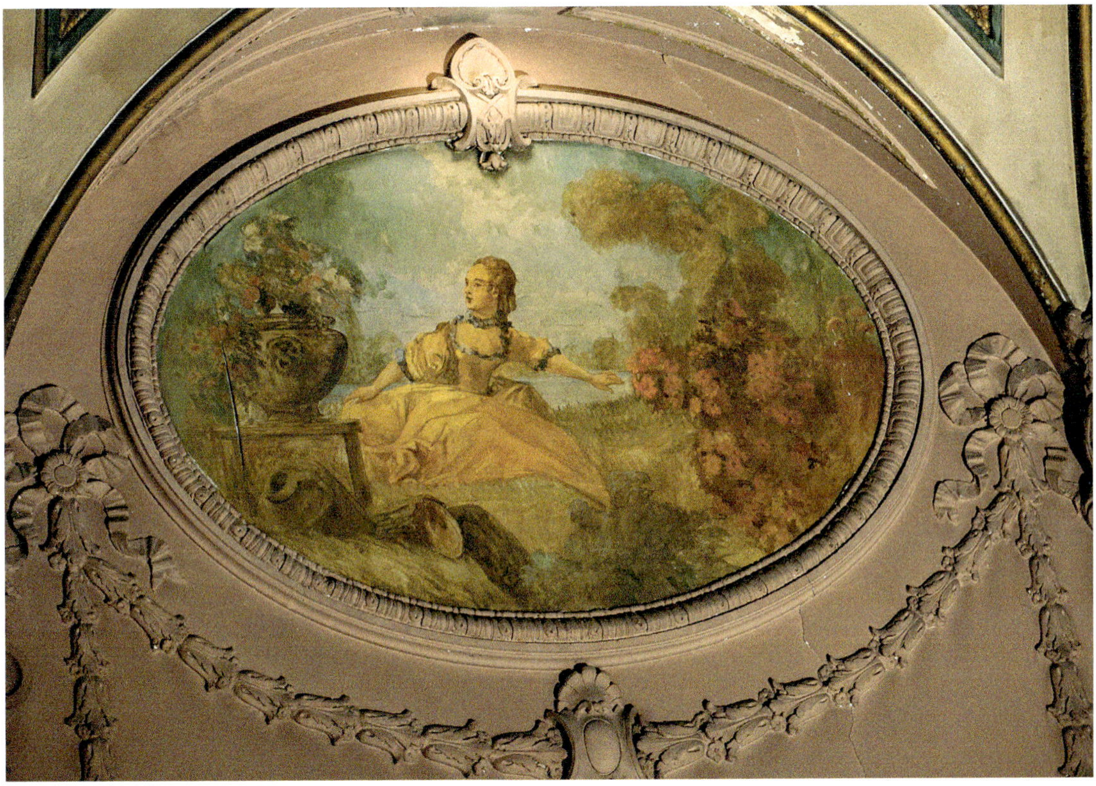

Ornate plasterwork acts as a frame around a Rococo style painting.

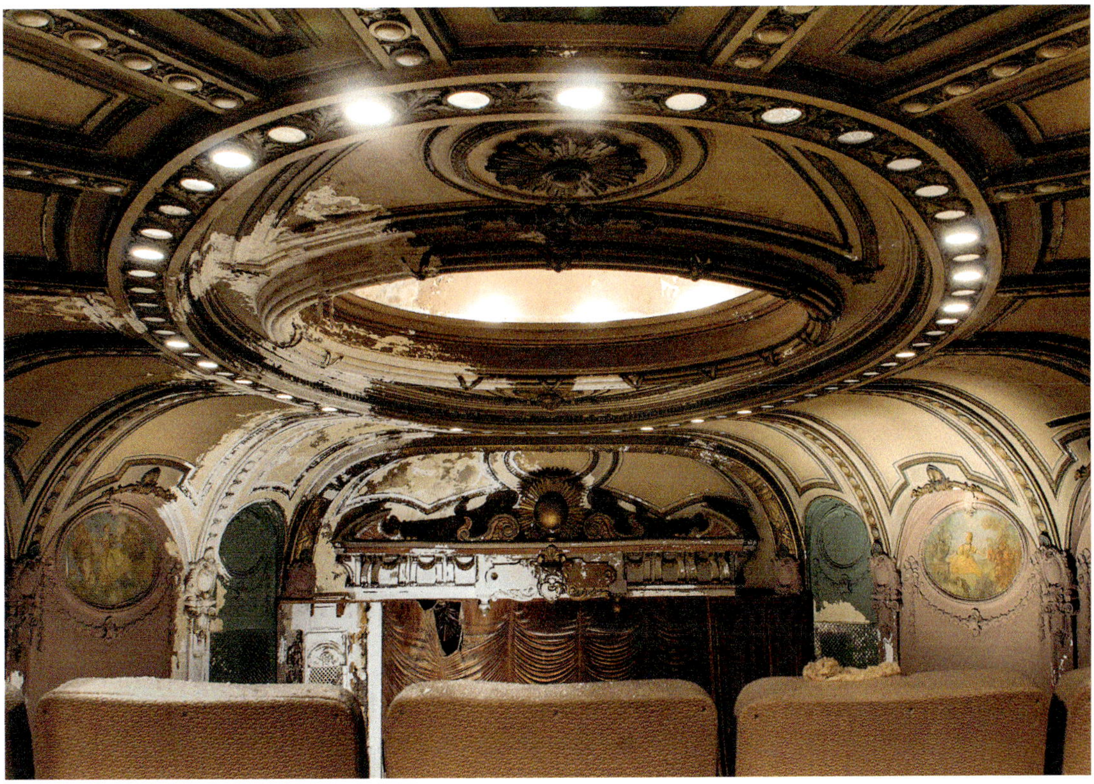

Patrons who sat in the upper balcony had a panoramic view of the magical lighting feature.

FOREST HAVEN ASYLUM, LAUREL

Forest Haven, a desolate 250-acre property with over twenty buildings in shocking stages of decay, resembles a ghost town more than a former institution for the developmentally disabled citizens of Washington, D.C. A silent reminder of their struggle, engraved on a plaque outside the administration building, reads: "Yet while I live, let me not live in vain."

Forest Haven's history, while not hidden, is not readily accessible either. According to descriptions from the time, the U.S. government built the facility in 1925 to banish from society, individuals categorized as "idiots." The term, frightening in its ignorance, pales when compared to the later, well-documented, appalling conditions the residents endured. The facility underwent a long slow decline from the beginning of the Great Depression until a federal lawsuit, in 1991, finally closed Forest Haven forever.

Today, as in the case of other abandoned hospitals and asylums, myths surrounding Forest Haven are plentiful, particularly among young explorers. A popular rumor claims Forest Haven is the site of an abandoned village deserted by government agents when an experiment backfired, killing the entire town. It is easy to see how such a rumor exists—it takes little to imagine Forest Haven this way. The dilapidated buildings—unhinged doors flung open, windows obliterated, water sloshing its way down impassable stairwells—are a great setting for a B-grade horror movie. Unfortunately, inside the buildings, evidence of the real-life horror remains intact, dispelling any truth in the abandoned town rumor.

Forest Haven may keep its secrets well, yet today any intruder can easily see former residents' medical records—stamped "confidential," strewn about the hallways. Medical equipment, not just small-scale blood pressure pumps and syringes, but sophisticated dental chairs, x-ray machines and laboratory testing materials fill room after room as though they are still waiting for the next patient to arrive.

Anne Arundel county residents have argued for the bulldozing of the property since its closure—but that was twenty-seven years ago. Forest Haven looks certain to remain a shameful wasteland, hiding the unmarked graves of the brave souls who endured inside its walls.

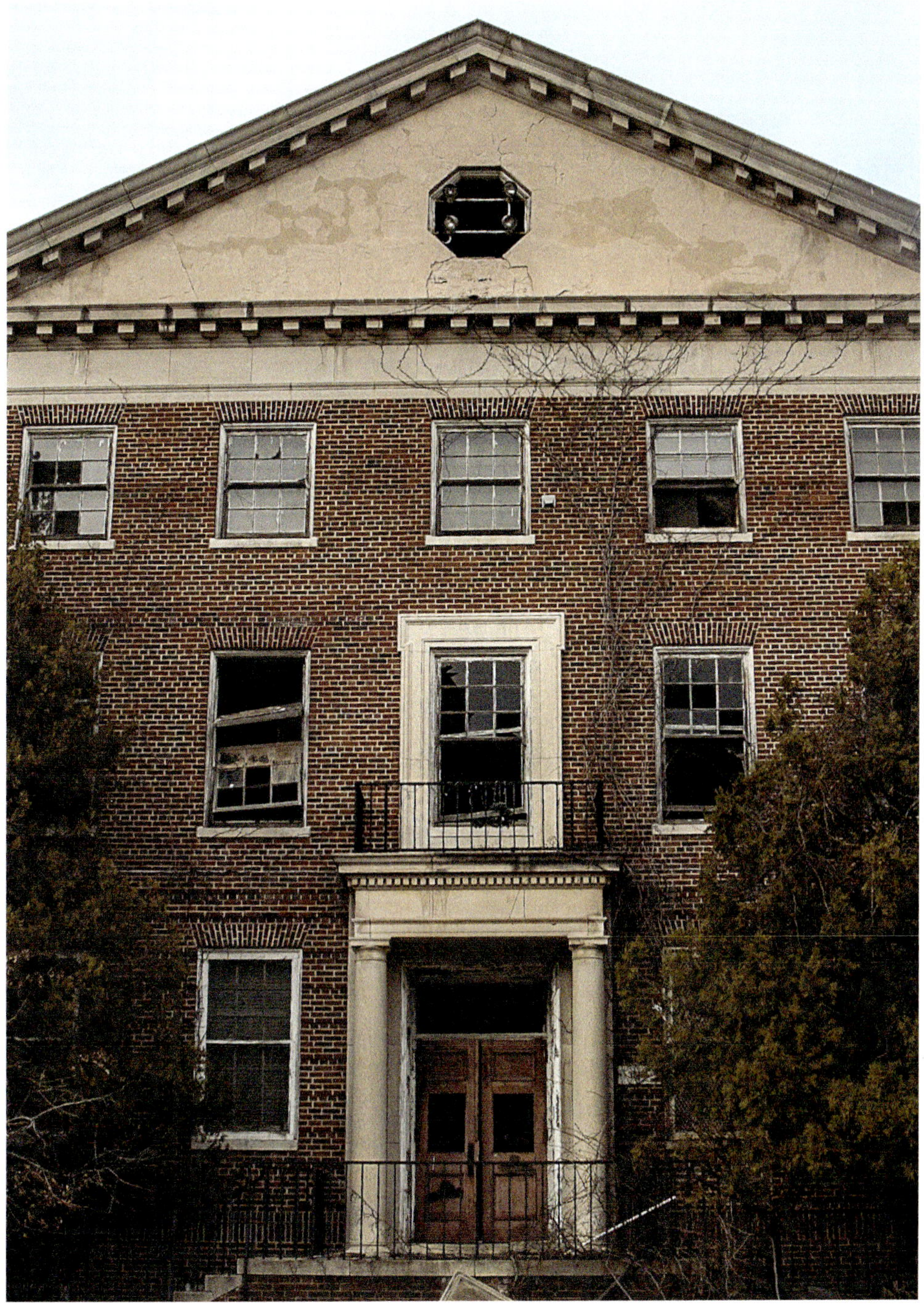

The hauntingly decrepit entrance to Forest Haven's main administration building.

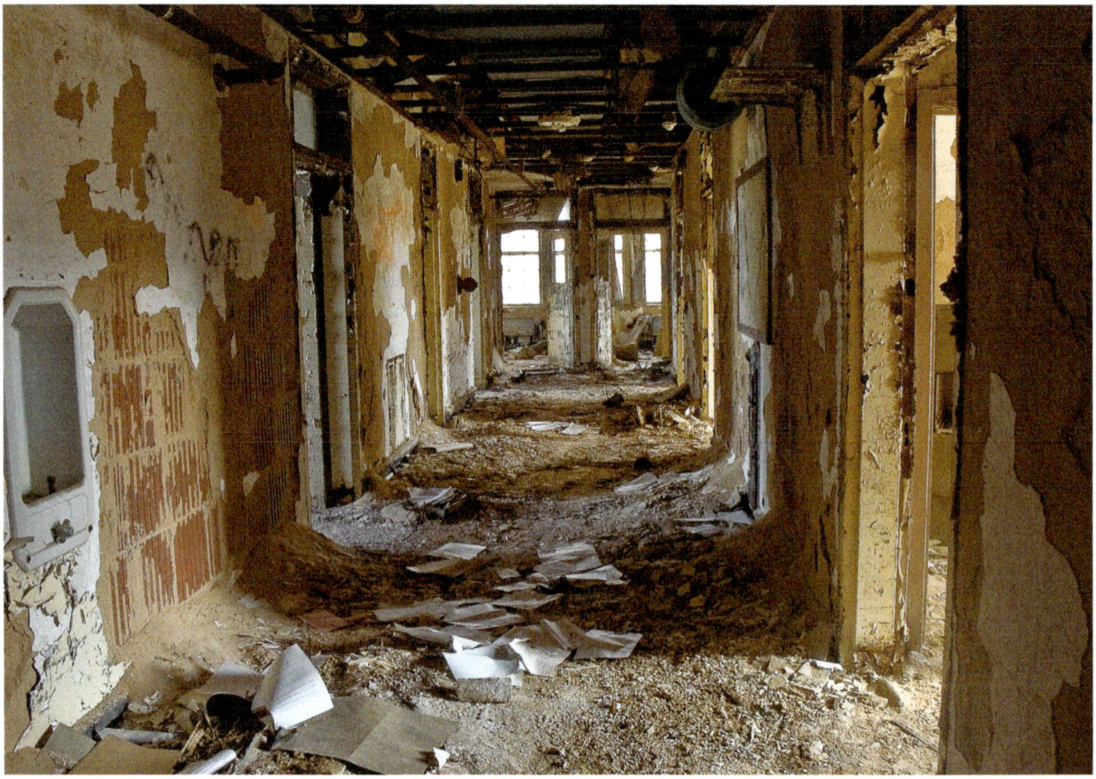

Floors thick with debris and paperwork fill every hallway.

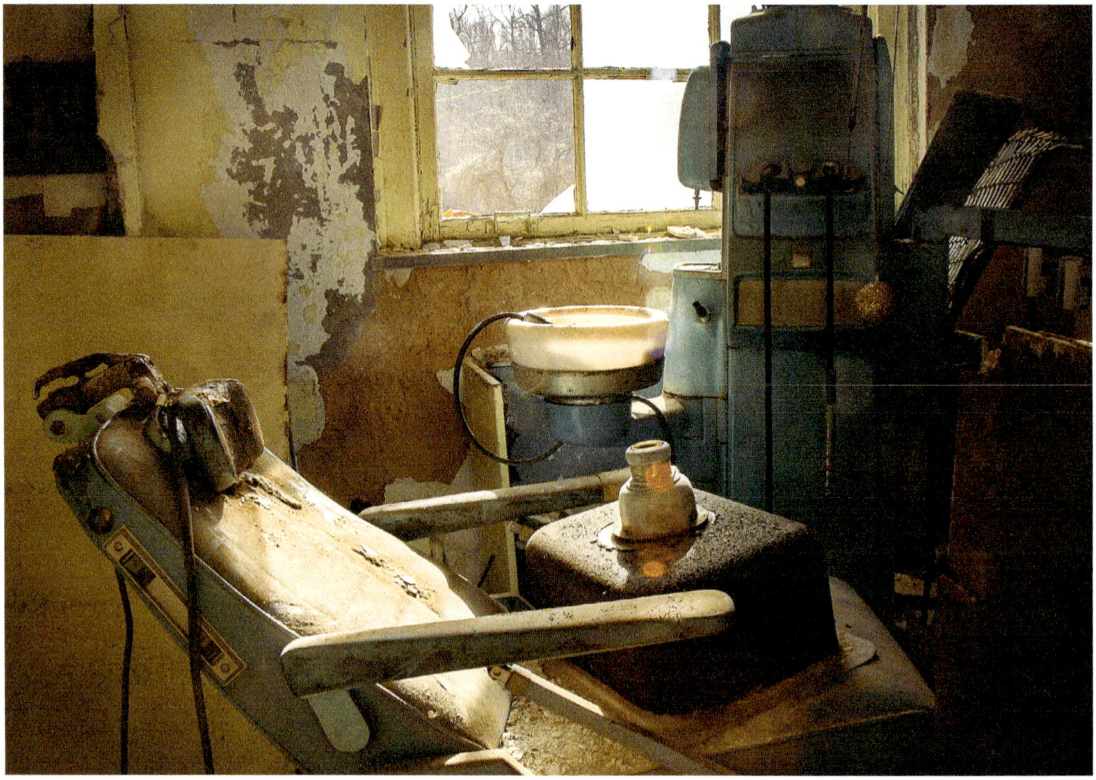

A rotting dental chair bathed in sunlight.

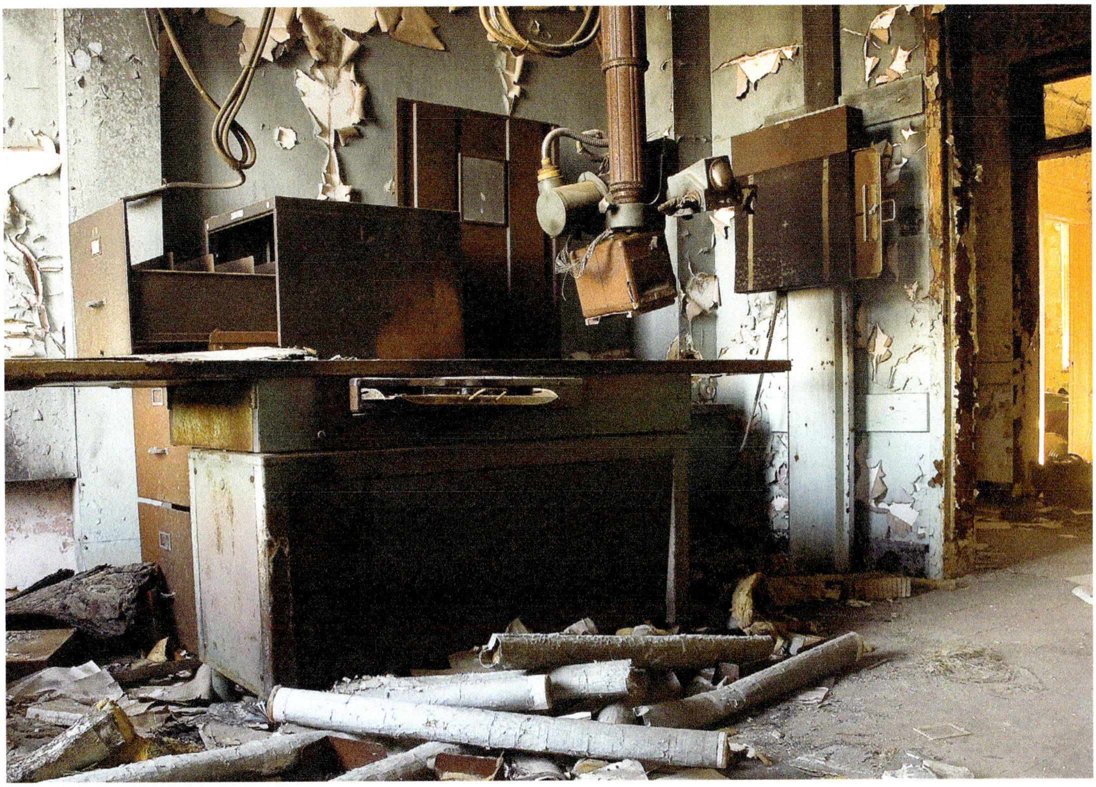

A rusting x-ray machine occupies a room next to a laboratory.

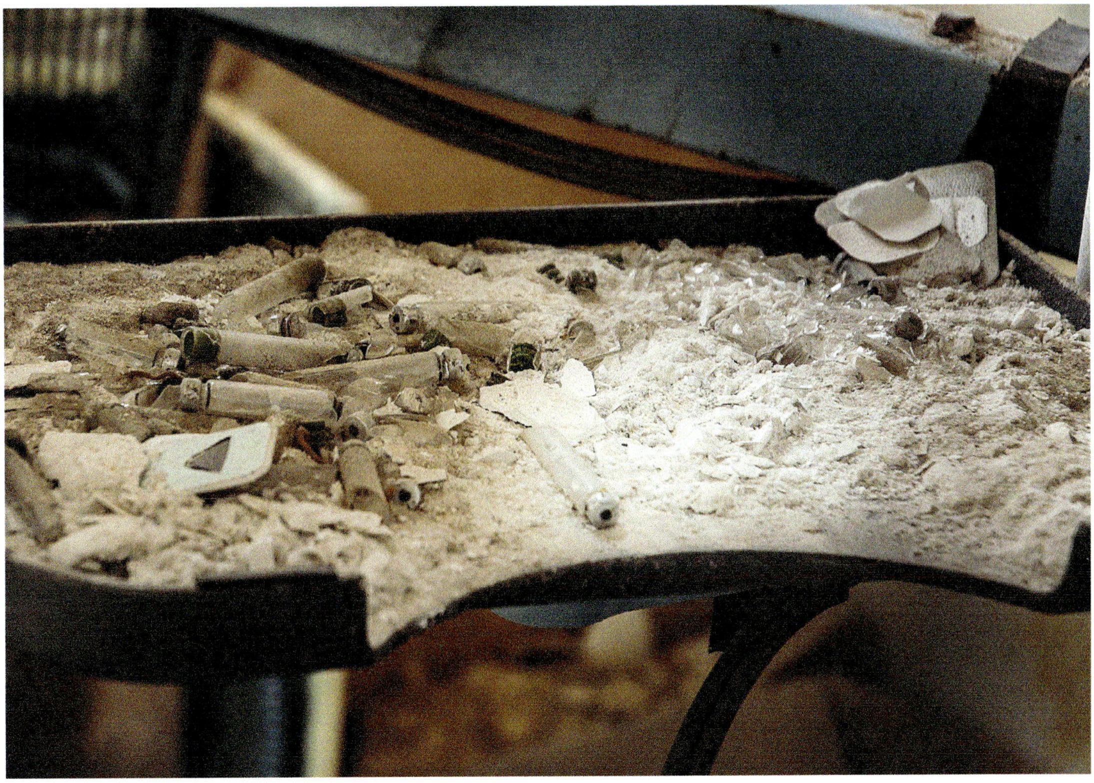

Discarded vials on a bed of ceiling plaster.

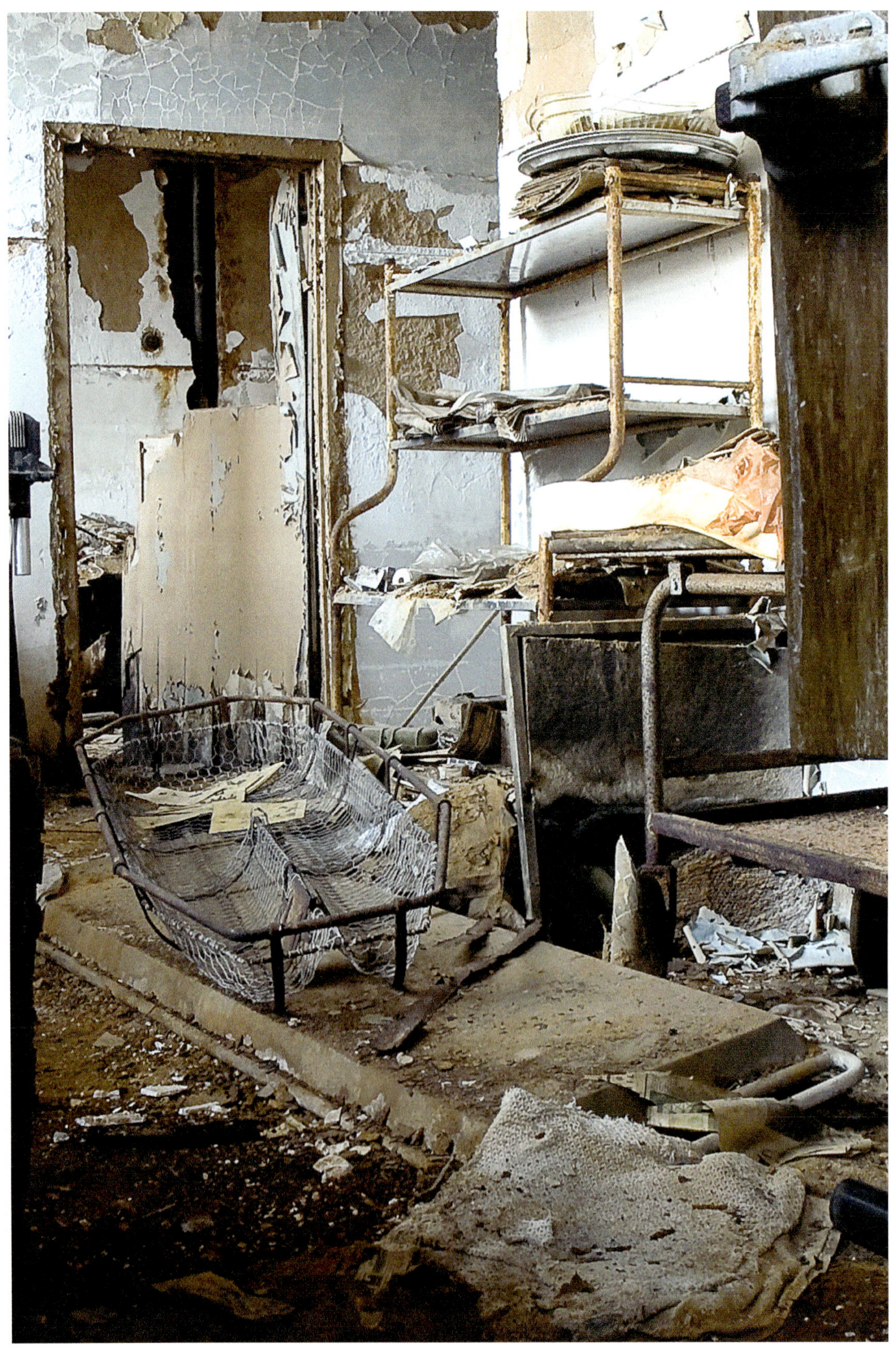

Forest Haven's morgue with a discarded stretcher.

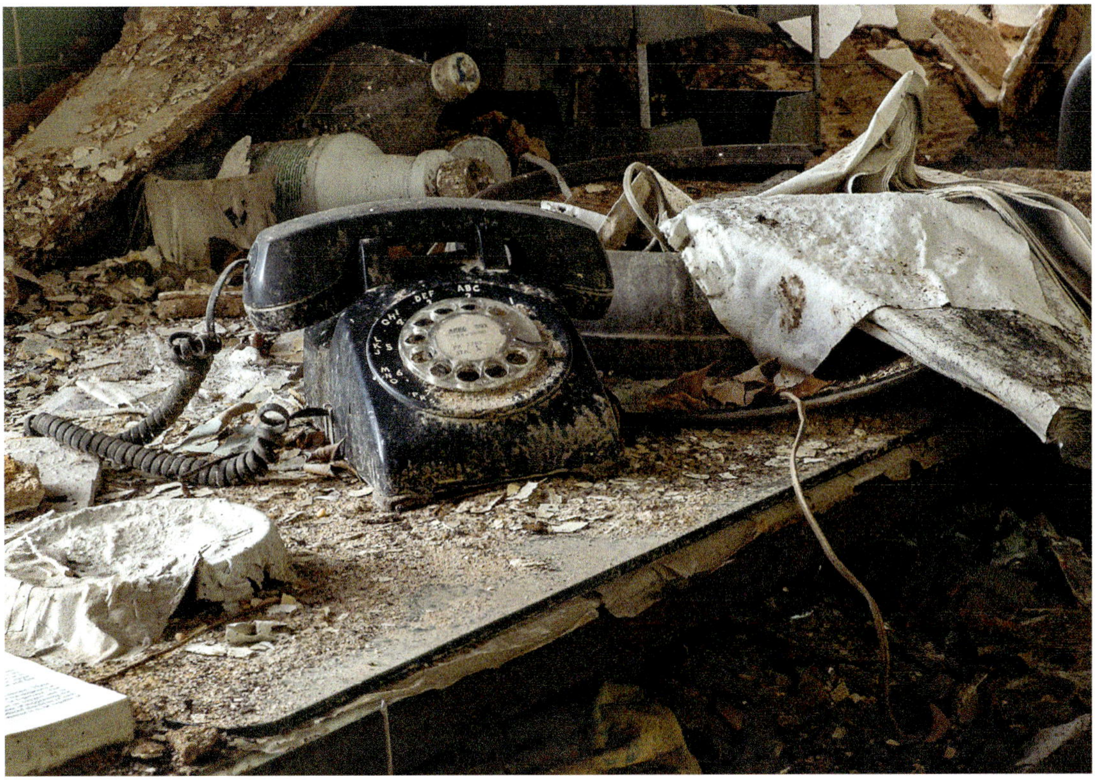

An old telephone surrounded by debris in a long-abandoned office.

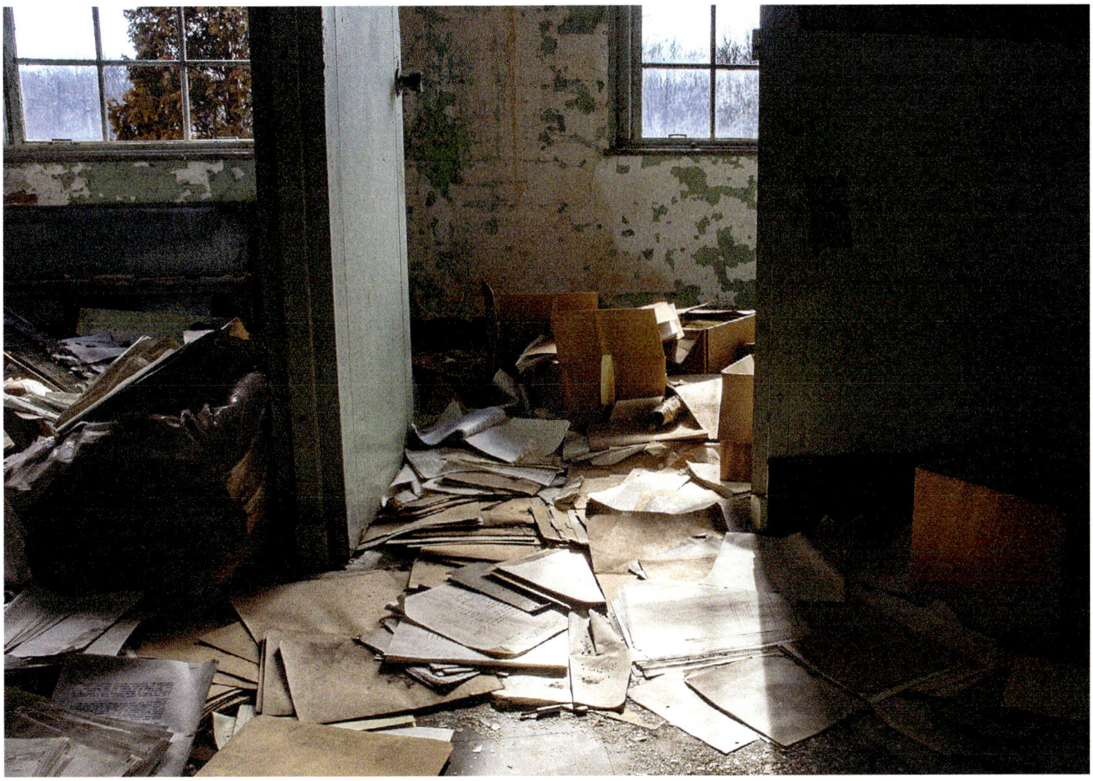

Former patients' medical records are strewn throughout the rooms and hallways of the main building.

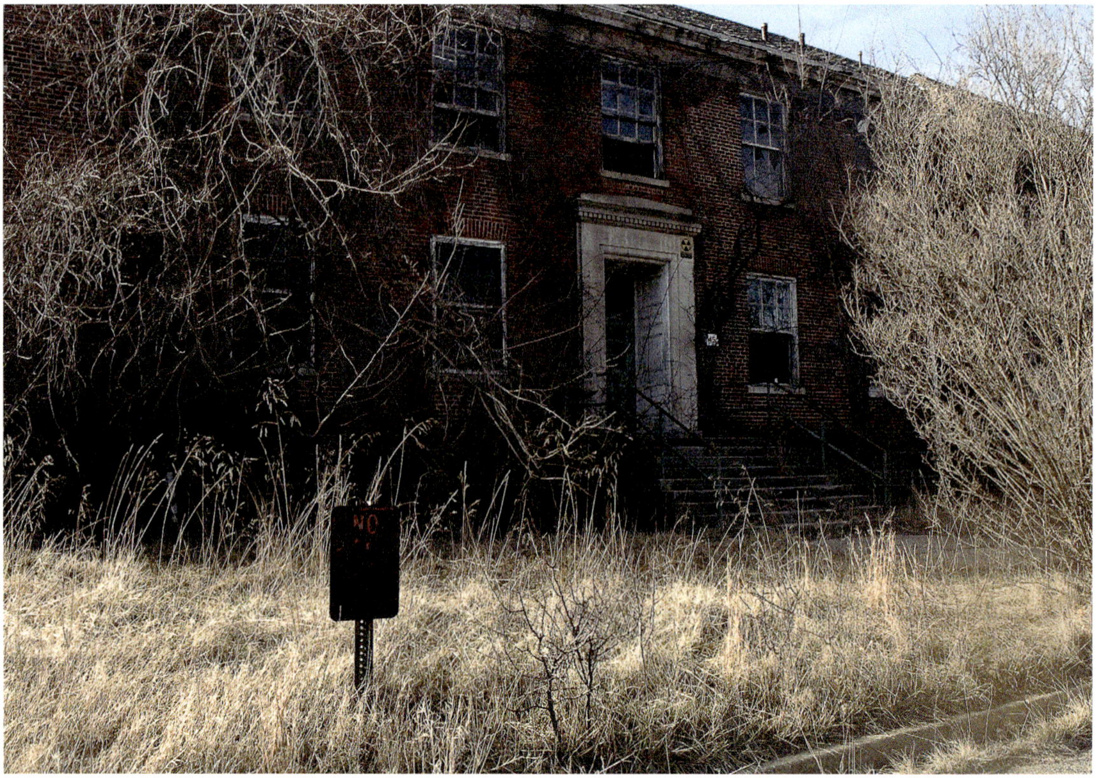

The overgrown exterior of a residence "cottage."

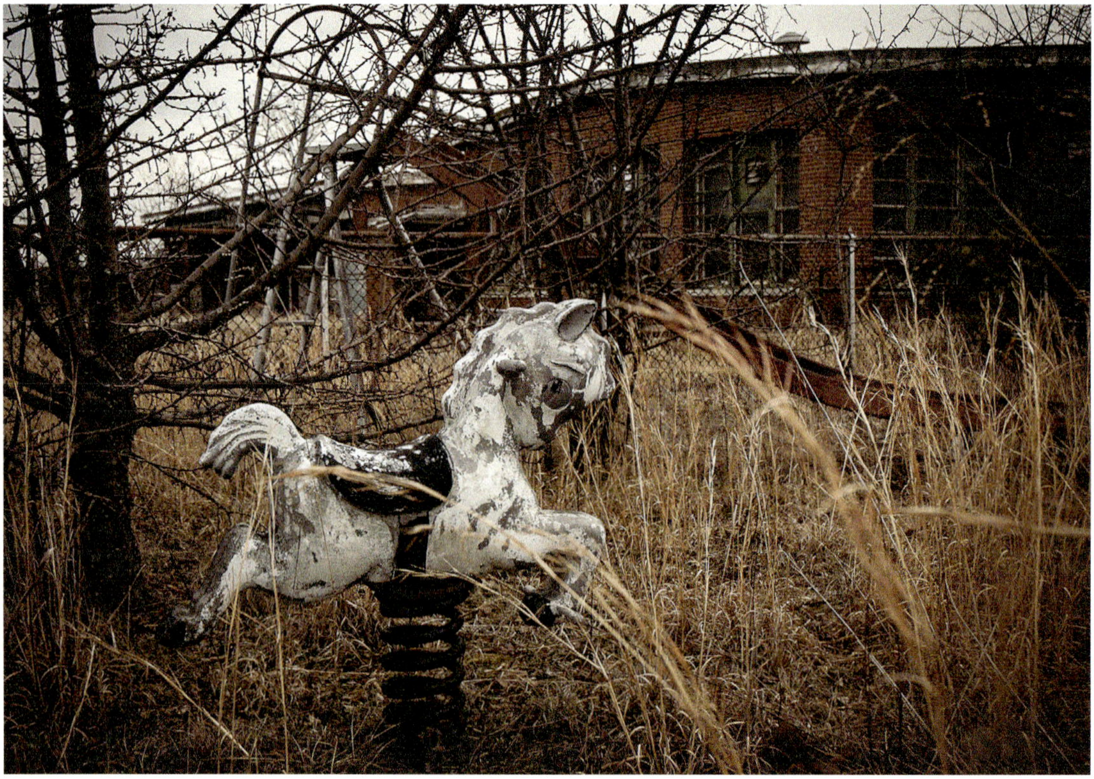

A playground in disrepair is a stark reminder of the children who spent their lives inside the grounds of the asylum.

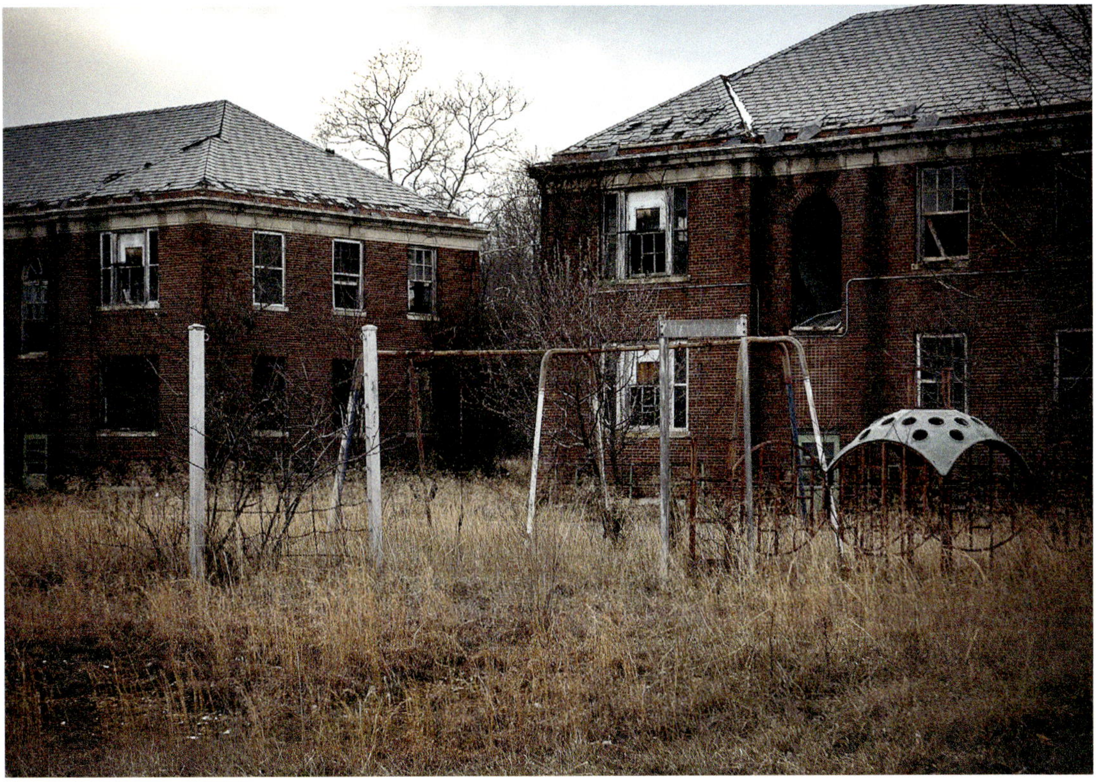

Neighboring residence cottages and their dilapidated playground equipment.

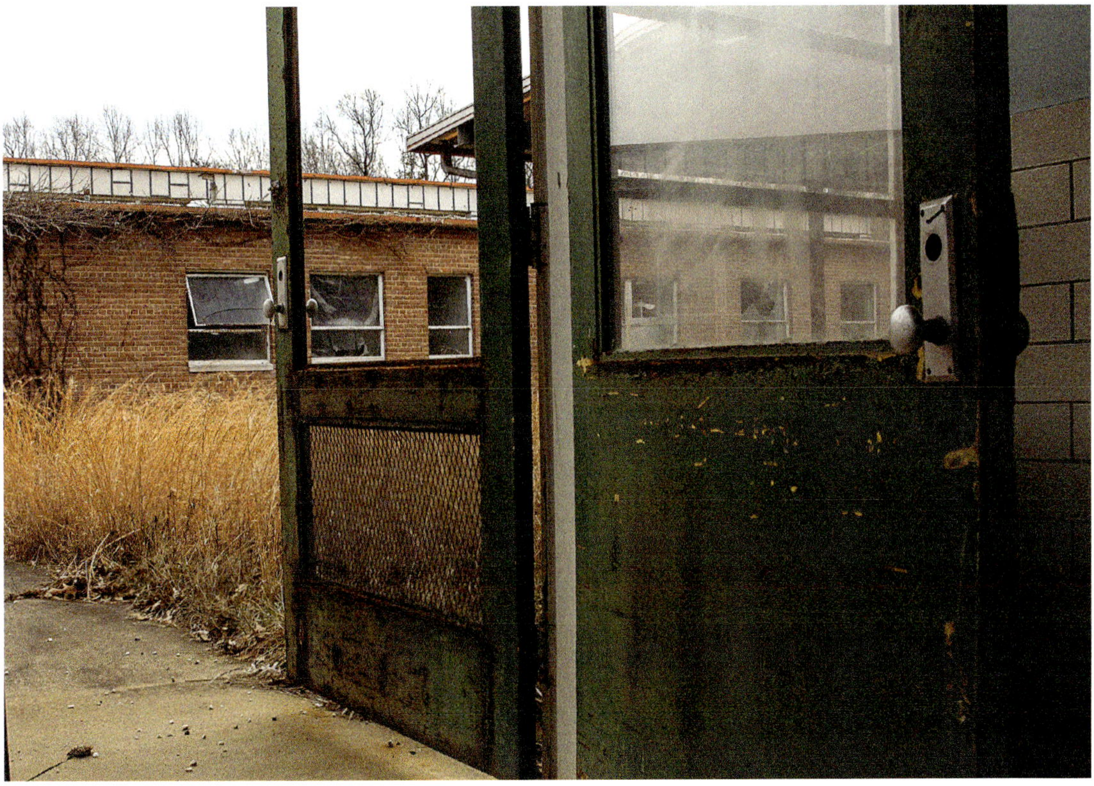

The classroom area of the grounds.

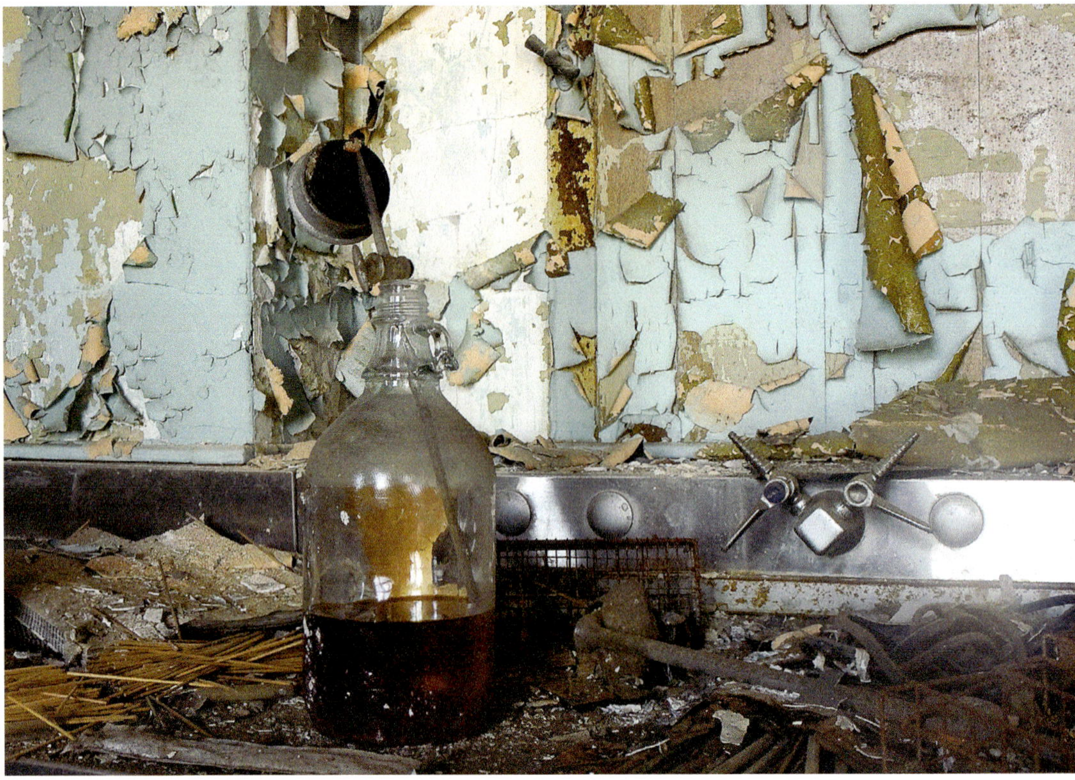

Unknown chemicals stagnate in large glass bottle.

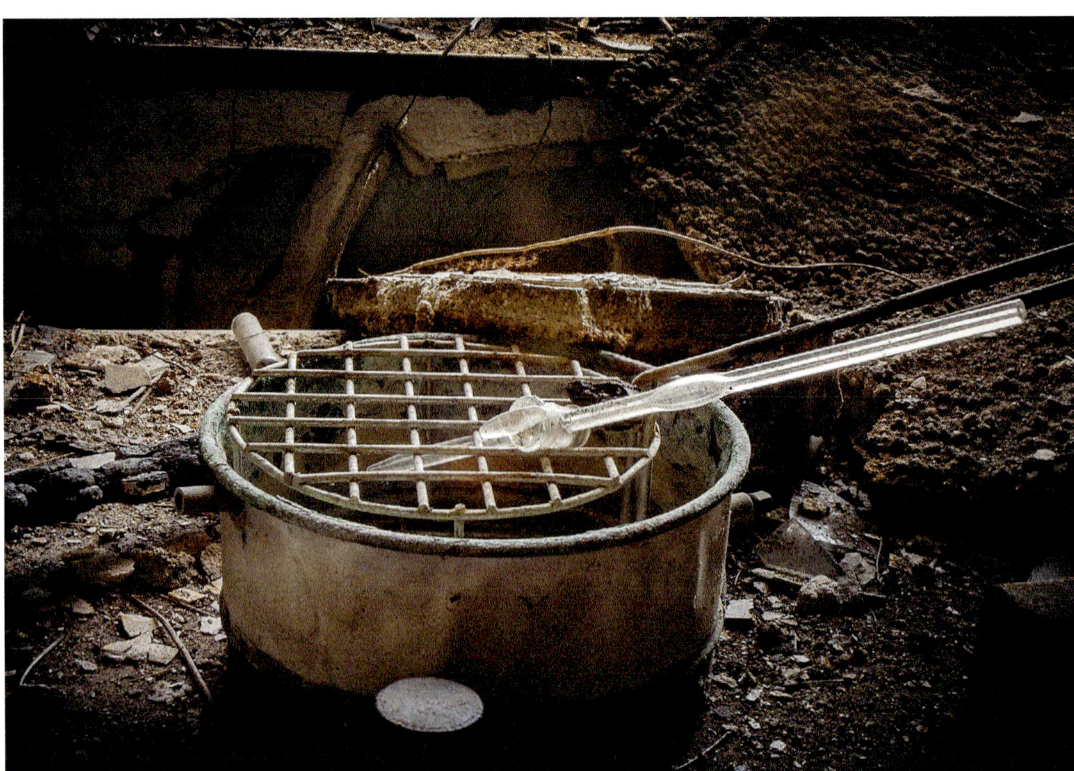

A glass pipette, or chemical dropper, and burner.

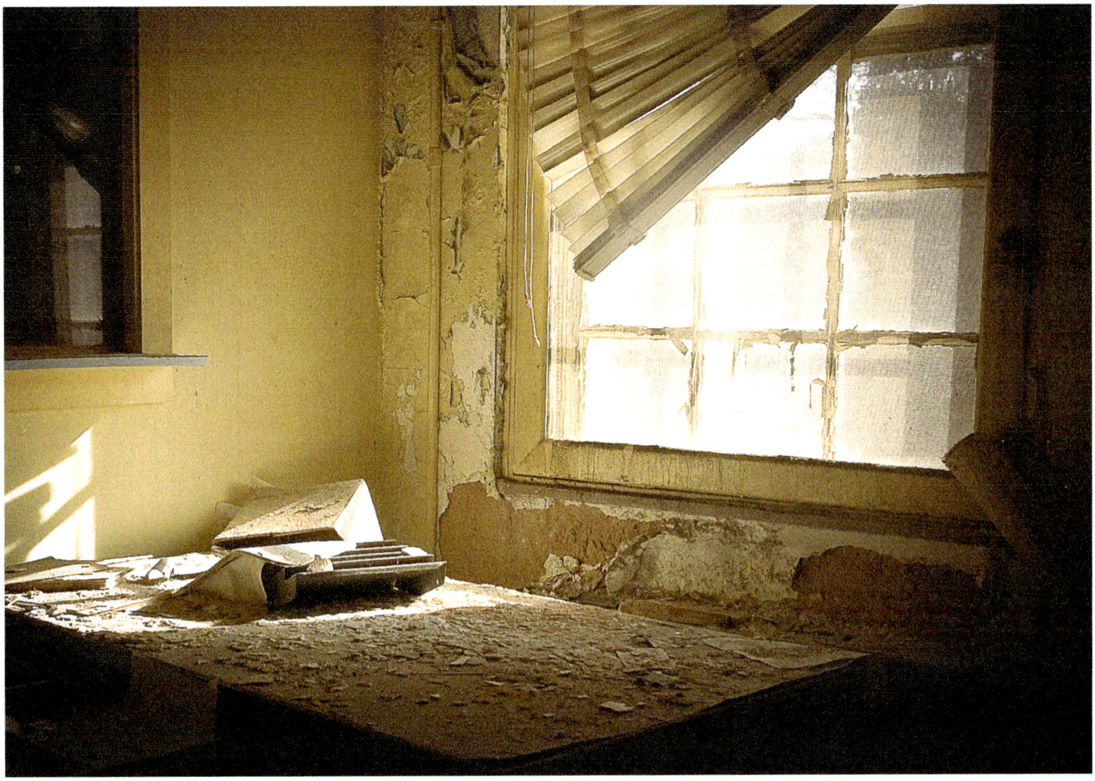

A discarded typewriter, saturated by sunlight, in an office in the main administration building.

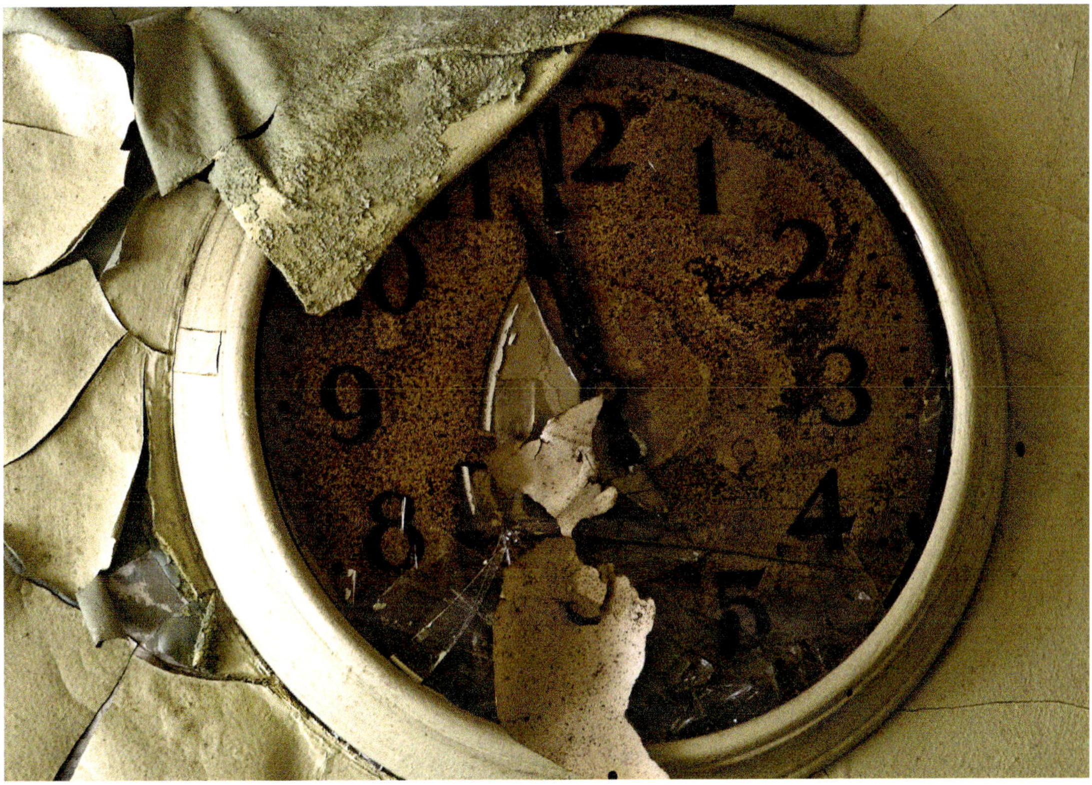

Peeling paint descends upon a shattered wall clock.

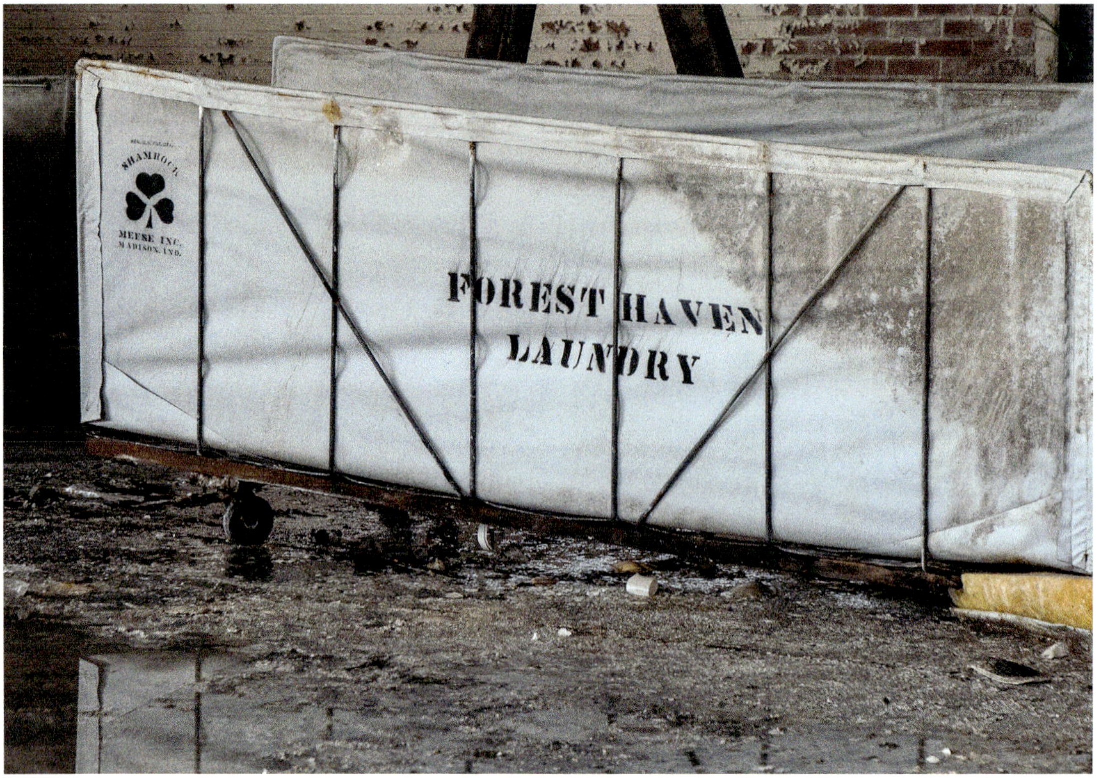

A large laundry cart discarded in the flooded laundry building.

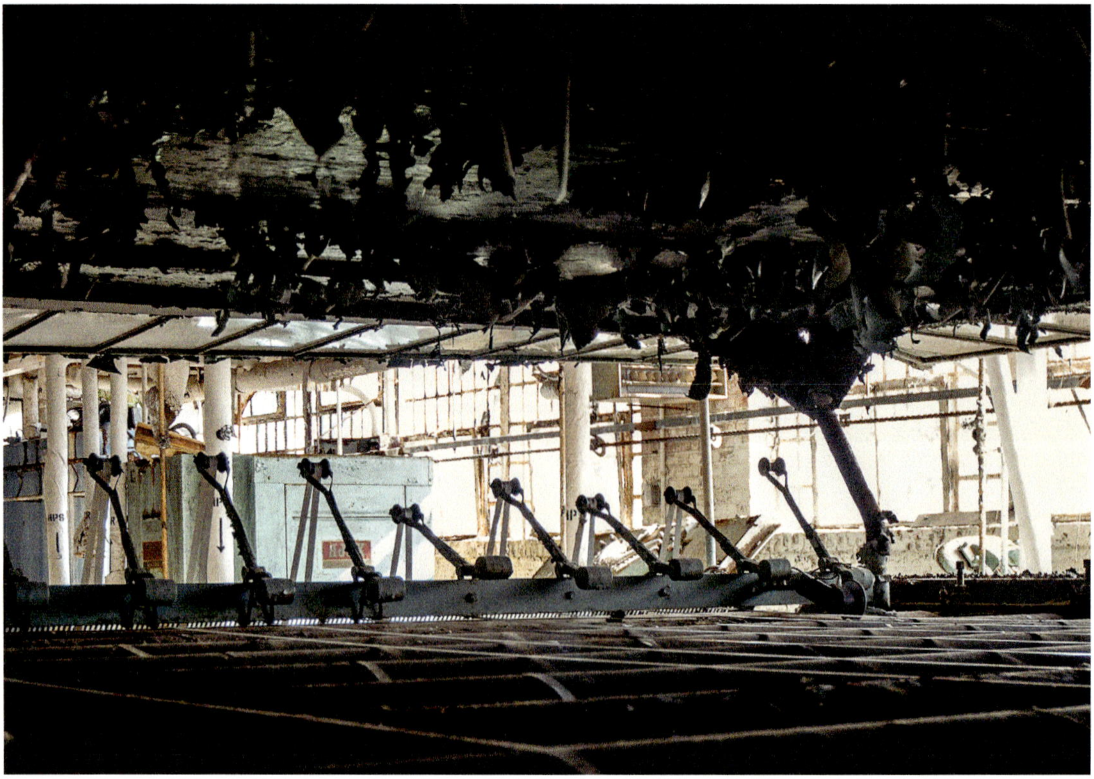

Thick layers of paint hang ominously over a long disused ironing machine.

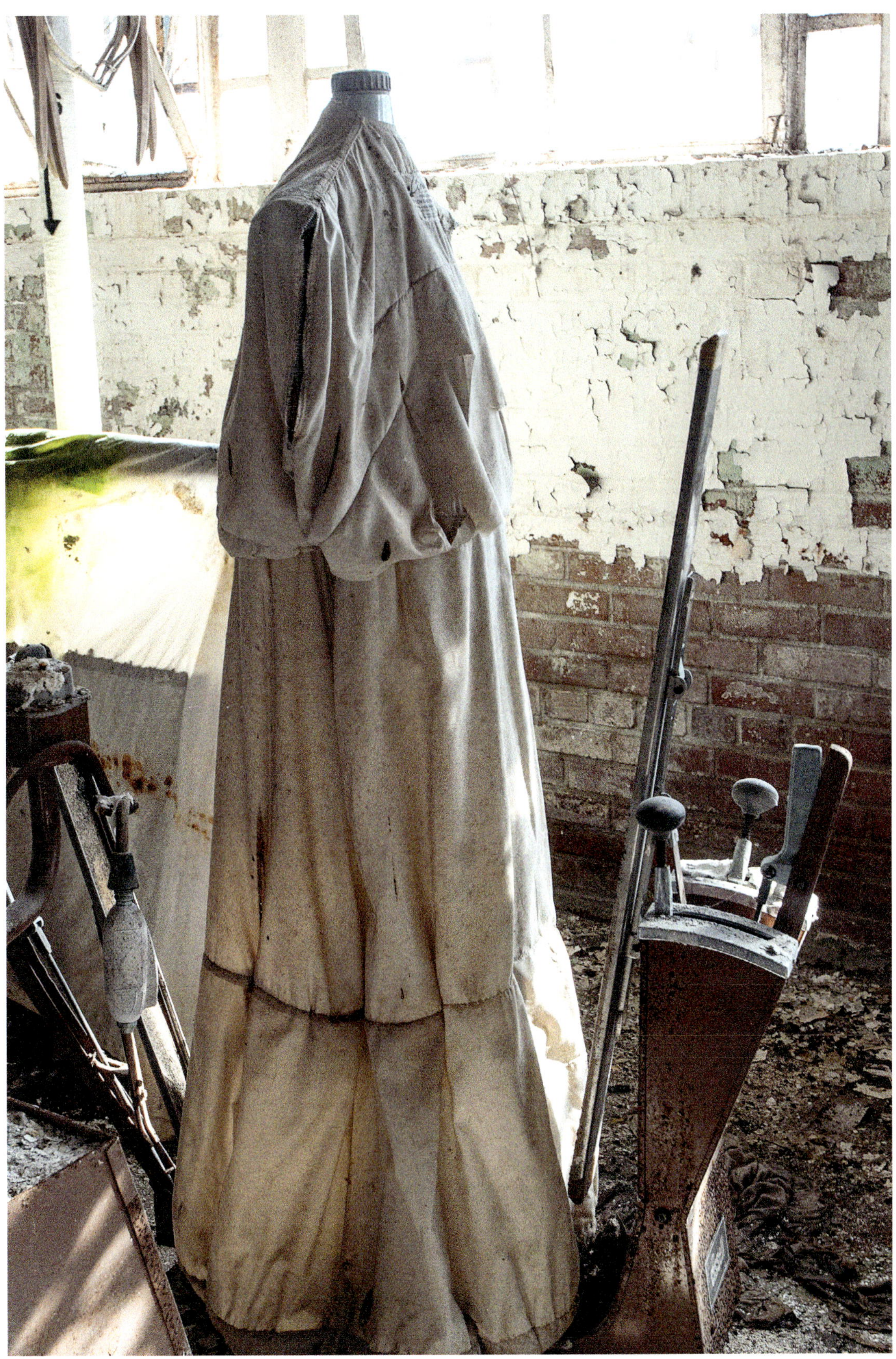

An automatic steam machine with clothing still intact.

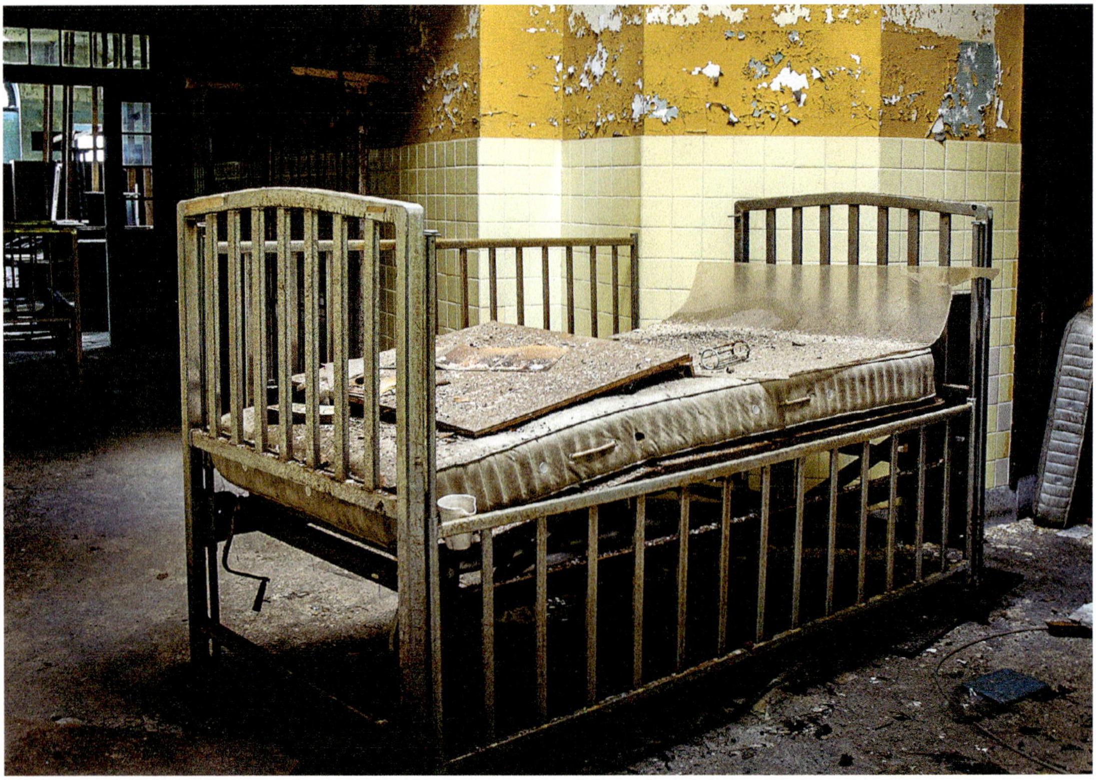

A hospital bed in a fire ravaged area.

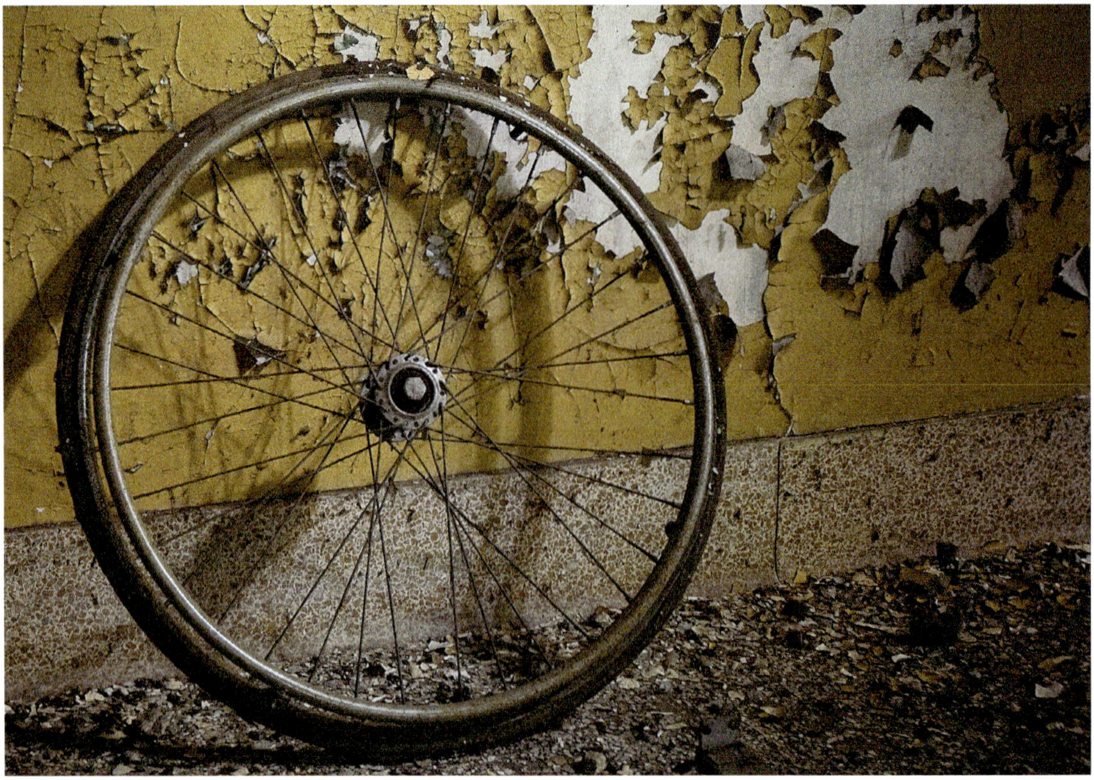

A wheel is all that remains of a resident's bicycle.

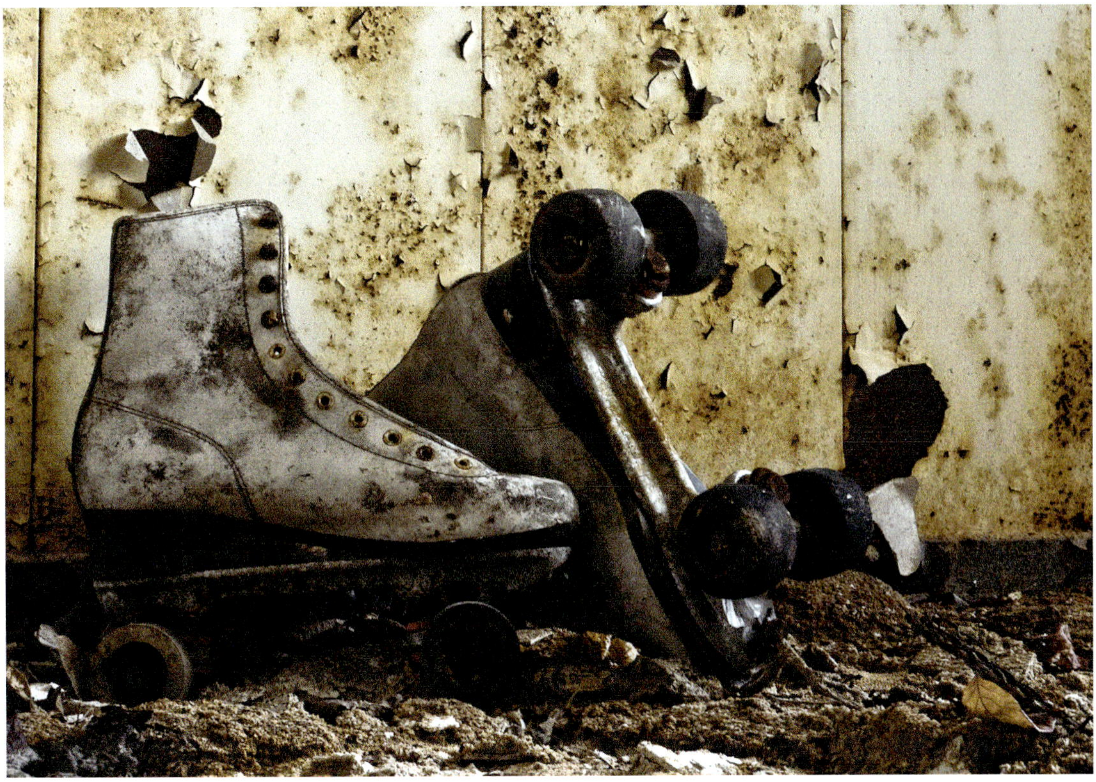

Personal items, like these roller skates, suggest patients enjoyed popular pastimes.

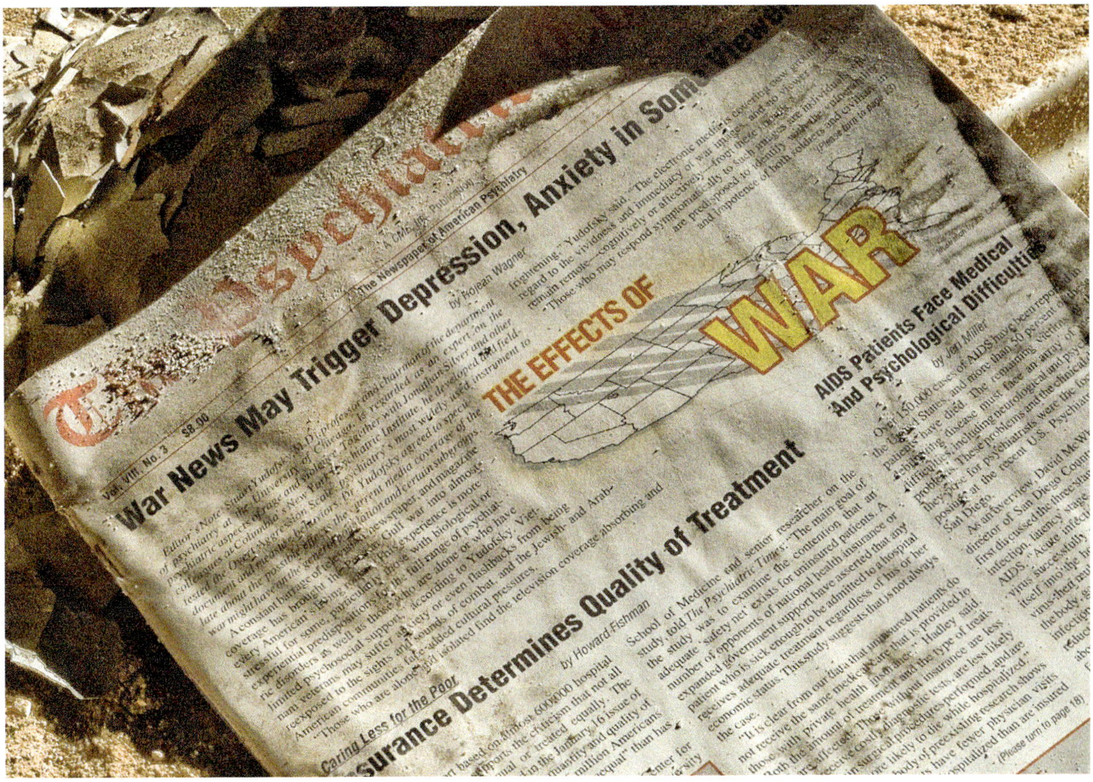

A March 1991 edition of *The Psychiatric Times*.

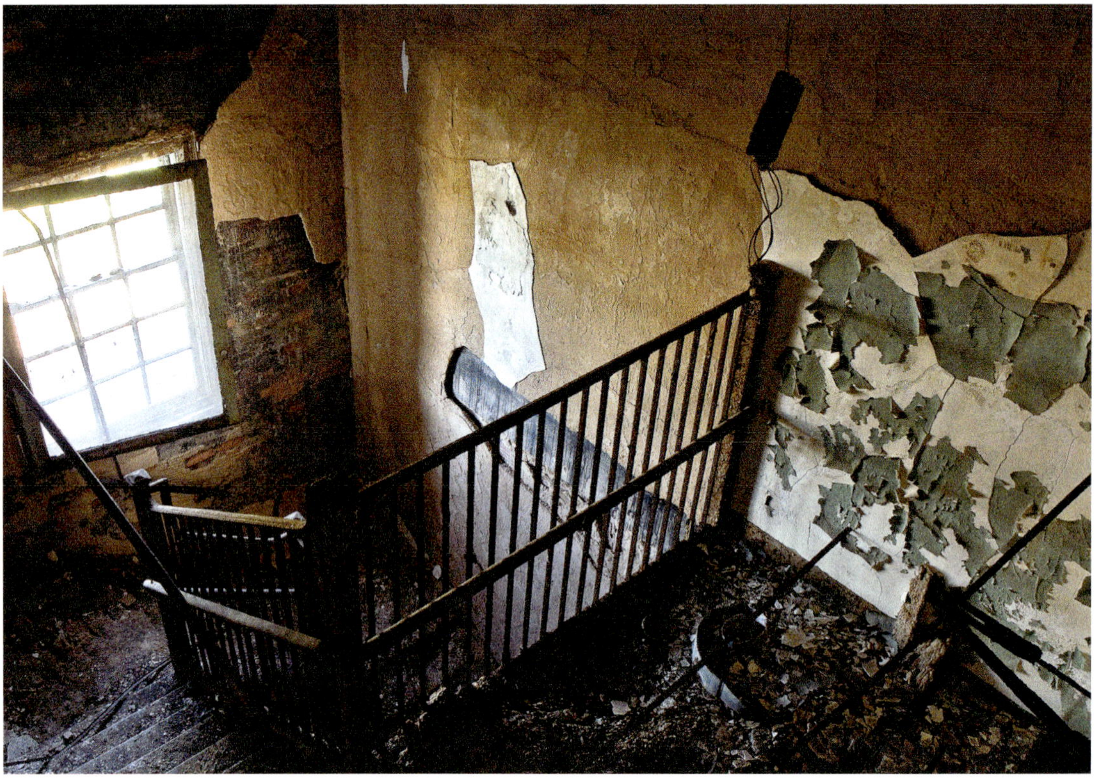

A crumbling stairwell, in the rear of the administration building.

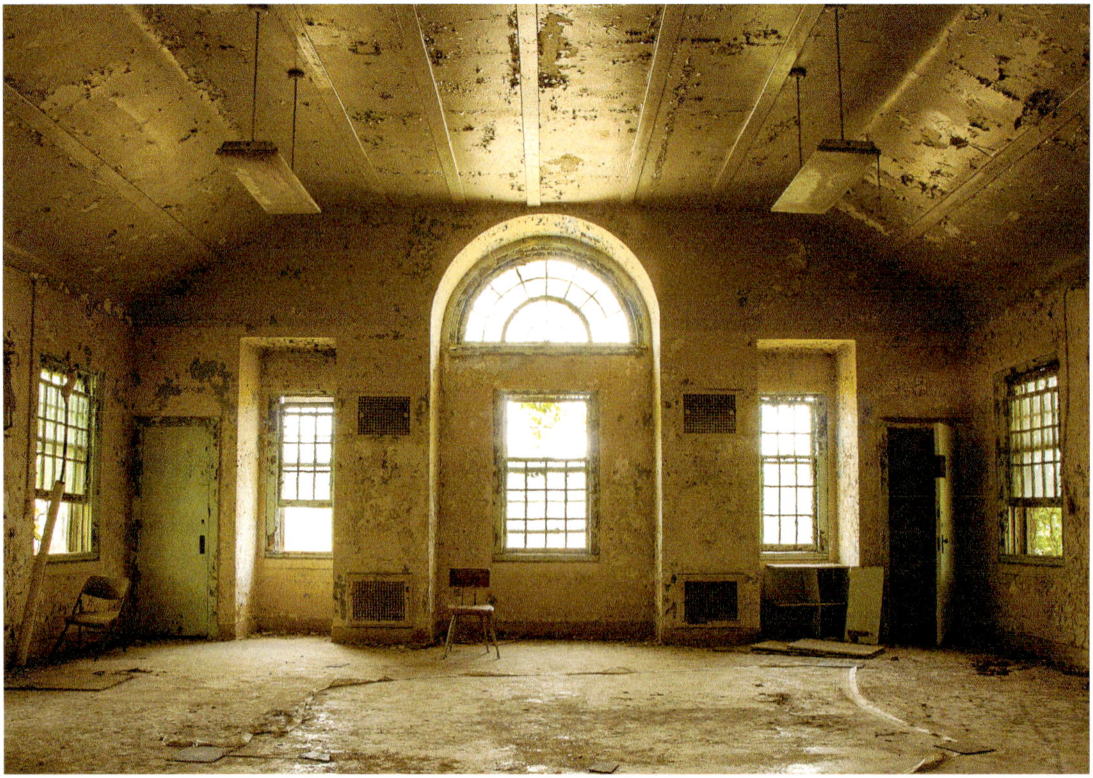

A group room in one of the recreational buildings.

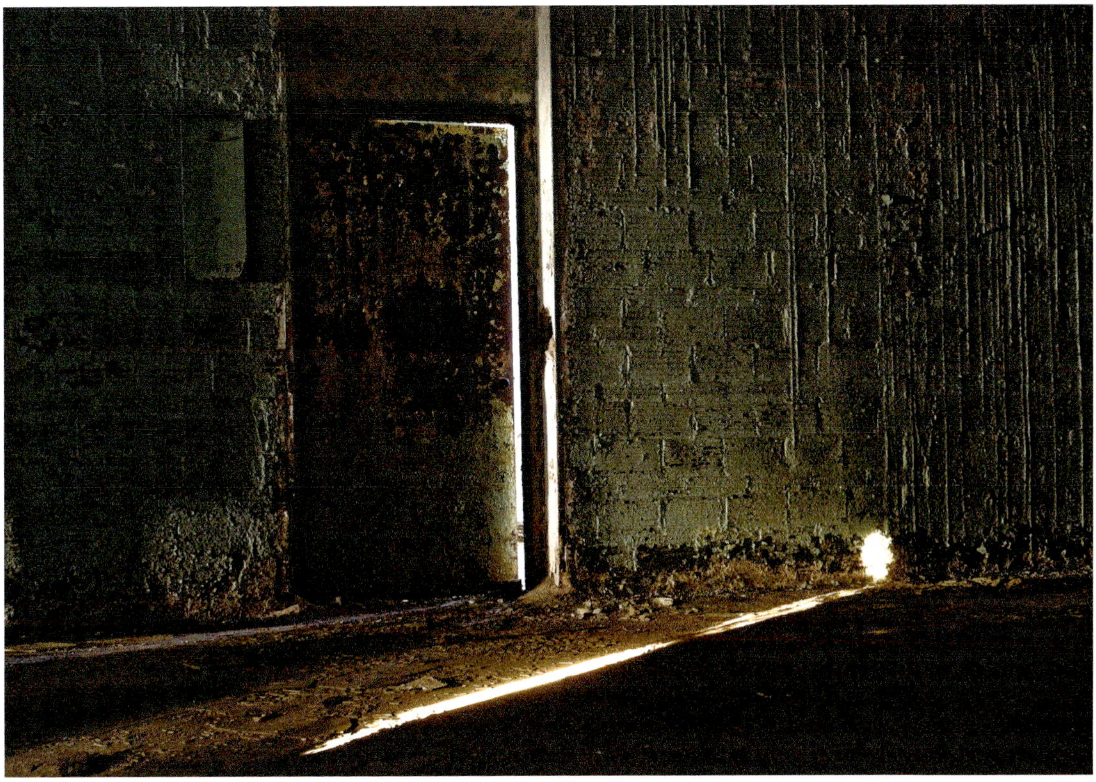

A slither of light in a damp and dark basement.

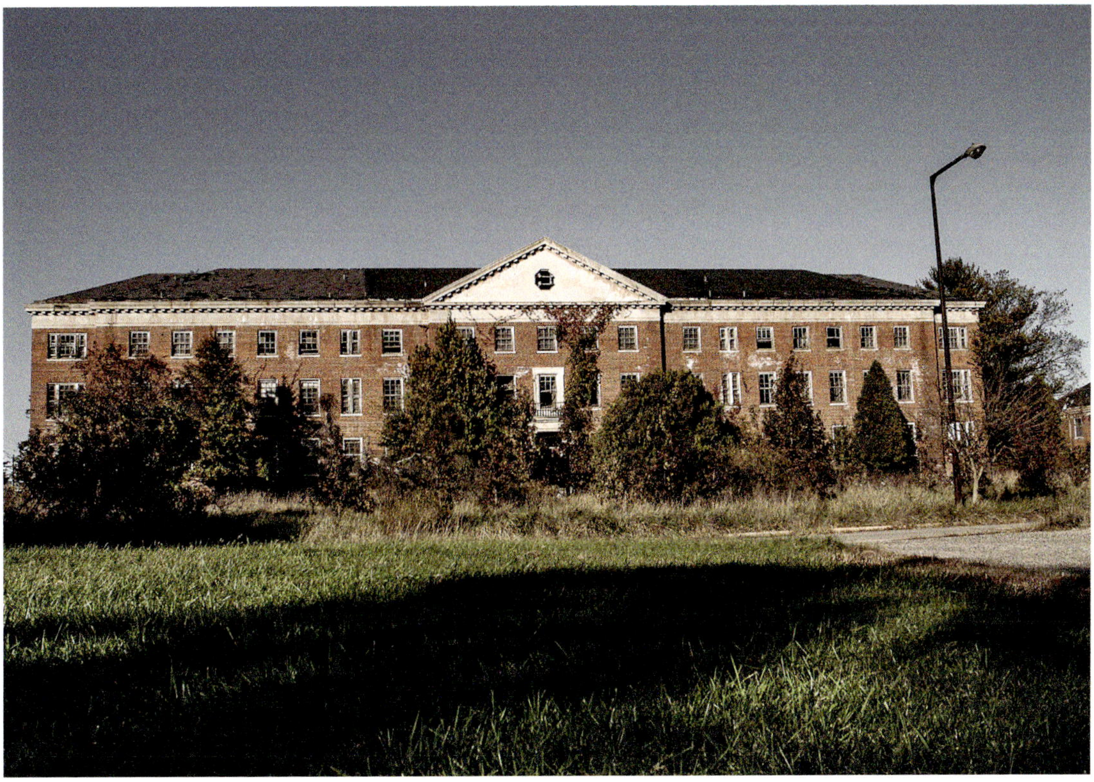

Shadows fall on Forest Haven's derelict Administration Building.

AMERICAN BREWERY, BALTIMORE

The golden-era of brewing in Baltimore ended around the middle of the twentieth century, however, many of the history-rich breweries still remain. The old American Brewery building in East Baltimore, with its unique architecture, remains an enduring symbol of Baltimore's illustrious brewing era.

Designed by New Yorker, and so called brewer's architect and millwright, Charles Stoll, the five-story brick building is unique in Baltimore and visible from blocks away. The American Brewery began its journey into history in 1863 as the J. F.Wiessner Brewing Company. There were twenty-one breweries operating when John Wiessner opened his brewery and although competition existed, demand was high. Baltimore played host to a large German population and a flourishing brewing industry. The brewery would undergo several periods of expansion under Wiessner's ownership. In the first year of operation, the brewery produced between 1,000–1,500 barrels, at its peak in 1919 under the Wiessner name, the brewery produced 110,000 barrels.

In 1920, the Volstead Act, formally known as the National Prohibition Act was passed, and the first golden age of Baltimore brewing came to an abrupt end. By the time Wiessner's last surviving son, Henry F., took over presidency of the company in 1925 the brewery had long since closed. All that remained for Henry to do was oversee the assets and physical plant. In January 1931, Henry sold what remained of his father's brewing empire to the American Malt Company.

With the repeal of Prohibition in 1933, the J. F. Wiessner and Sons Brewing Company, now owned and operated by the Fitzsimmons family, reopened as the American Brewery. During the second period of its brewing history, this Baltimore icon produced such popular brews as American Pilsner, Nut Brown Ale and Brewer's Best Beer. By the late 1960s, the smaller Baltimore breweries found themselves in danger of being swallowed by larger national companies. In 1972, the American Brewery succumbed, like so many others, to the consolidation of the brewing industry—the architectural wonder's days as a brewery ended.

Preservationists and government officials now see the American Brewery building as the cornerstone of a rejuvenation effort aimed at revitalizing a drug ravaged and deteriorating East Baltimore neighborhood. The former brewery provides an anchor site and contains offices, and job training space. The developer's respect for the historic significance of the building—characterized by the successful inclusion of valuable brewing equipment into the floor plan and faithful reconstruction of the facade—will guarantee the American Brewery and its proud brewing history will live on well into the twenty-first century.

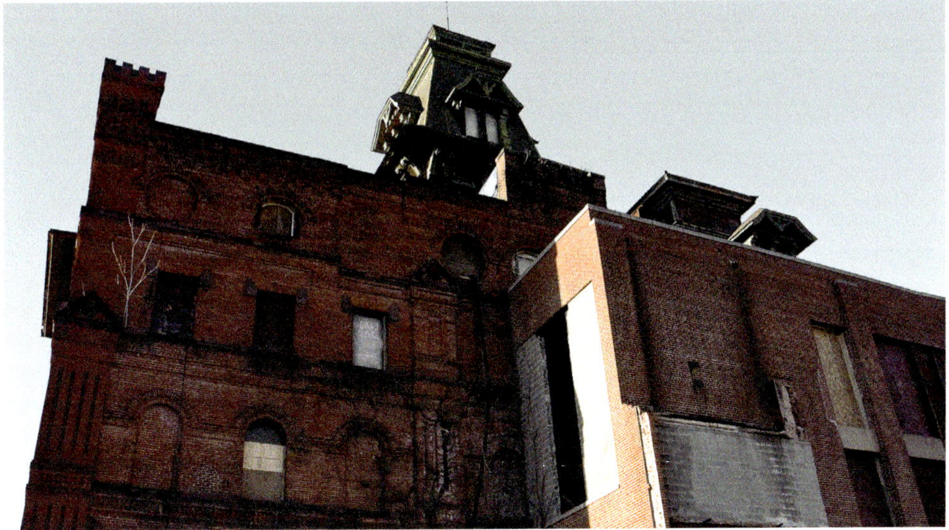

The rear of the main brewery building during the renovation.

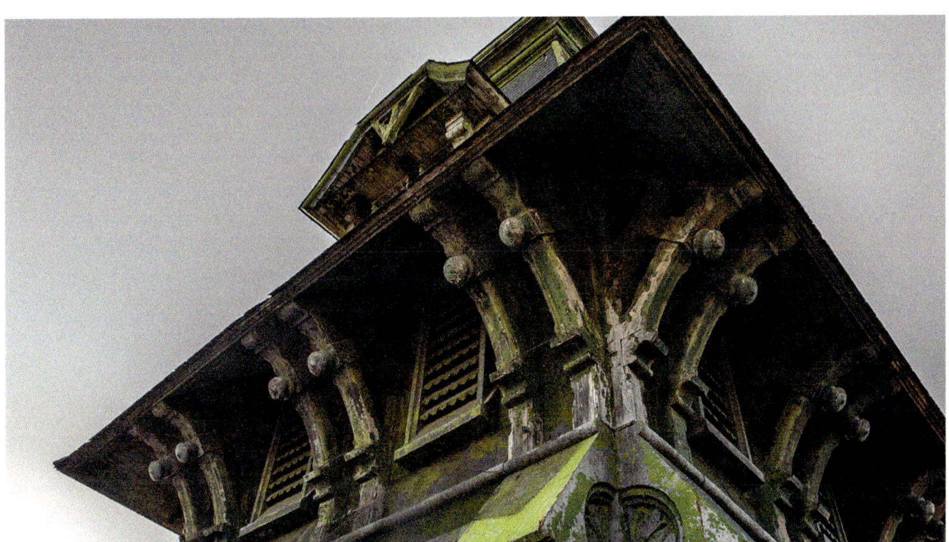

The decorative corbels supporting the upper roof.

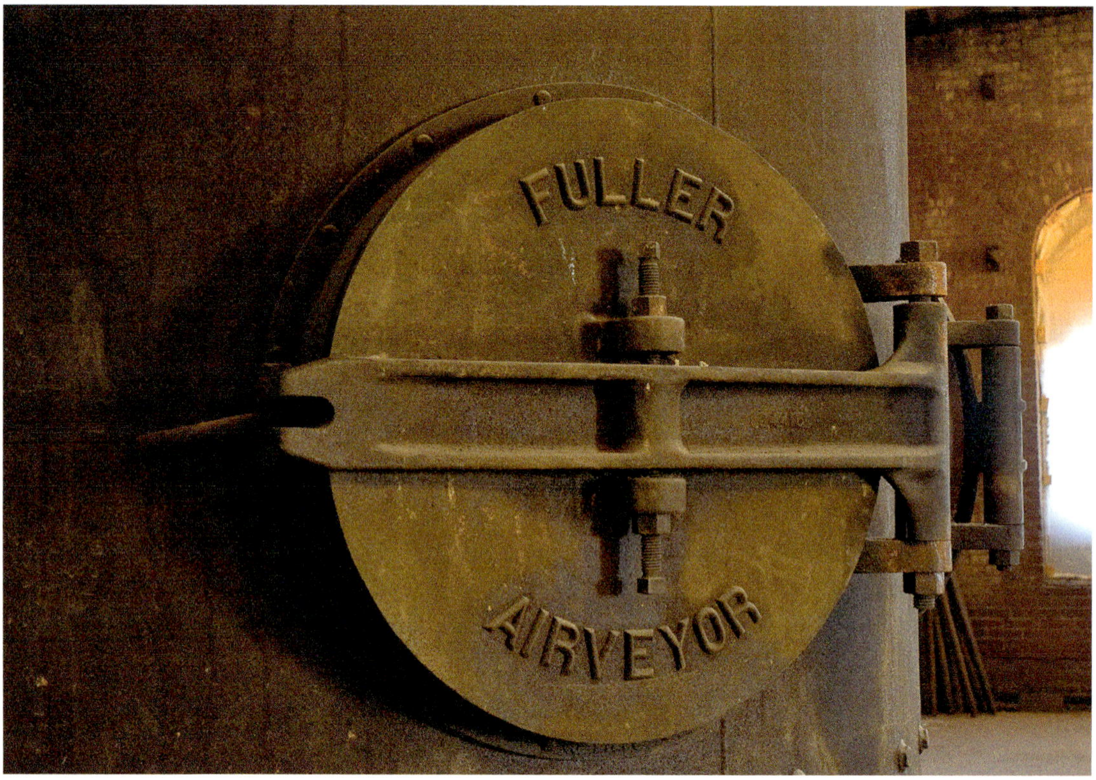

The Fuller Airveyor seal on the hatch.

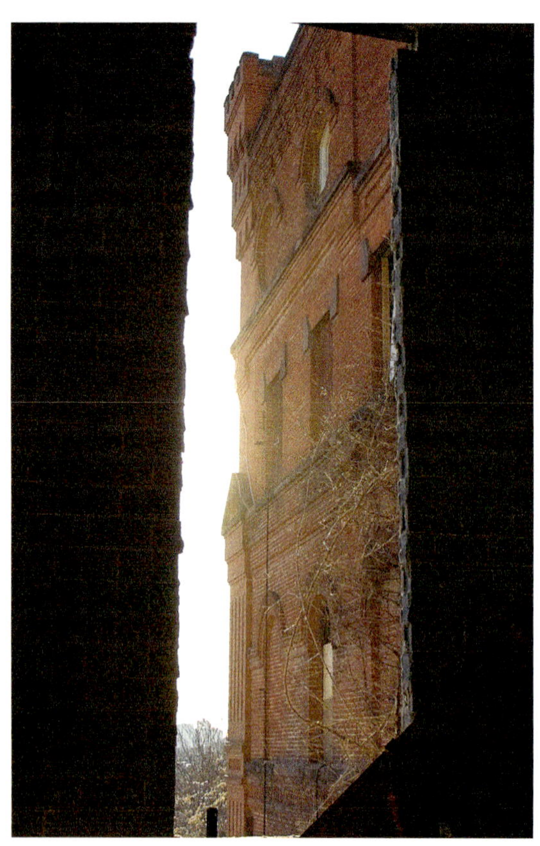

Afternoon sunlight streams through a gaping hole in the side of the building.

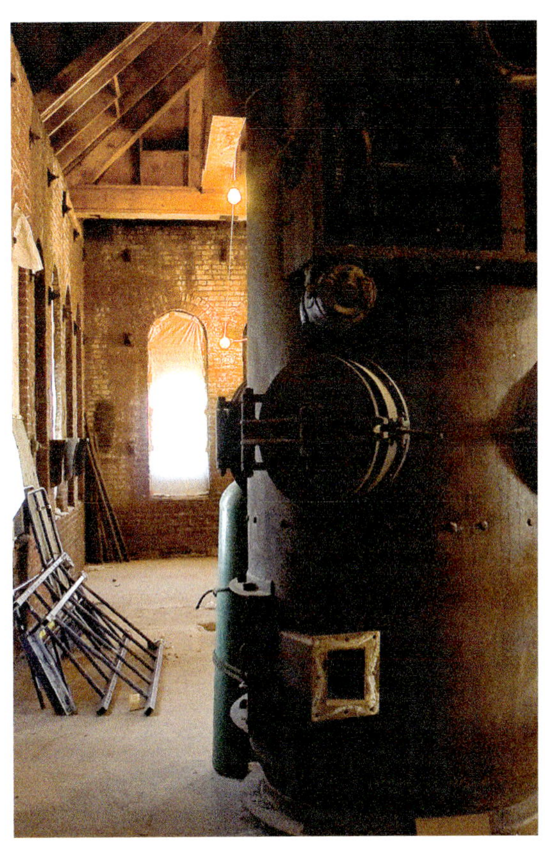

During the brewing process, grain was once blown through the airveyor.

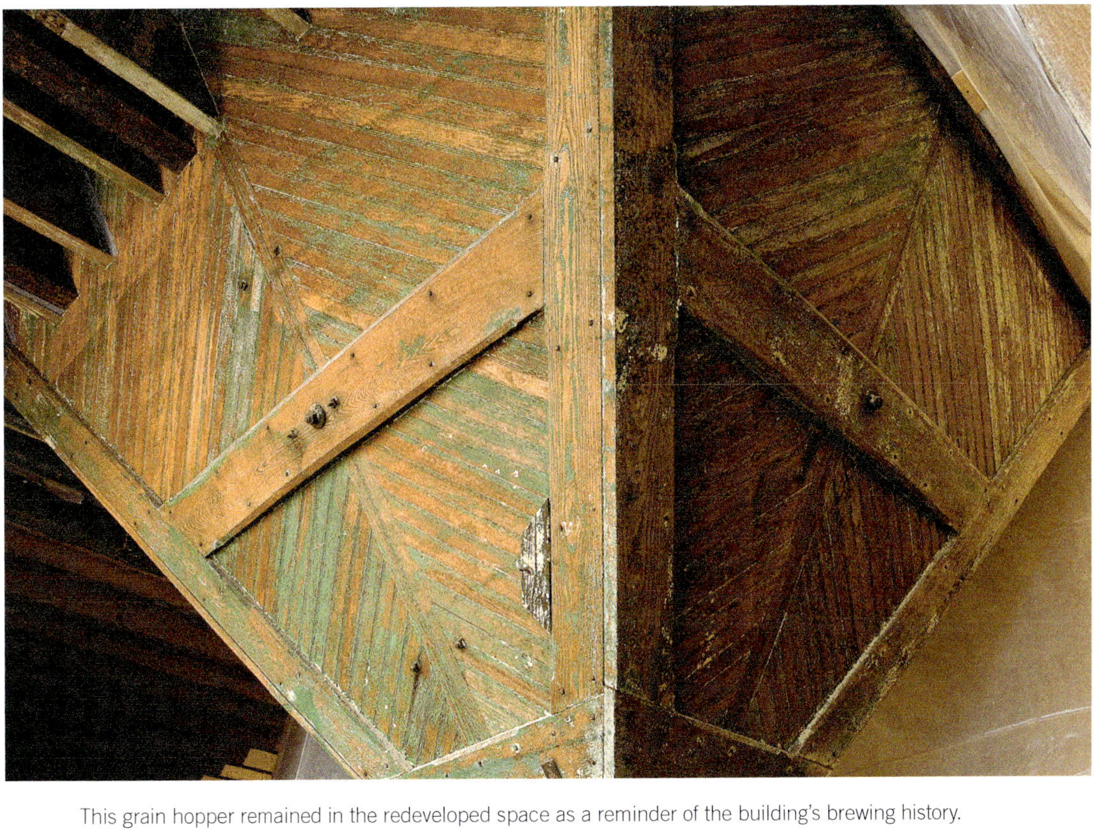

This grain hopper remained in the redeveloped space as a reminder of the building's brewing history.

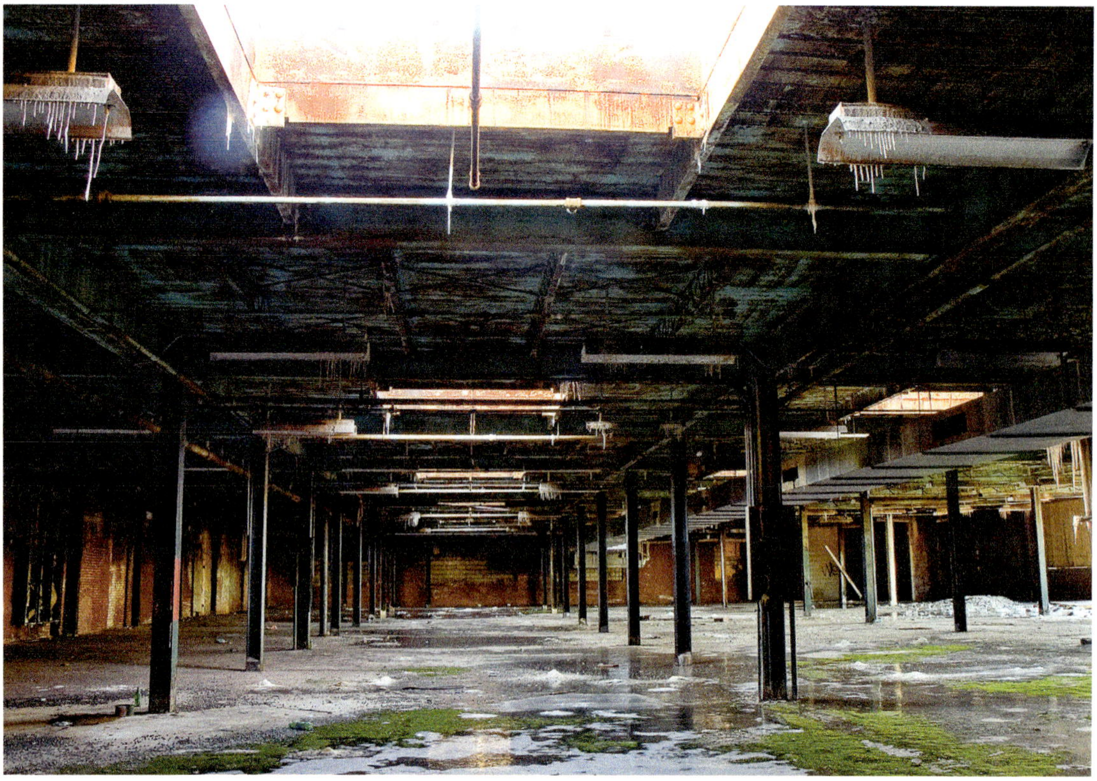

A thin sheet of ice covers the third floor of the disused bottling house on Gay Street.

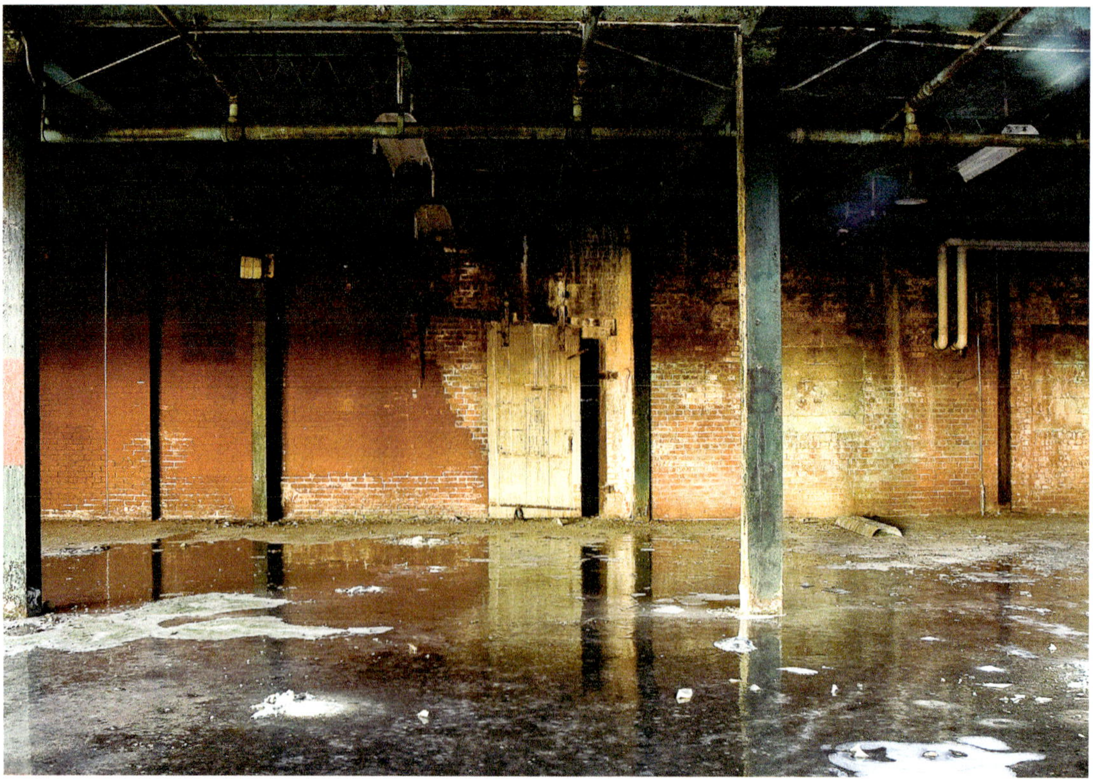

An eerie reflection of a fire door in the bottling house.

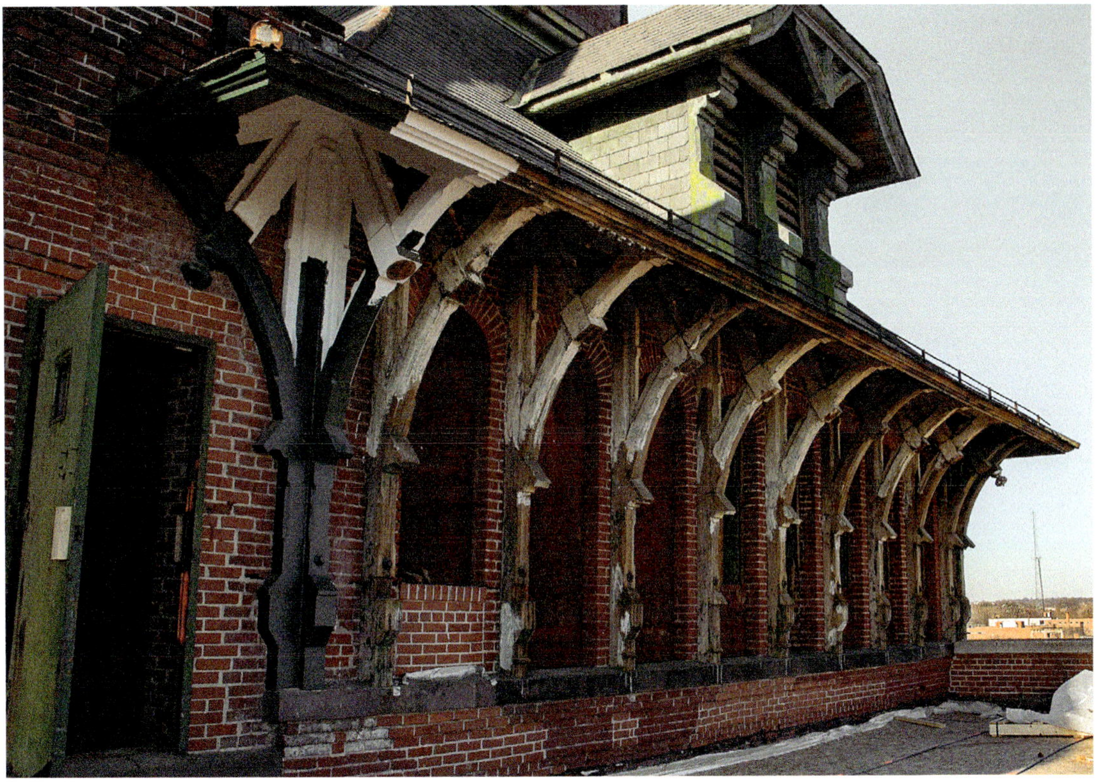

The rooftop area where the ornate woodwork was fully restored and retained.

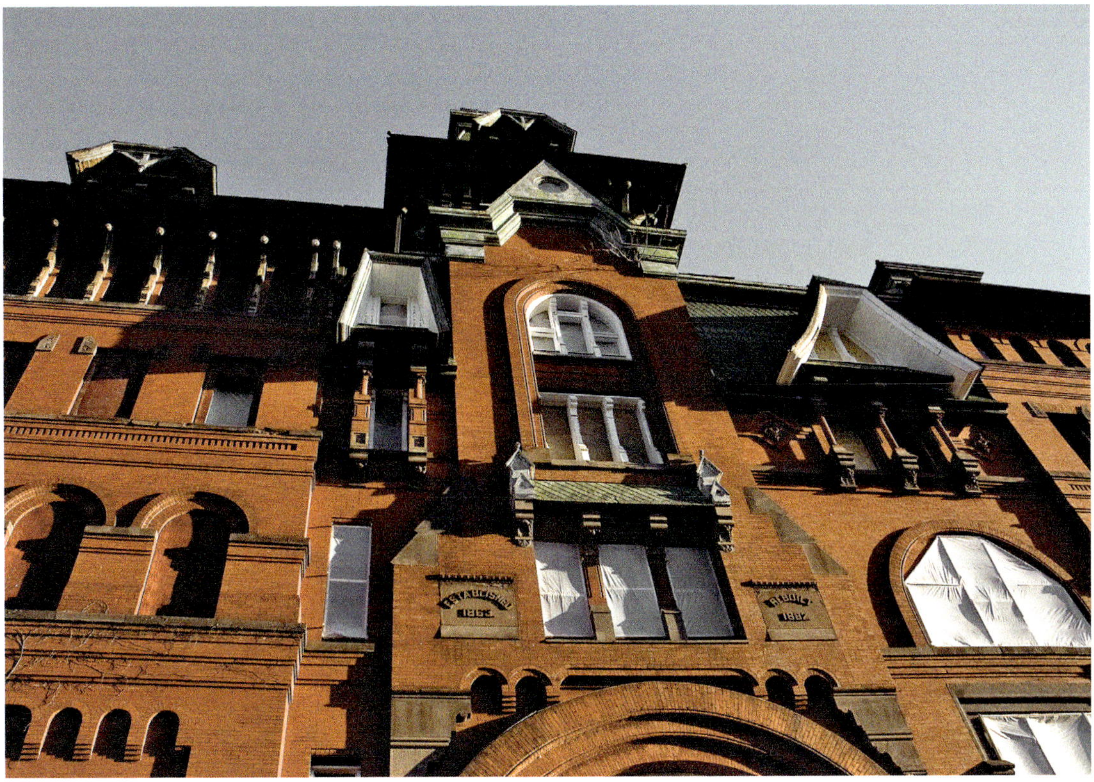

Plastic sheeting and plywood act as stand-ins for the long-ago destroyed windows.

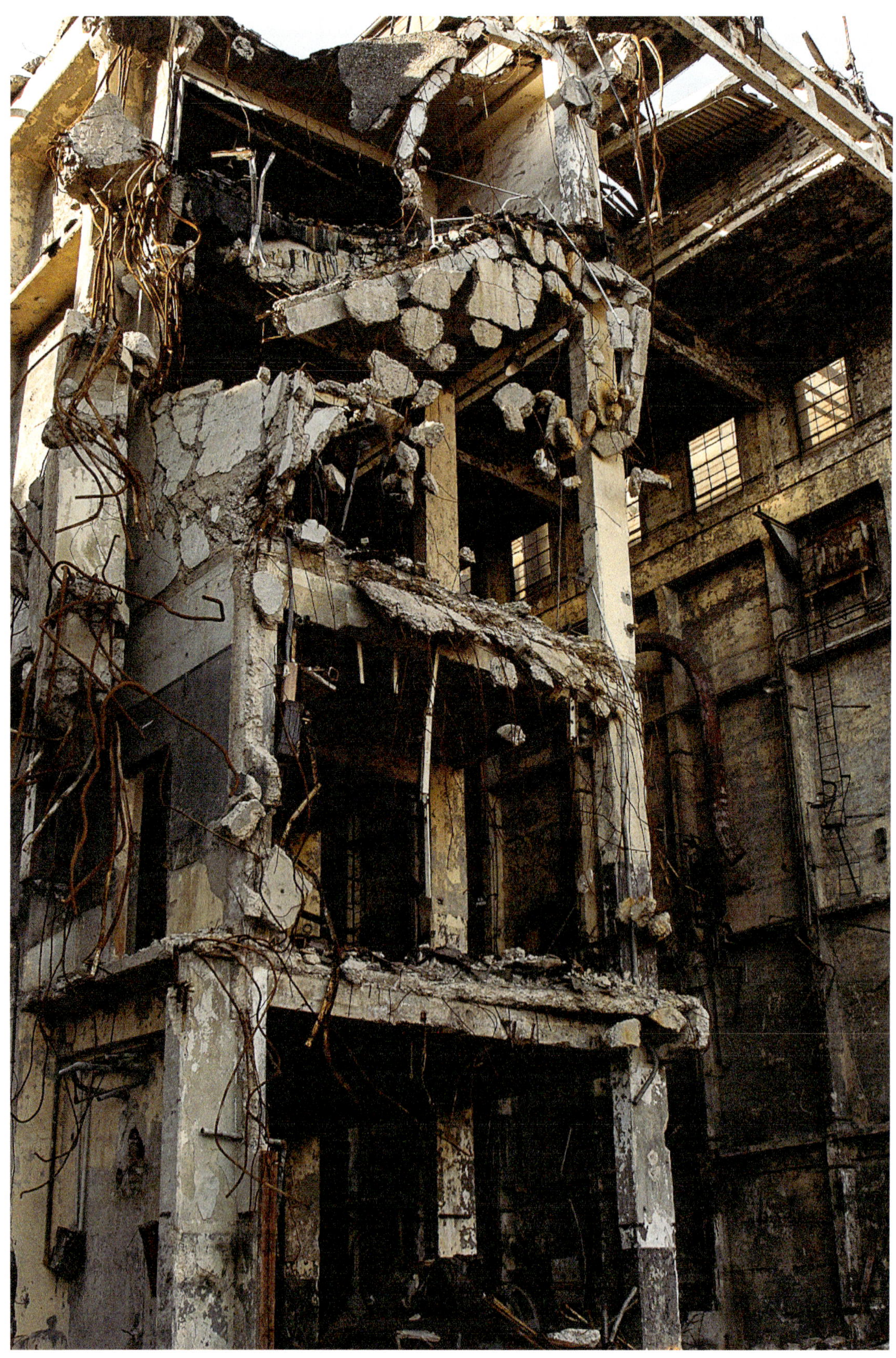

Westport Power's massive crumbling structure looms over workers below.

WESTPORT POWER, BALTIMORE

Like so much of Baltimore's brawny industrial past, the former Westport BGE power station, abandoned in the early 1990s, succumbed to the wrecking ball in 2008. The deafening sound of steel crashing into the plant's massive walls, over and over again—every day, for months on end—become the area's audio signature.

Originally opened in 1906, by Consolidated Gas Electric Light & Power Company, the power station was the largest reinforced concrete station in the world. Built on 23 waterfront acres, the building boasted impressive proportions—it was 255 feet deep by 115 feet wide and 70 feet high. With memories of the Great Baltimore Fire of 1904 still fresh, Consolidated Gas Electric used concrete and steel exclusively. In a booklet, they released about the opening of Westport they explain, "Not a stick of wood is used in the construction of the building nor will there be any wood anywhere when it is finished." Even the framing for the windows consists of solid steel. The carefully planned construction of Westport contributed to its century-long survival and become a major factor in the slowness of the demolition—Westport was not built to come down.

It required a Herculean effort to raze a building designed to never collapse. Daily, hordes of workers assembled, blowtorches in hand, to break down tons and tons of solid steel framing and to disassemble mammoth turbines that once powered Baltimore City. The steel and iron, once reduced to manageable sizes, was shipped to New Orleans and then to China. Other laborers arrived to complete the dangerous task of removing asbestos and a multitude of other hazardous materials. Incredibly, the immensity of the demolition and clean-up process did not deter those with dreams of redevelopment.

Situated on the last remaining stretch of Baltimore's highly coveted waterfront property, its demise, at the hands of developers, was inevitable. With the popularity of the Inner Harbor, Canton, Fells Point and Harbor East, it had to follow that the only parcel of undeveloped land with water and city views could not be left as an industrial wasteland.

A decade later, plans for the "new" Westport have yet to be realized. The 2008 economic downturn halted the original developer's plans for 2,000 residences, a sixty-five-story skyscraper, offices, a stadium, a beach, a kayak launch area and running paths. Years of legal battles and bankruptcy filings ended in 2015 with the purchase of the land, for a mere 6 million, by Under Armour's billionaire CEO Kevin Plank.

The waterfront site, where the monolithic power station, built never to come down, once stood, remains a muddy wasteland. The powerful turbines have long been silent—just as the current land owner is—there are no signs of the promised redevelopment.

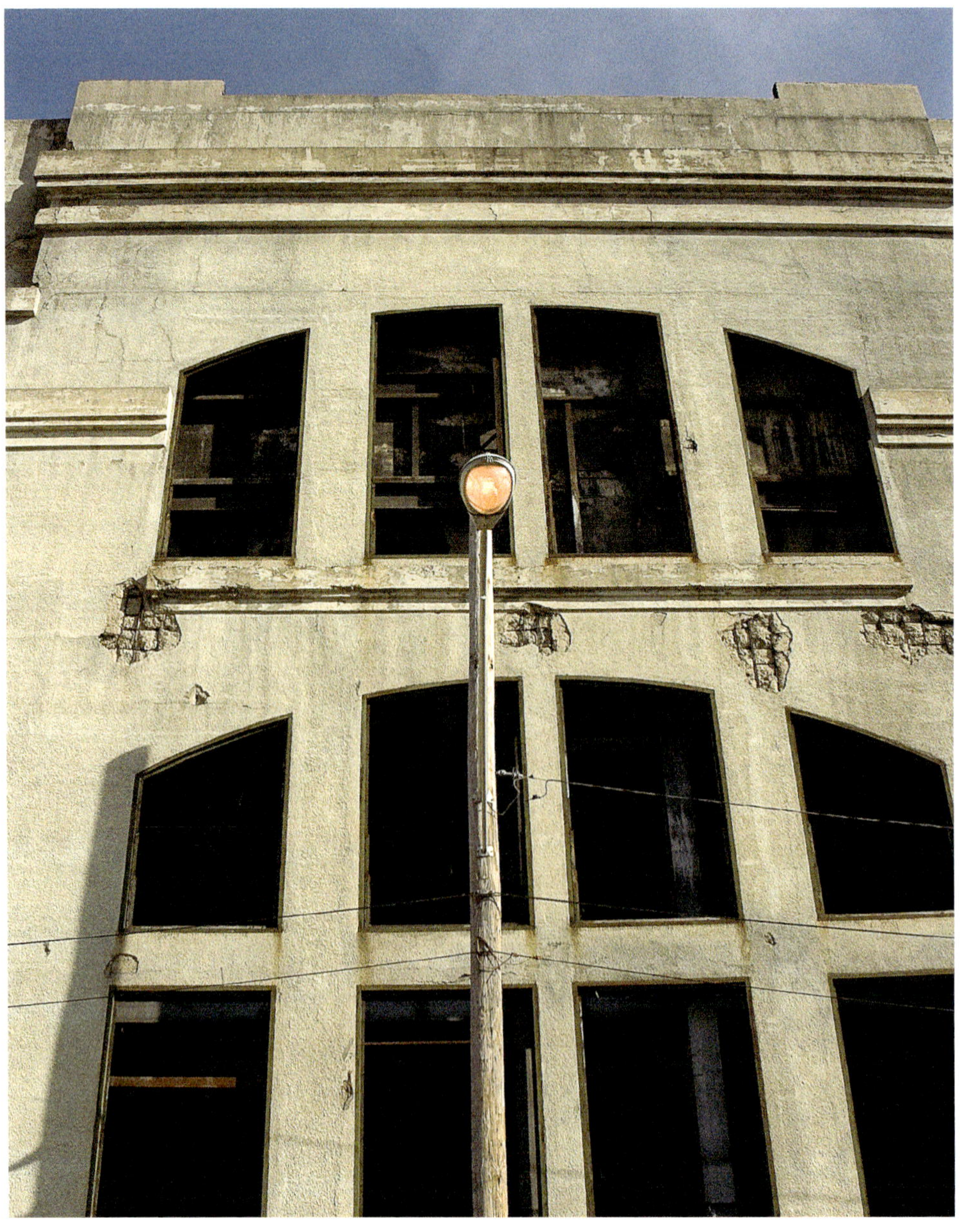

The Kloman Street entrance to the power plant.

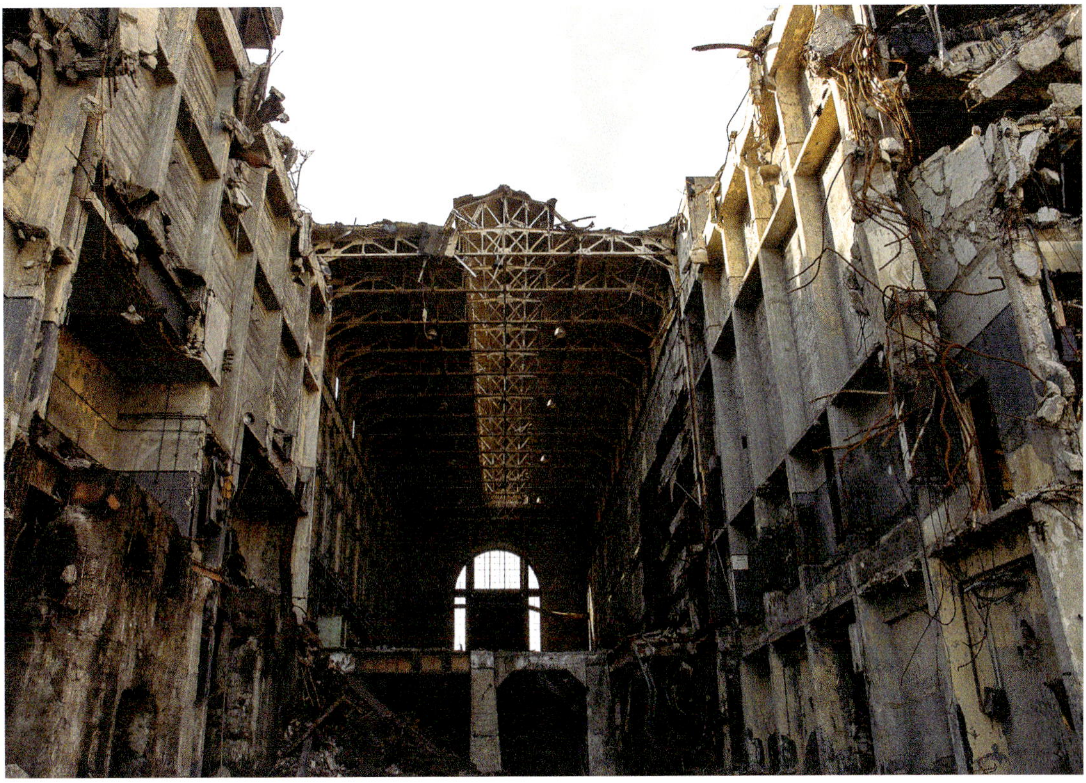

The skeleton of the structure becoming exposed.

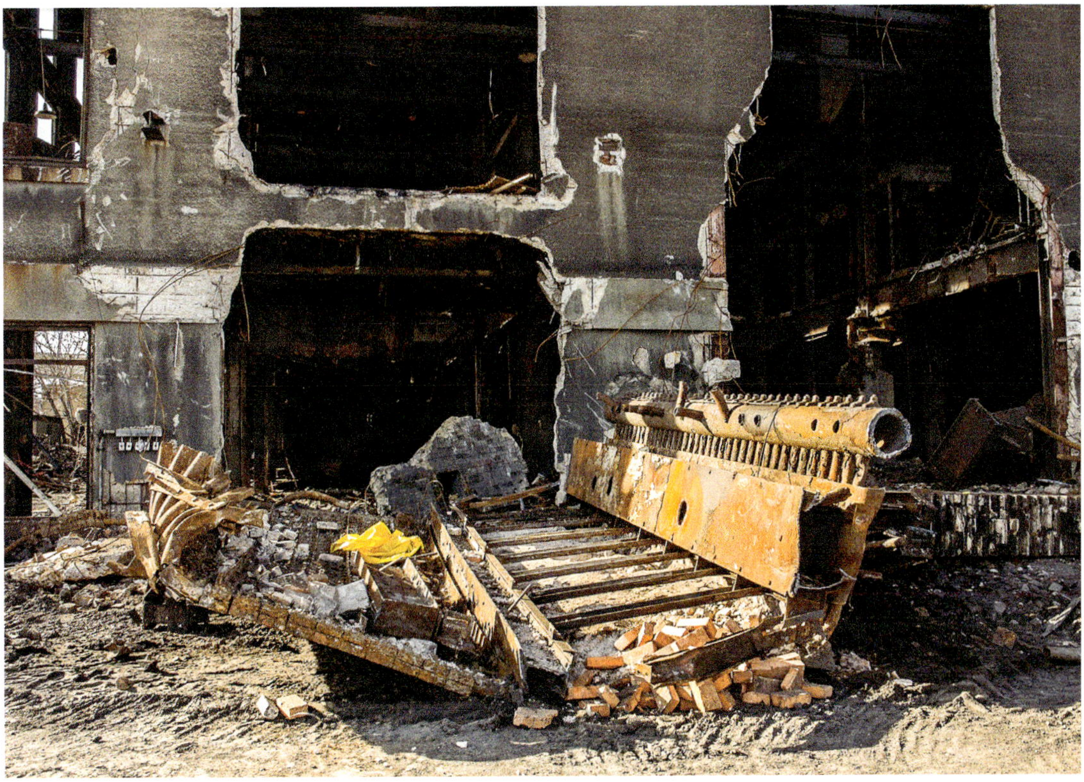

Massive pieces of iron and steel surround the former power plant waiting to be reduced to a more manageable size.

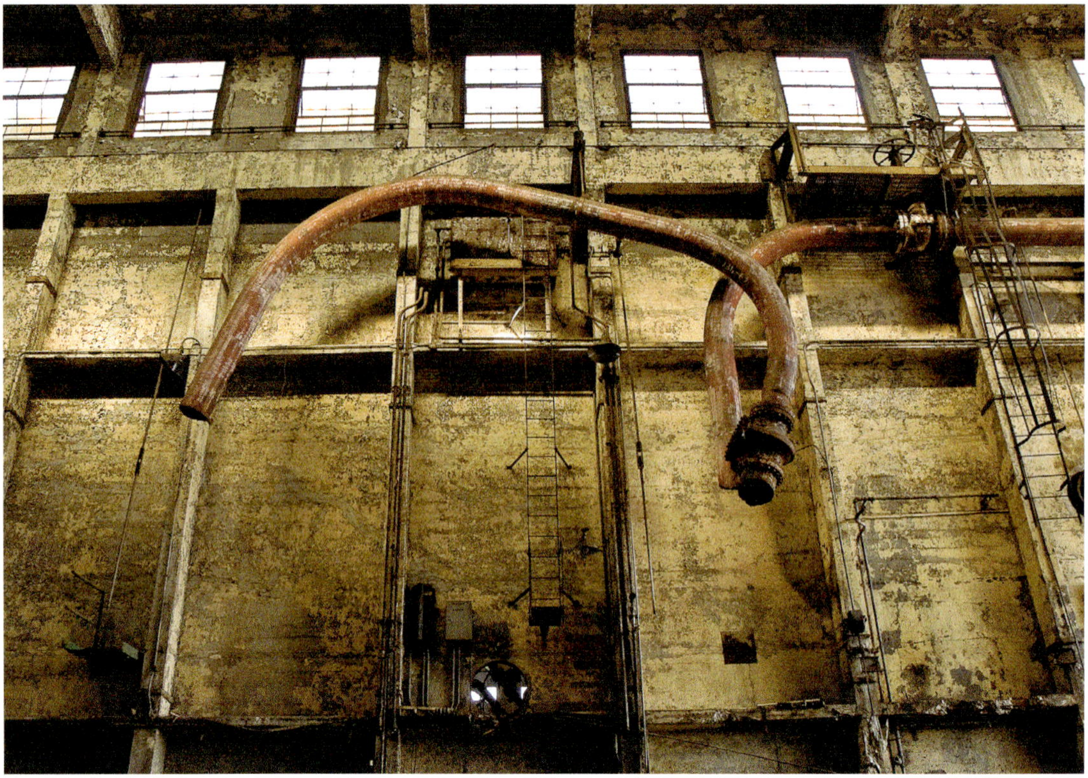

Dangling steam pipes appear suspended by air, they once wound their way throughout the power plant.

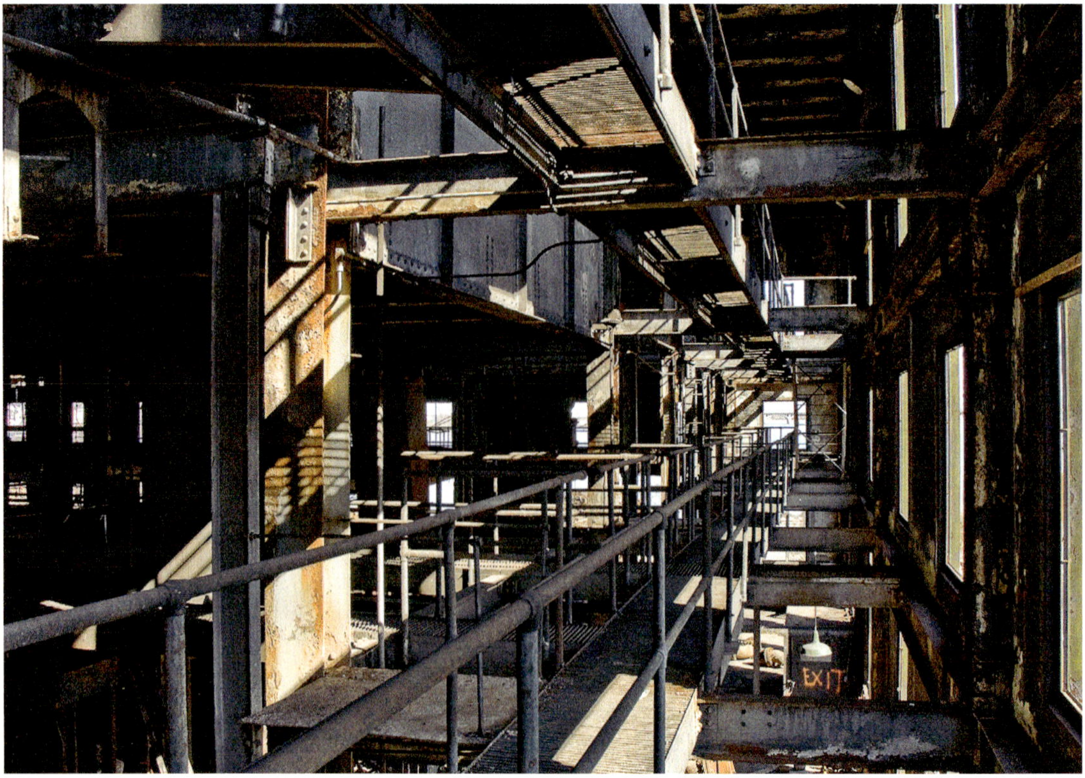

An interior upper-level walkway exposed to sunlight.

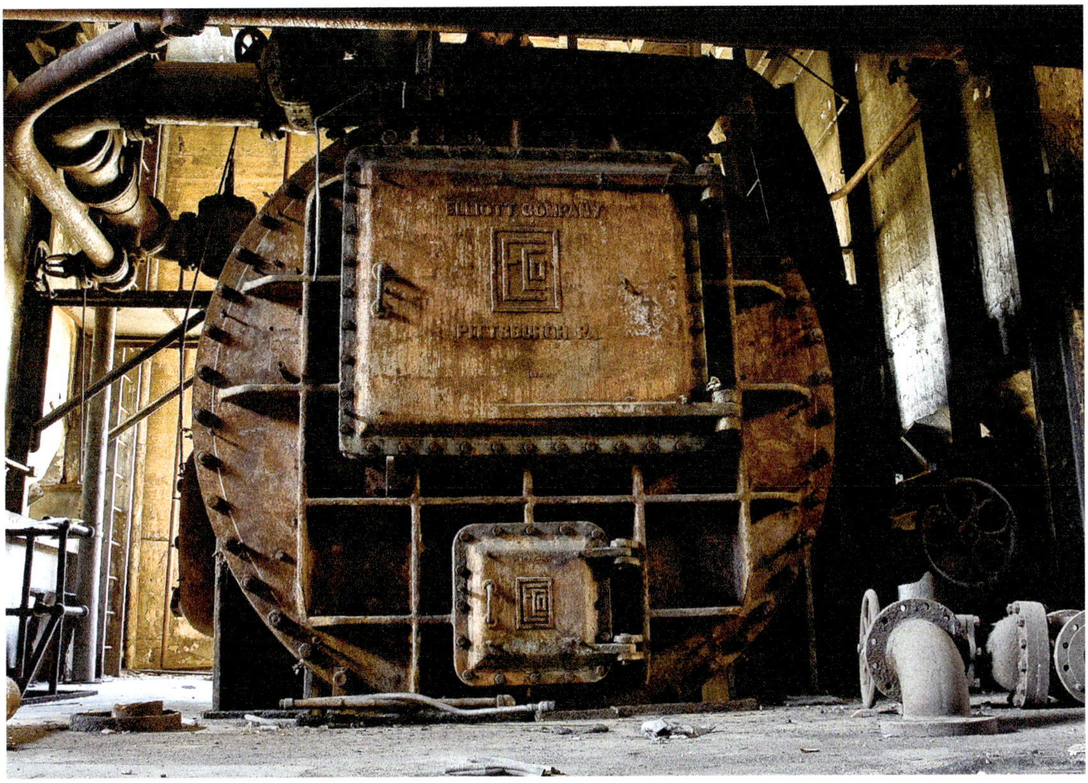

An immense boiler, still intact—its fate the same as the rest of the building.

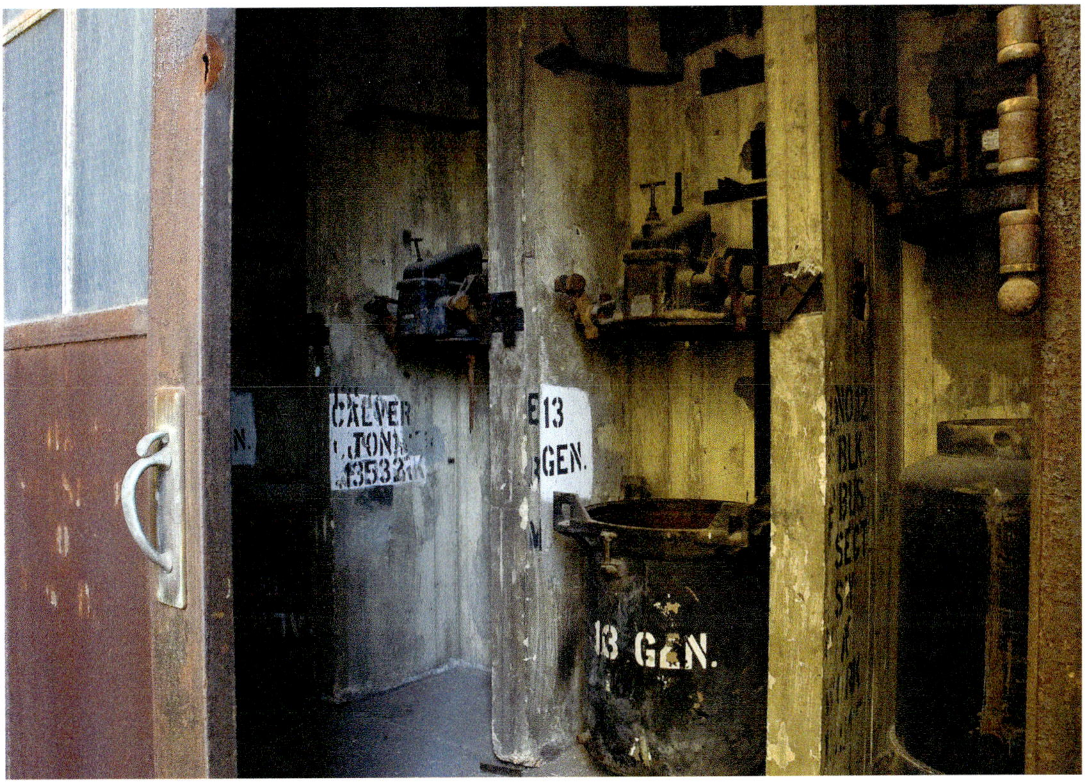

The air compression tank area.

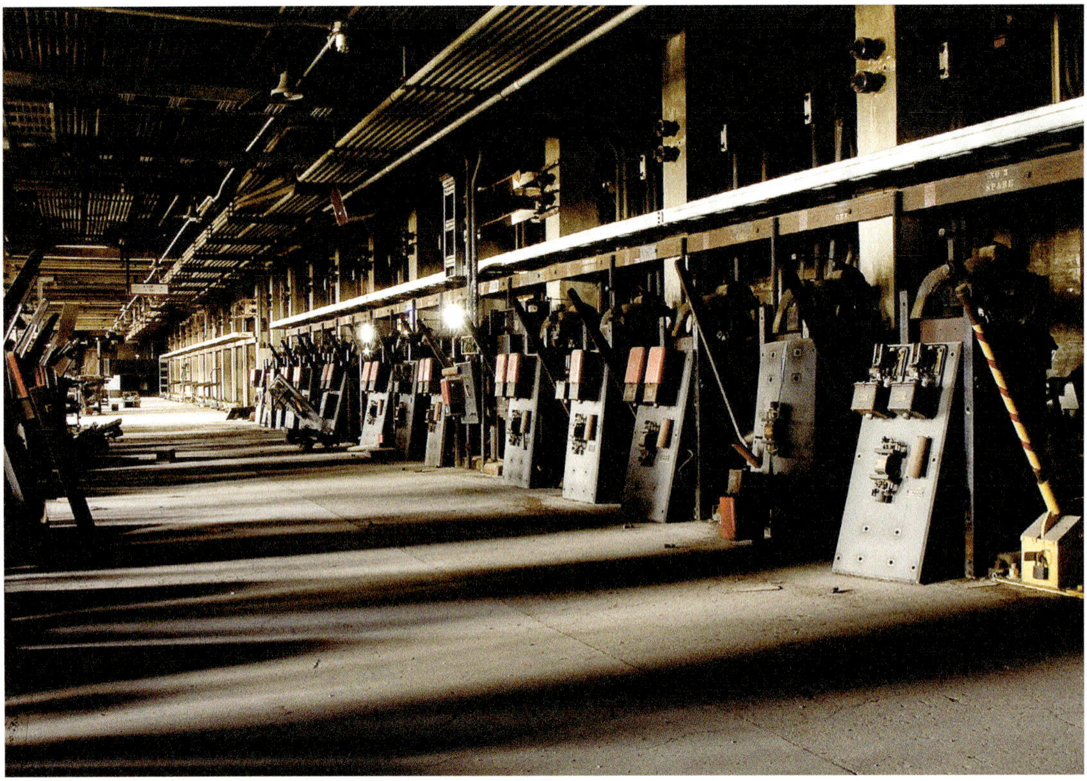

Switches used to control electricity flowing out of the power plant.

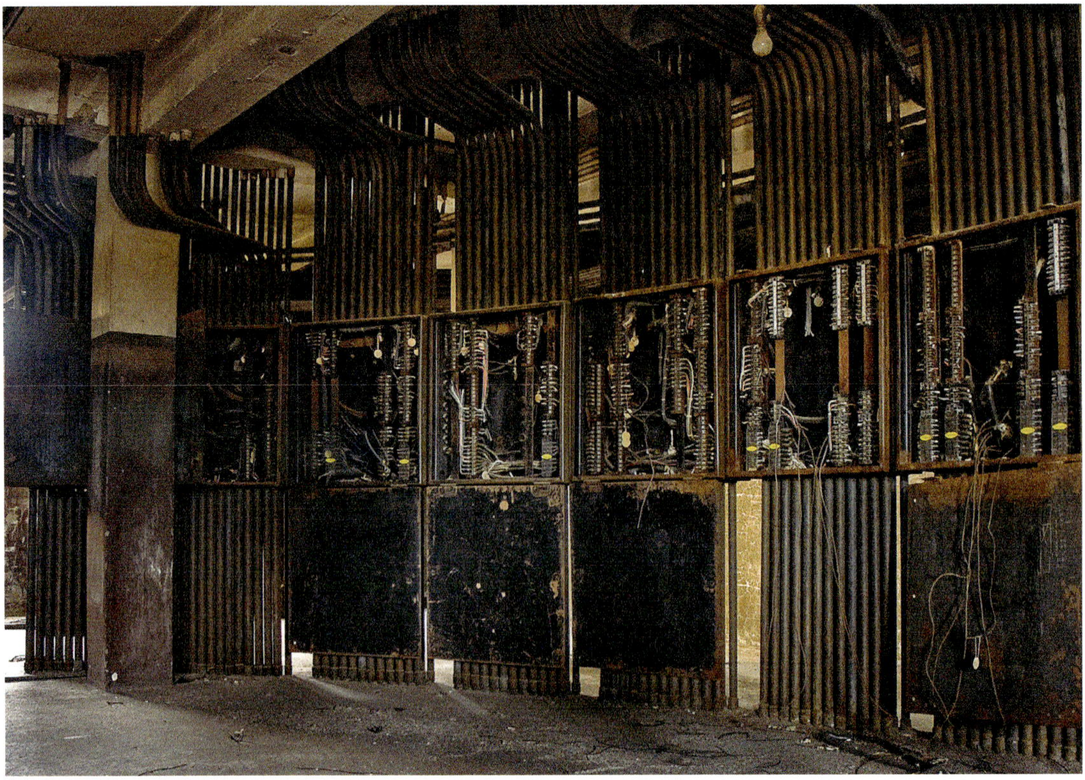

Disused electrical bus panels in the power distribution room.

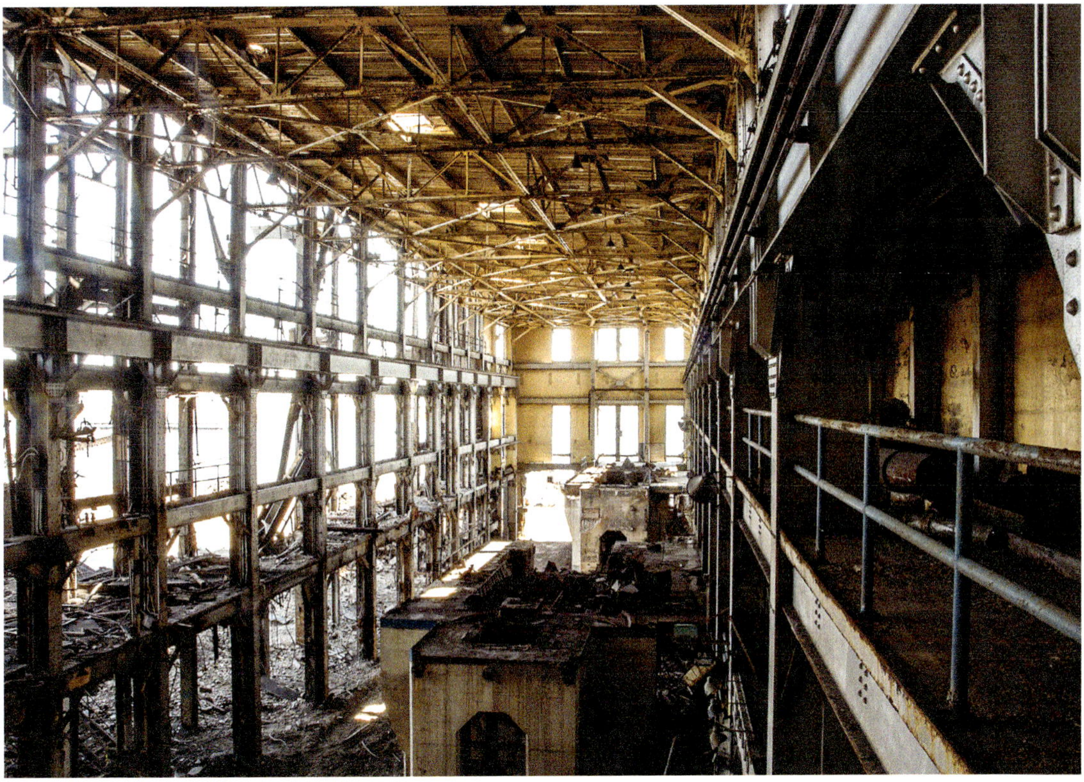

Southeast view, from the massive turbine building, of the enormous concrete piers that held the turbines.

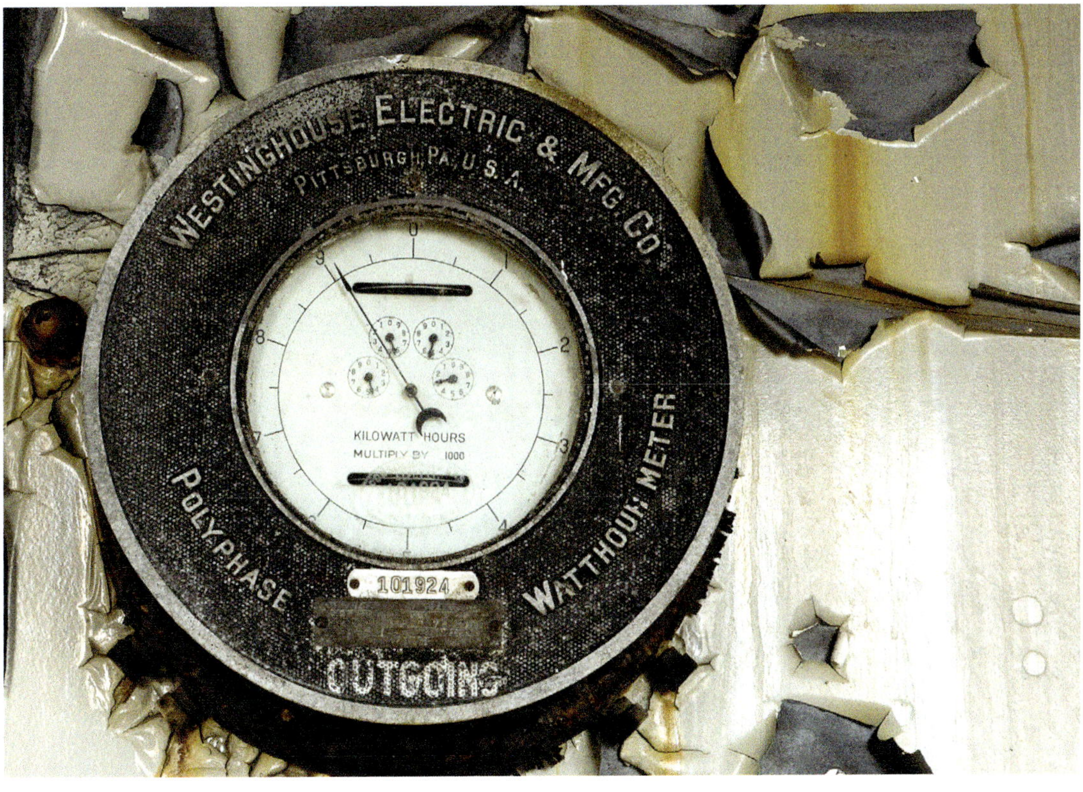

Electric meters measured power flowing out from the generators.

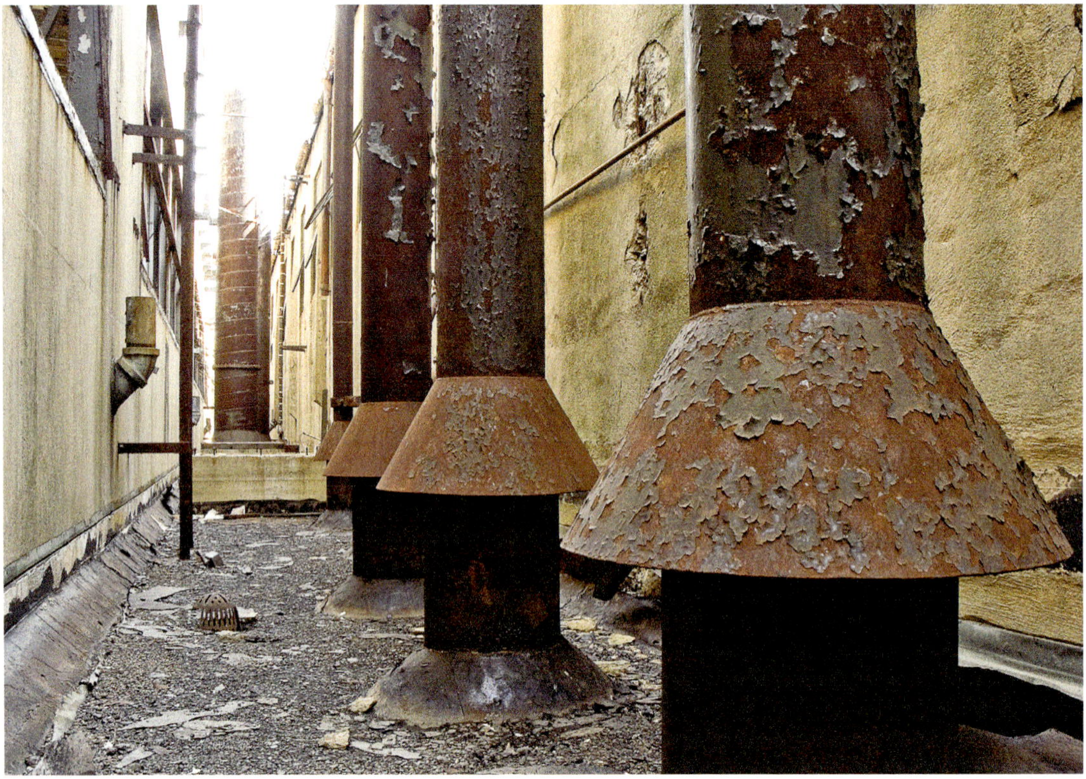

Vent stacks align repetitiously on the rooftop.

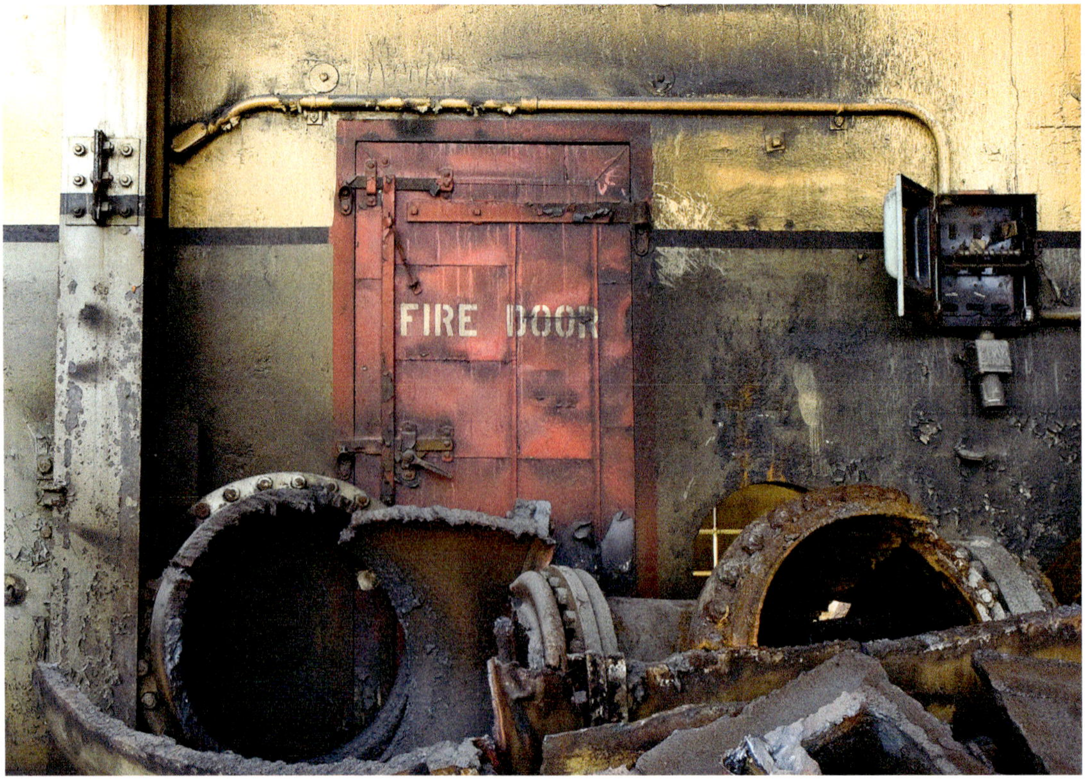

A fire door blocked by pieces of severed pipe.

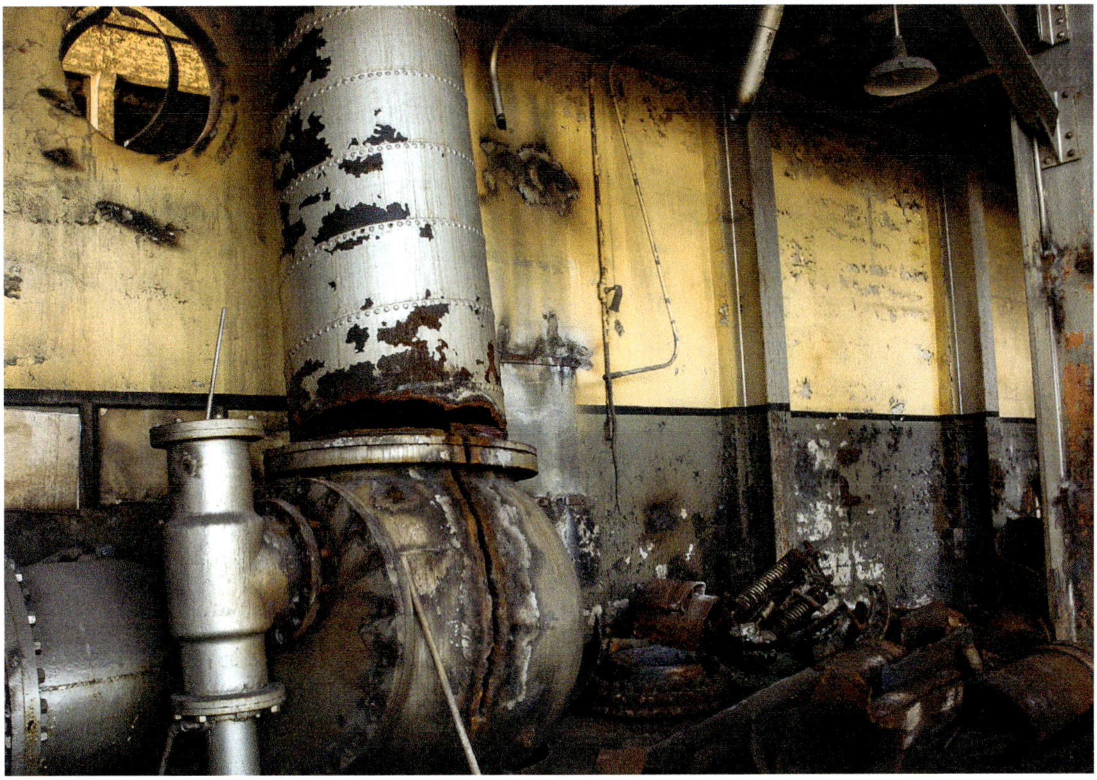

Pipes in the process of being dismantled have been separated by a grinder.

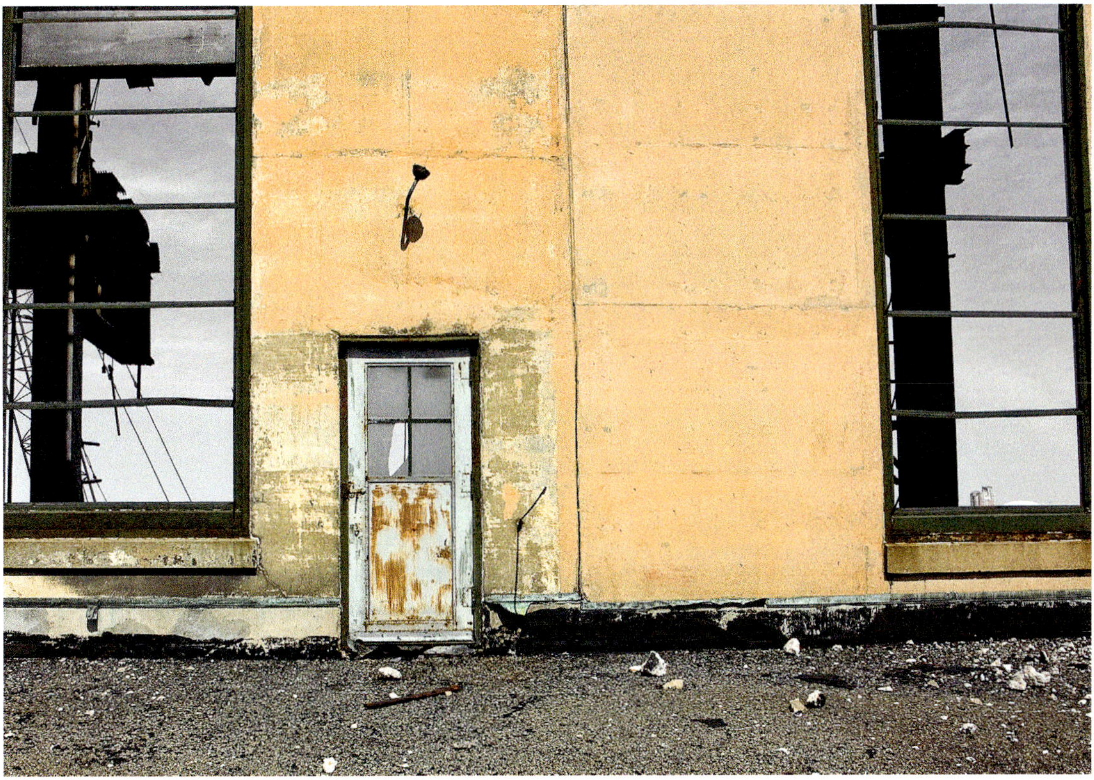

A door, at the south end of the plant, opens to nothing but what remains of the steel frame.

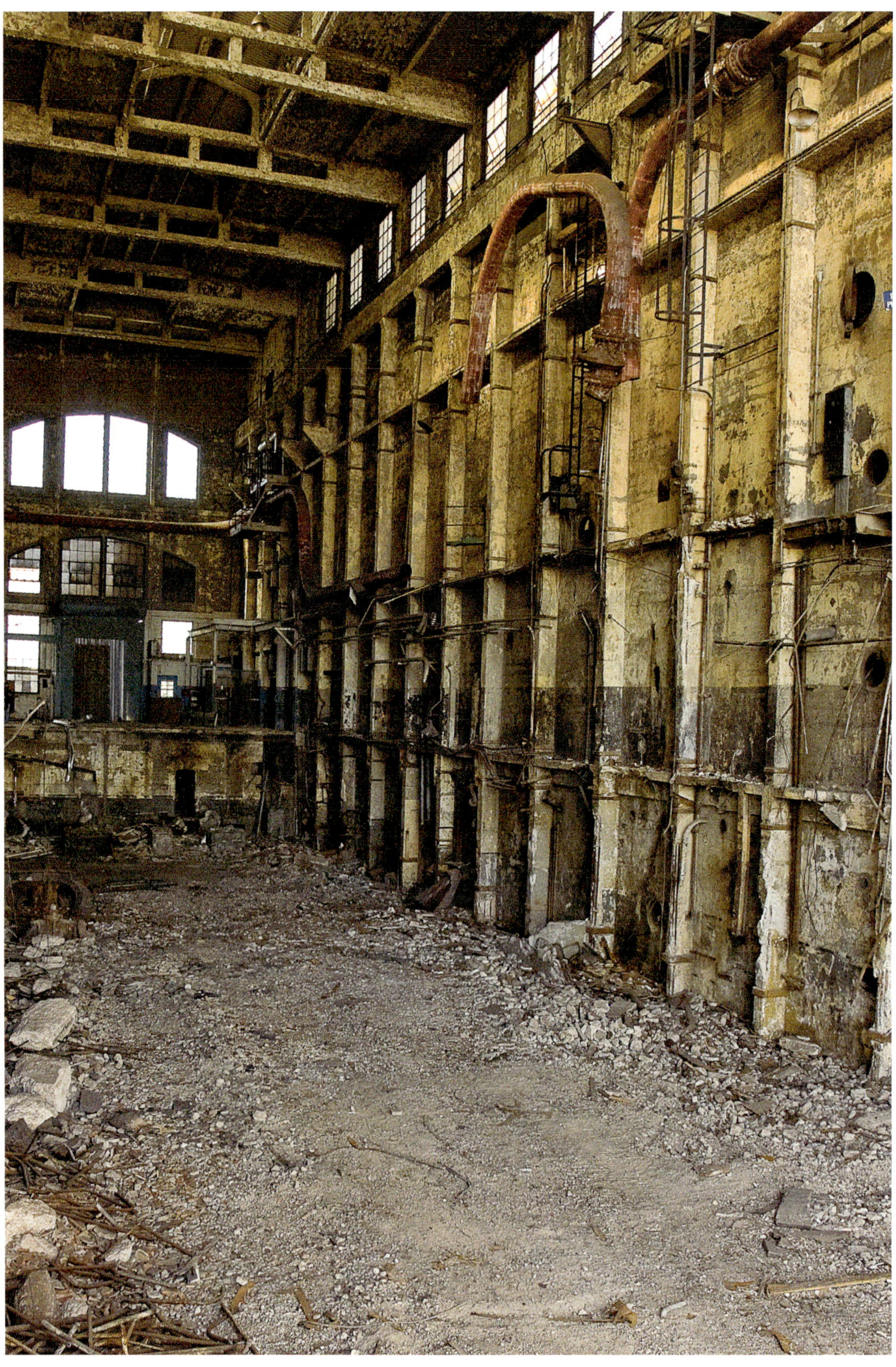

Severed pipes hanging precariously in the gutted central area of the plant.

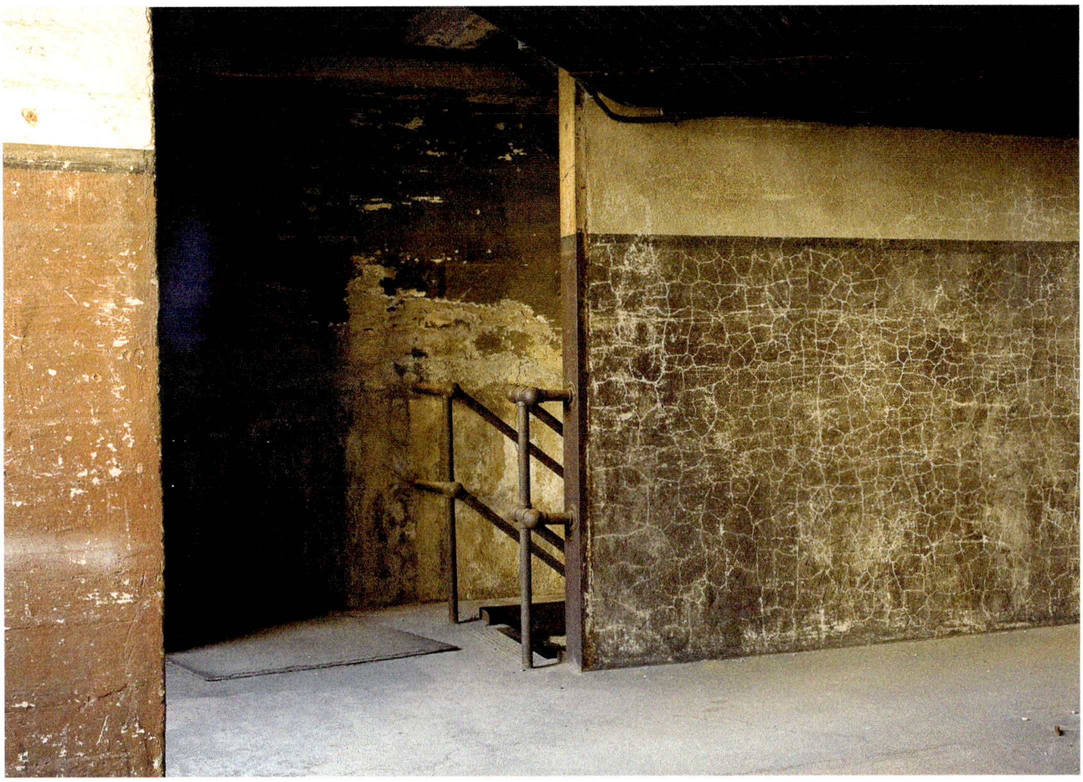

A stairway leading down to the power distribution room.

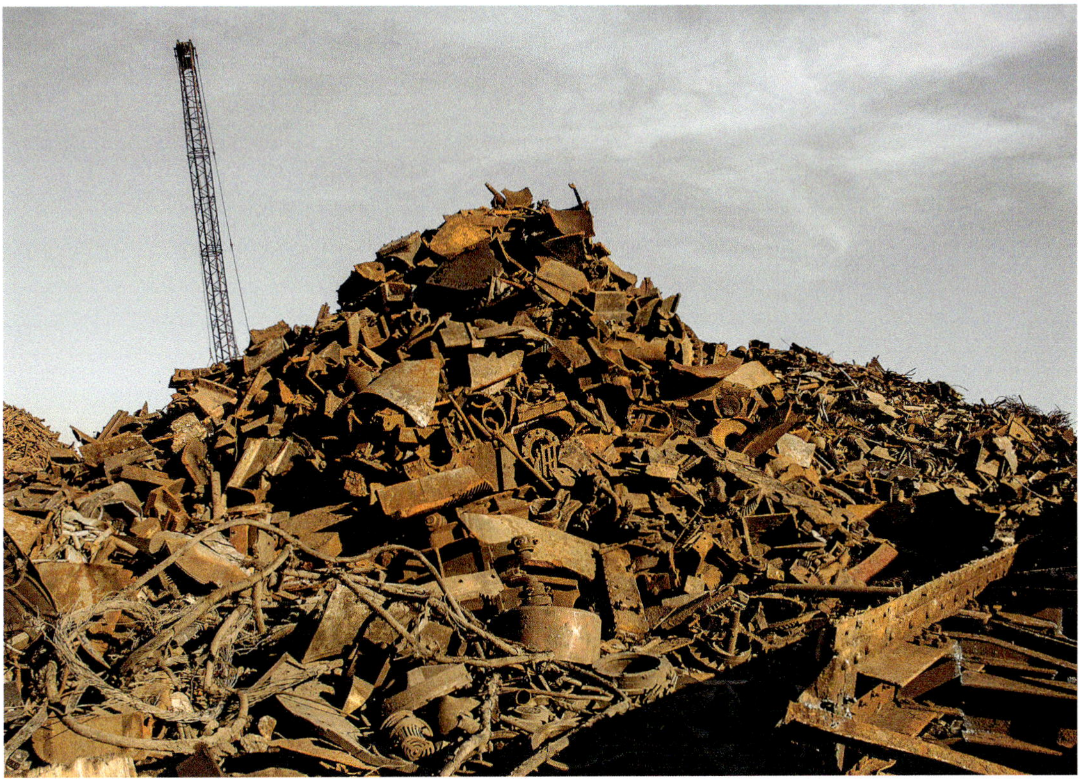

A massive heap of cut down iron awaiting removal by ship to New Orleans, where it will be recycled and sent to China..

THE ENCHANTED FOREST, ELLICOTT CITY

Infectious laughter and squeals of joy, from both young and old, once reverberated through the woods of the Enchanted Forest in Ellicott City. What more could a child wish for than to be surrounded by beloved fairy tale and nursery rhyme characters—come to life—and how liberating for adults to be charmed and entertained by memories of magical tales?

Sadly, the Enchanted Forest, once a make-believe playground for children and adults, no longer exists as an engaging land of fantasy. The grounds now lay silent, the background hum of traffic, from an adjacent shopping mall, replacing the laughter. The constant honking of geese, who now call Little Toot the Tugboat's lake home, is no substitute for the musings of Mother Goose guiding her goslings.

The Enchanted Forest opened on August 15, 1955, a month after Disneyland. Driven by passion and imagination, Howard E. Harrison, Sr., and his son created the Enchanted Forest to fulfill a promise they made to Howard Junior's children—to bring to life the children's much-loved nursery rhyme and fairy-tale characters. Under the watchful eye of popular local designer, Howard Adler, a team of workers constructed the charming creations using papier-mâché, cement and fiberglass.

With no mechanical rides, for thrill seekers, the Enchanted Forest boasted such timeless characters as the Three Little Pigs, Humpty Dumpty, The Dish and The Spoon, Miss Muffet and her Spider, Goldilocks and the Three Bears, Snow White and the Seven Dwarfs, the Crooked House, Little Toot, the Old Woman who lived in the Shoe, with, of course, her shoe, and many, many more cherished characters from what now seems like a bygone era.

The park originally occupied 20 acres, later expanding to 52 acres, and then was reduced to 32 acres to make way for the Bethany Woods Housing development. Operating for just over thirty years, at its peak, the Enchanted Forest thrilled some 350,000–400,000 visitors each season from May to October.

In 1988, after the Enchanted Forest's closure, JHP Development purchased the site and bulldozed the eastern side to construct a typically unappealing shopping mall. Today very little remains. Cinderella's castle resembles an ancient ruin, precariously balanced on a rotting foundation, the turrets irreparably cracked and falling. Hansel and Gretel's cottage, now defaced by graffiti, welcomes those who ignore the no trespassing signs, with a giant, crumbling ice-cream cone on the roof, and dirty but still brightly colored walls.

There will be no reopening or restoration of the Enchanted Forest, but happily, many of the figures have been rescued. Thanks to the dedicated efforts of Martha Clark, the enchanting characters have been restored, and given a new home at Elioak Farm. Today, beloved figures such as the Black Duck, Mother Goose and her gosling, Snow White, Sleeping Beauty, Robin Hood and many more, now, once again, delight and enchant visitors. While this is not the happy ending the Harrison's would have wished for the Enchanted Forest, some solace can be found in knowing these wonderful reminders of a more innocent time now have a new home—safe from any further destruction.

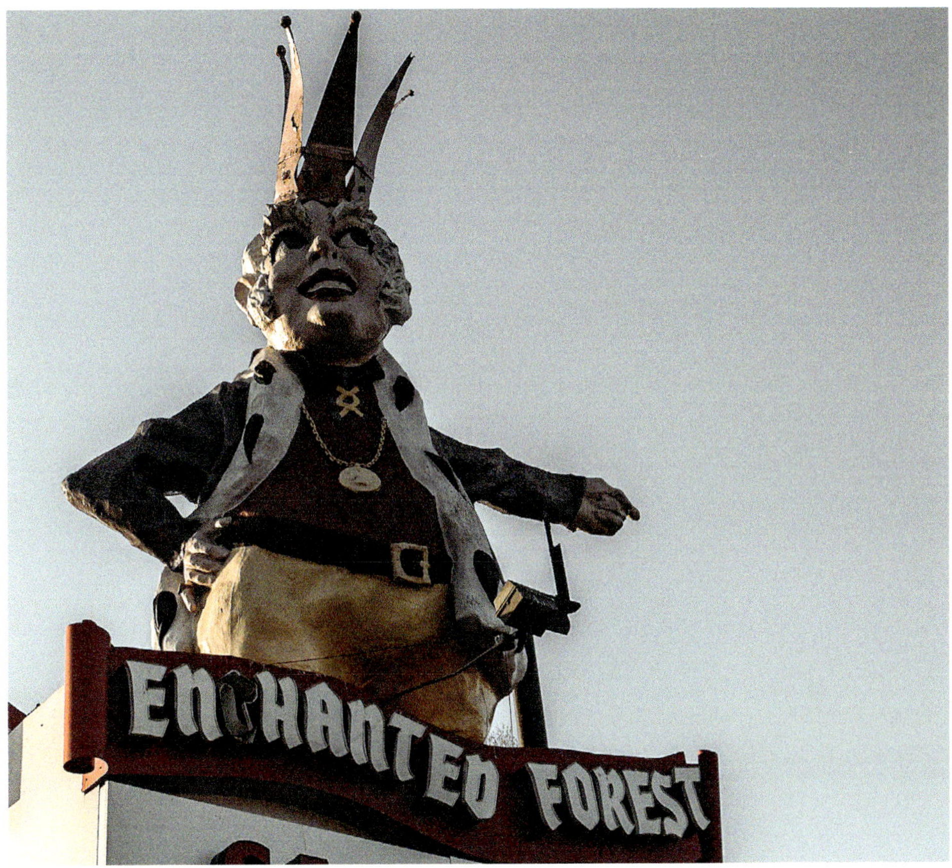

Old King Cole stands atop the Enchanted Forest sign on Route 40 in Ellicott City.

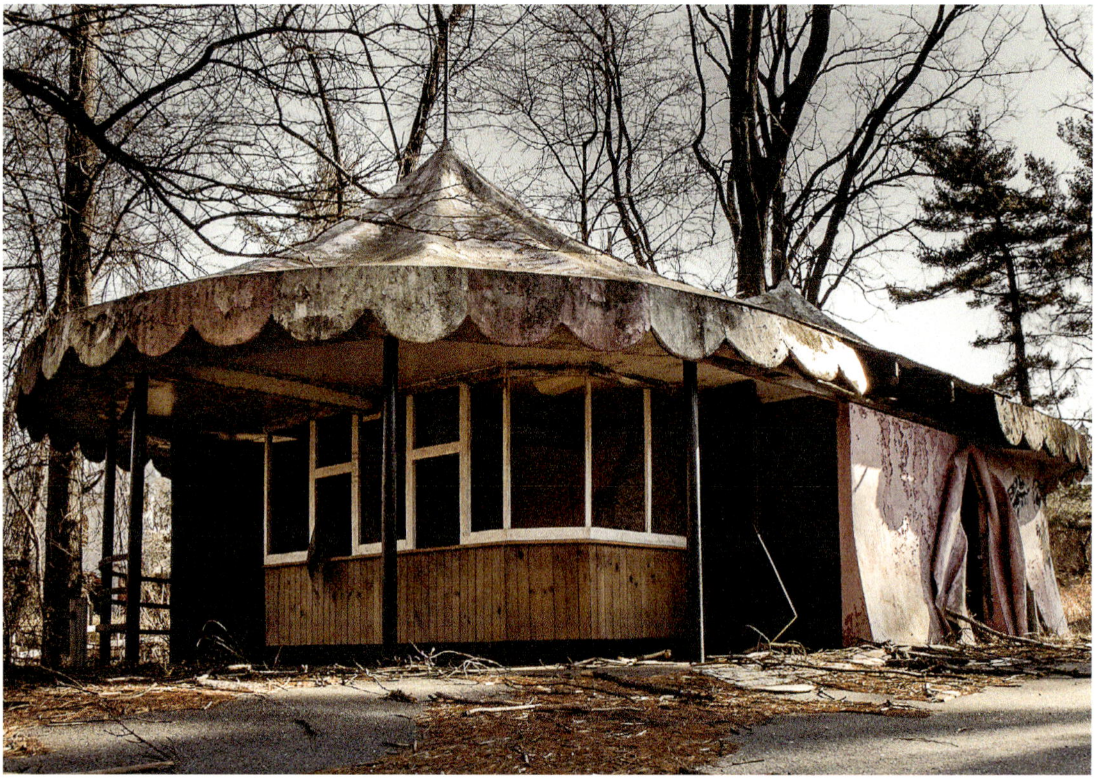

A crumbling concession stand near the main entrance of the park.

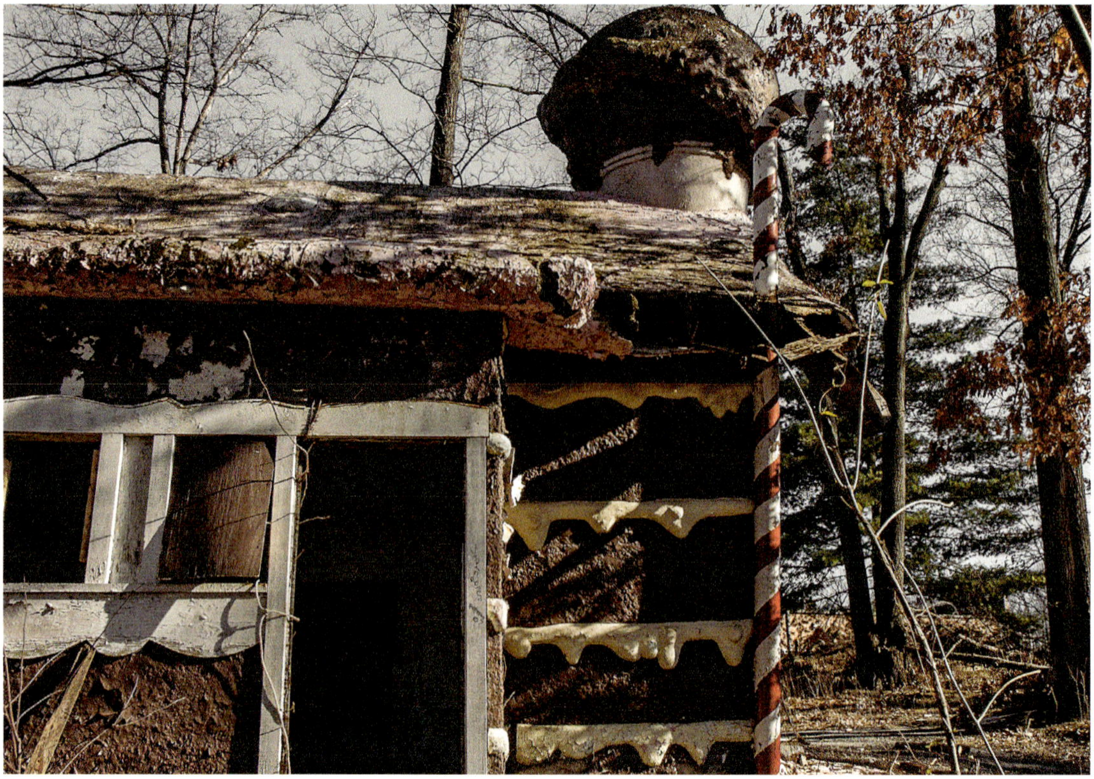

Hansel and Gretel's gingerbread house with a giant ice-cream cone at the entrance.

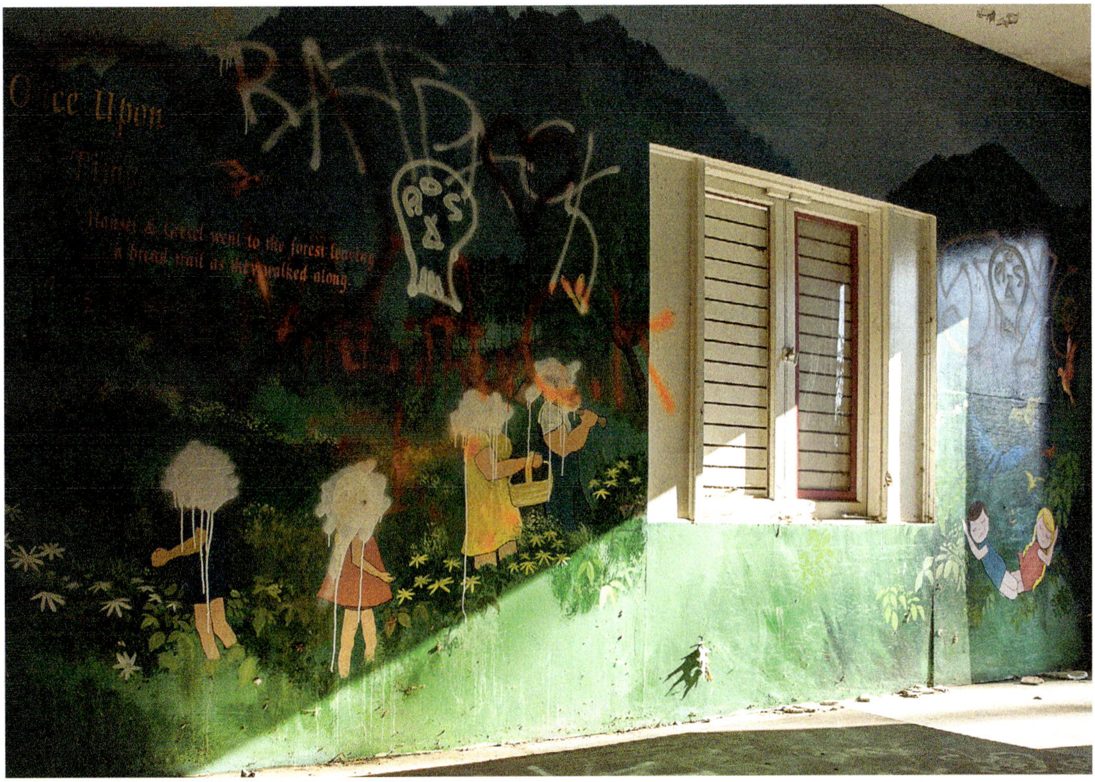

The interior of Hansel and Gretel's cottage, defaced by vandals.

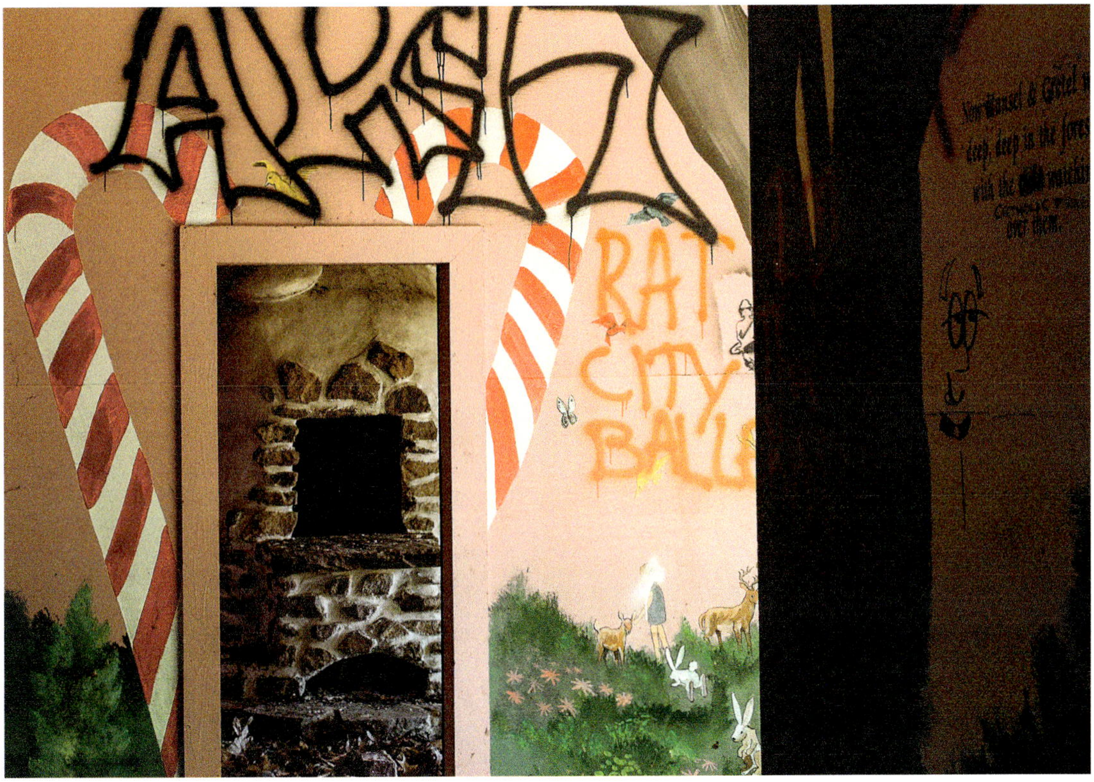

A doorway inside Hansel and Gretel's cottage leads to the oven.

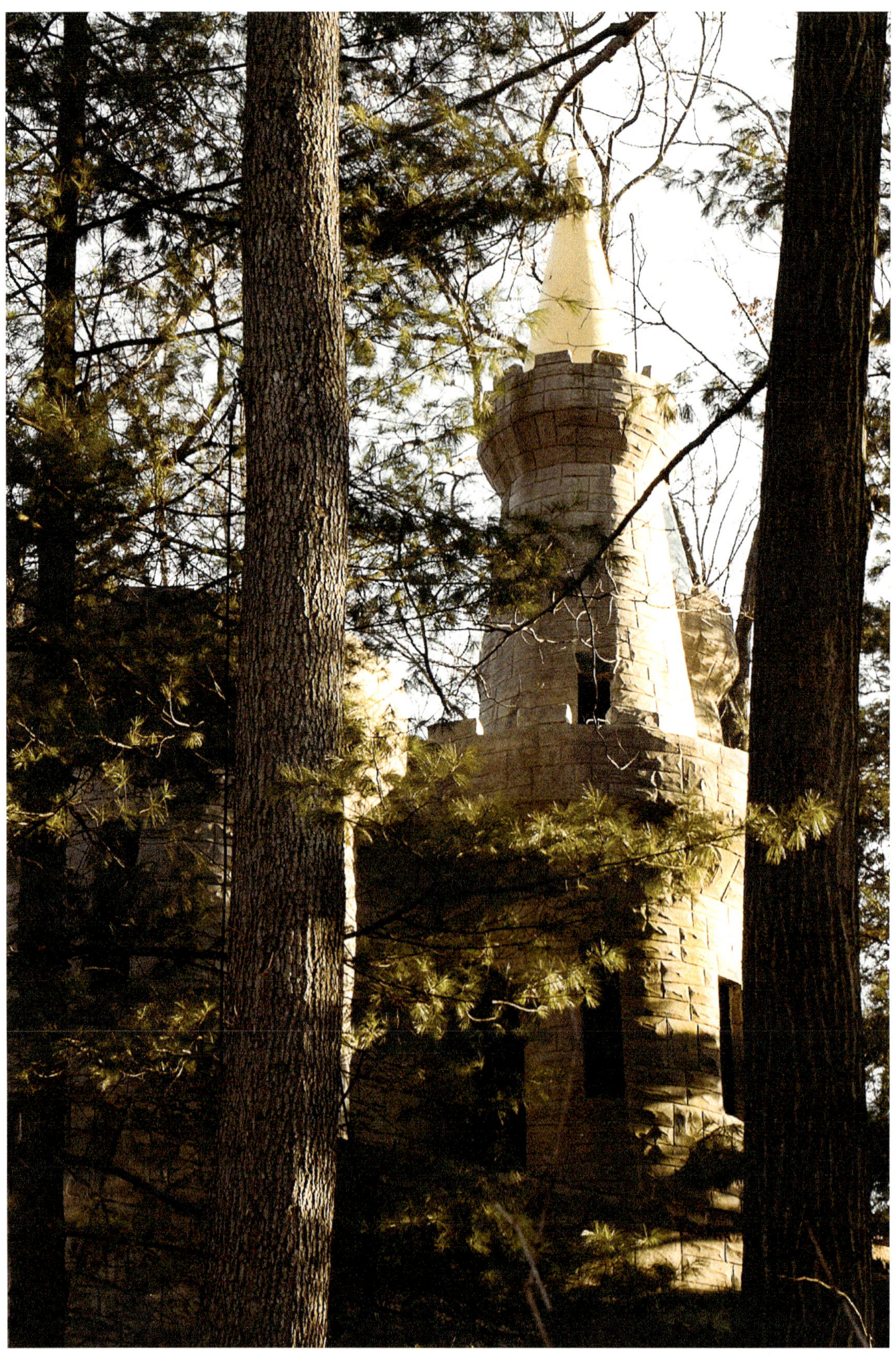

A turret, part of Cinderella's castle, surrounded by trees.

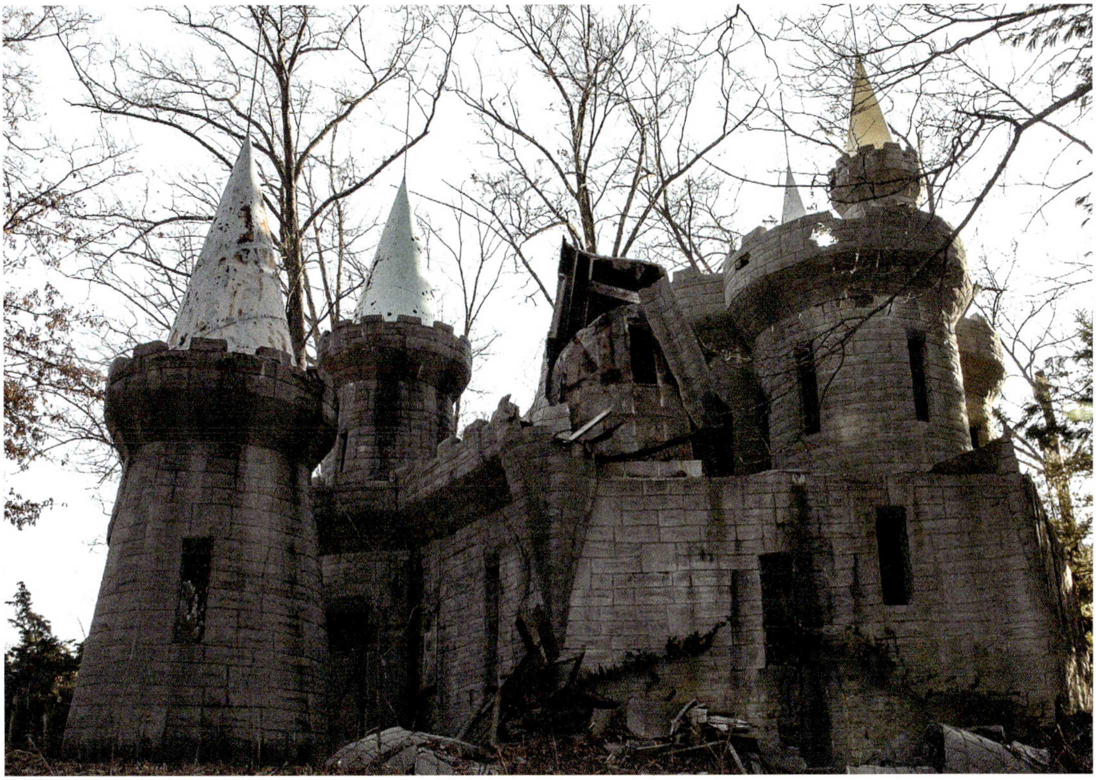

Cinderella's castle collapsing in on itself.

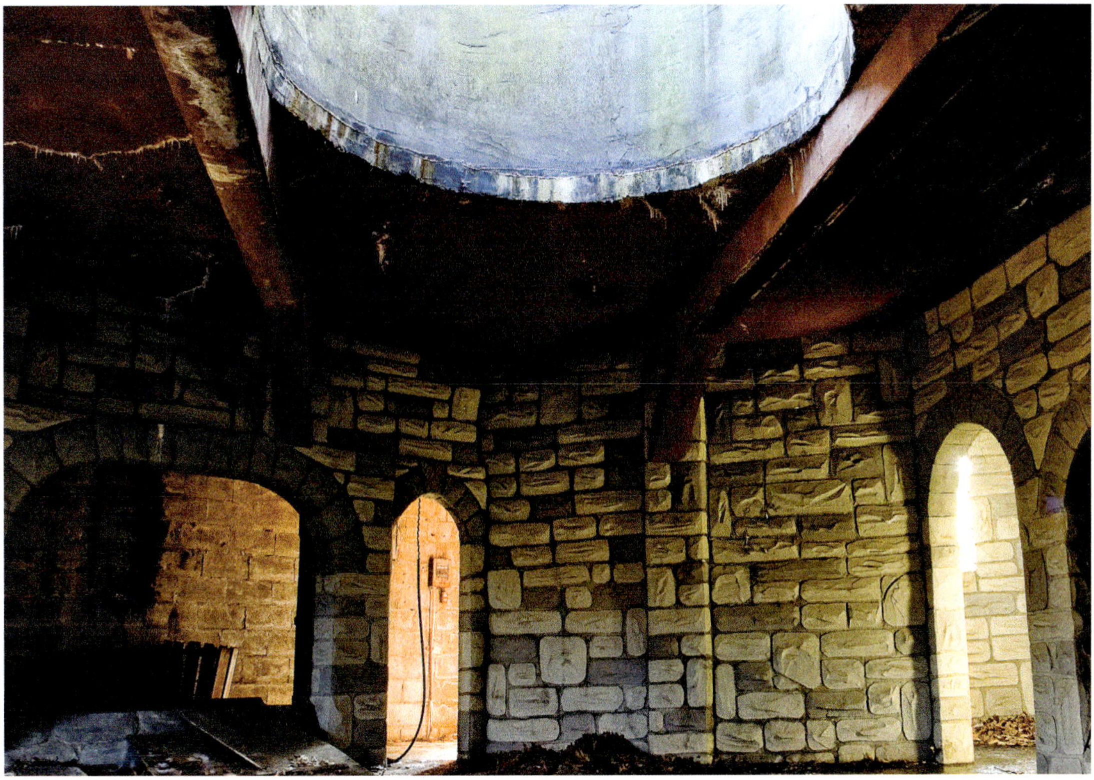

A ghostly light illuminates the interior castle walls.

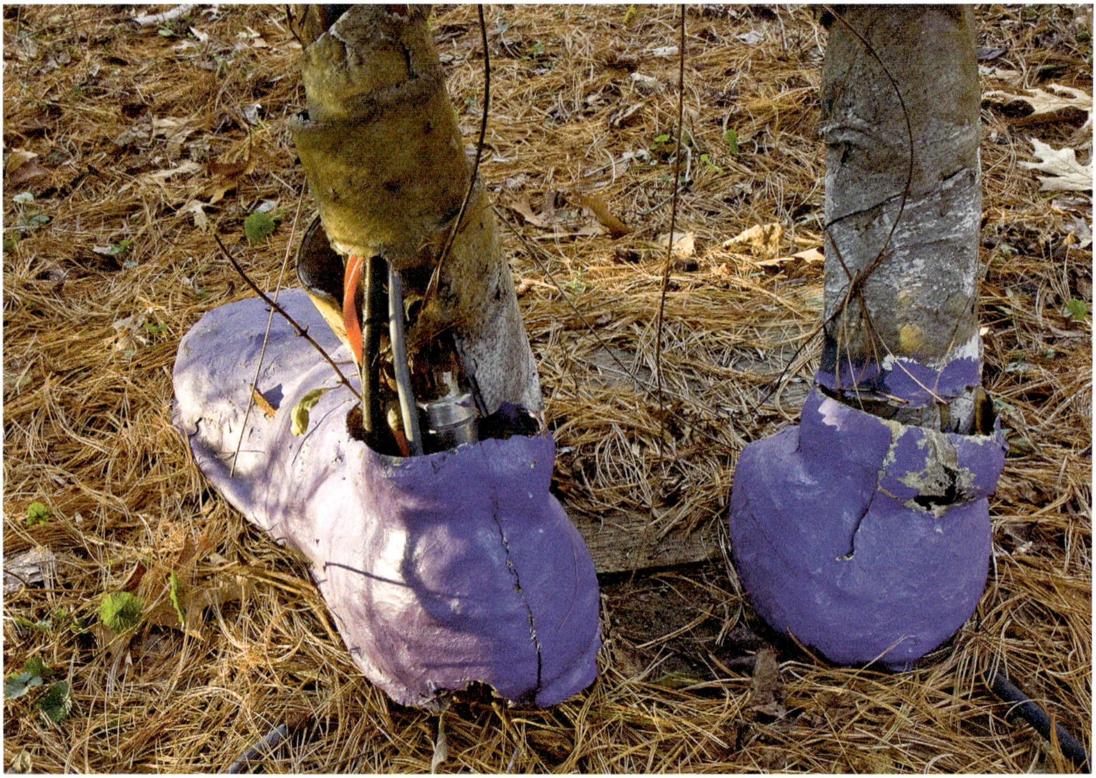

Big purple shoes filled with torn plaster legs exposing wires and a piston.

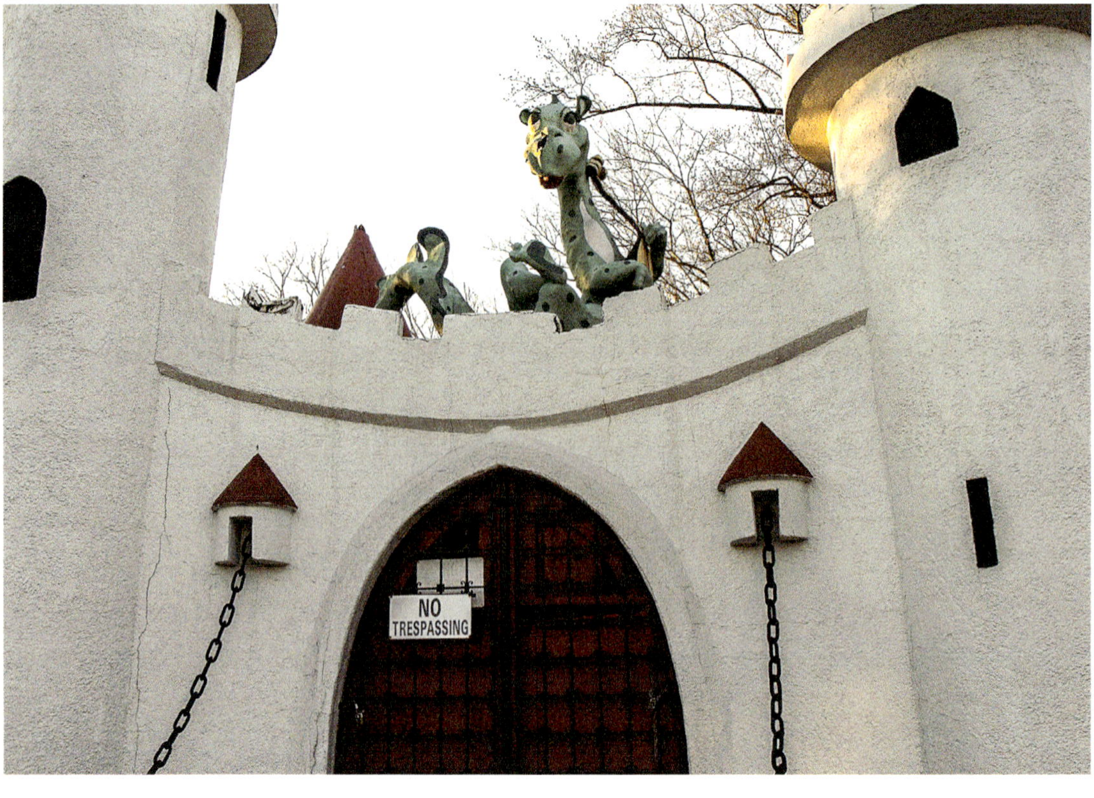

A friendly dragon welcomed visitors to the park, long before an unwelcoming no trespassing sign was posted.

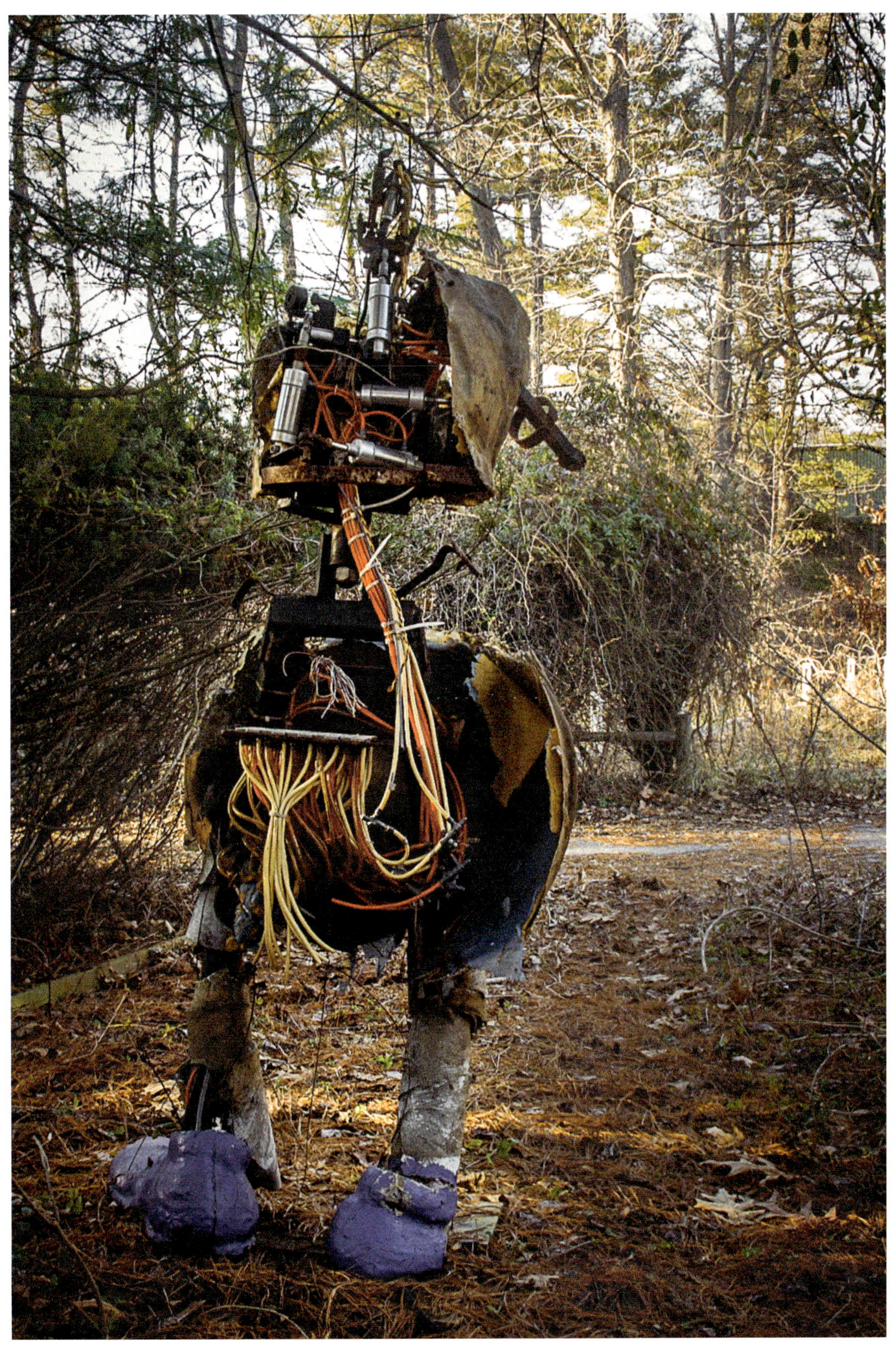

A robotic frame is sadly all that remains of this once loved character.

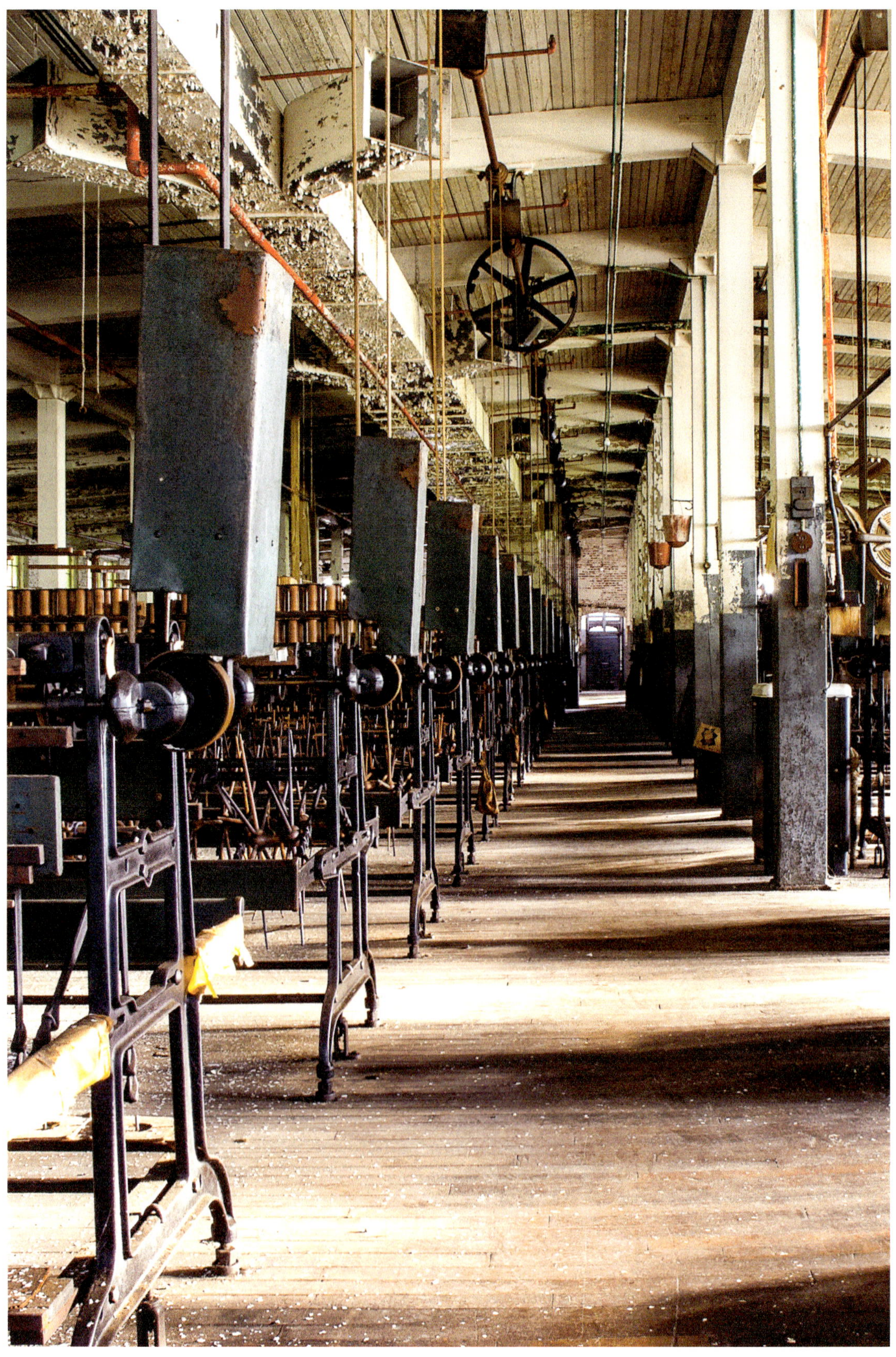

The main floor of the Lonaconing Silk Mill stands silent and unmoved since the workers left in 1957.

KLOTZ THROWING COMPANY, LONACONING

Time travel belongs to the narrative of fantasy and sci-fi literature, yet wandering through the wide-open floors of Klotz Throwing Company, in Lonaconing, visitors cannot help but feel as though they have traveled back to 1957; there is even an original calendar in place to remind you of the year you have arrived in.

Built between 1905 and 1907, at a cost of $100,000, the silk mill operated for fifty years before closing in the summer of 1957. A history of labor strikes plagued the unionized mill and a final walk-out in 1957 caused the company to close the once bustling mill permanently. What remains today is a time capsule of America's industrial heritage.

Row upon row of century-old winding machines stacked with thousands of spools wait silently for the workers who will never return. Personal items are tucked in storage nooks and a powder case marks what was once a supervisor's work station. Bright red fire buckets hang on pillars at the end of each machine row, a reminder of how primitive worker-safety protections once were.

A closer look at the structure reveals that time has, in fact, not stood still. Sadly, the roof is in need of repair and the constant attack by nature's forces is taking a toll. Areas of the floor are in danger of collapsing as wind, rain and snow enter through the damaged roof and broken windows. Owner, Herb Crawford, has worked stoically for more than forty years to preserve the mill, but he fears time may run out. The cost to repair the roof will be far more than what Herb can raise from photo tours and the occasional movie location fee. Preservation Maryland has visited the site and agree with Crawford of the historic significance of the mill, yet no offer to help with restoration has been forthcoming. It will be a tragedy if America's last intact silk mill, a vestige of another era, does not post-exist as a monument to manufacturing processes of the industrial age.

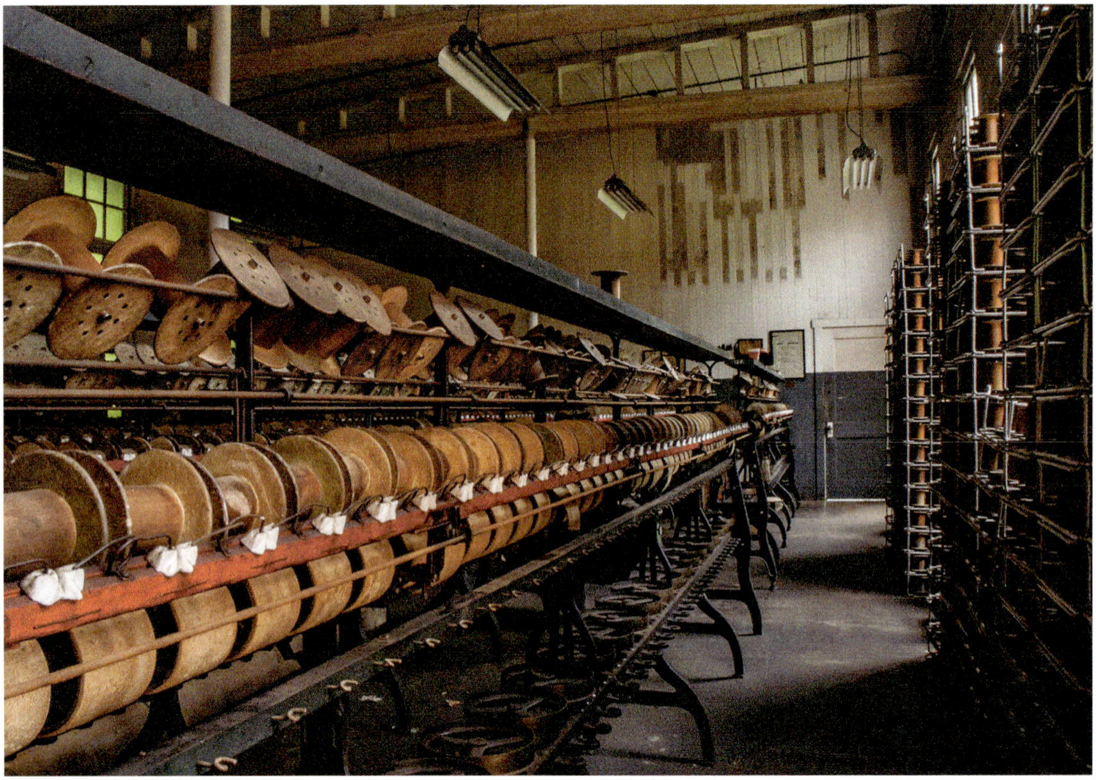

Empty silk spools line the walls and winding machines.

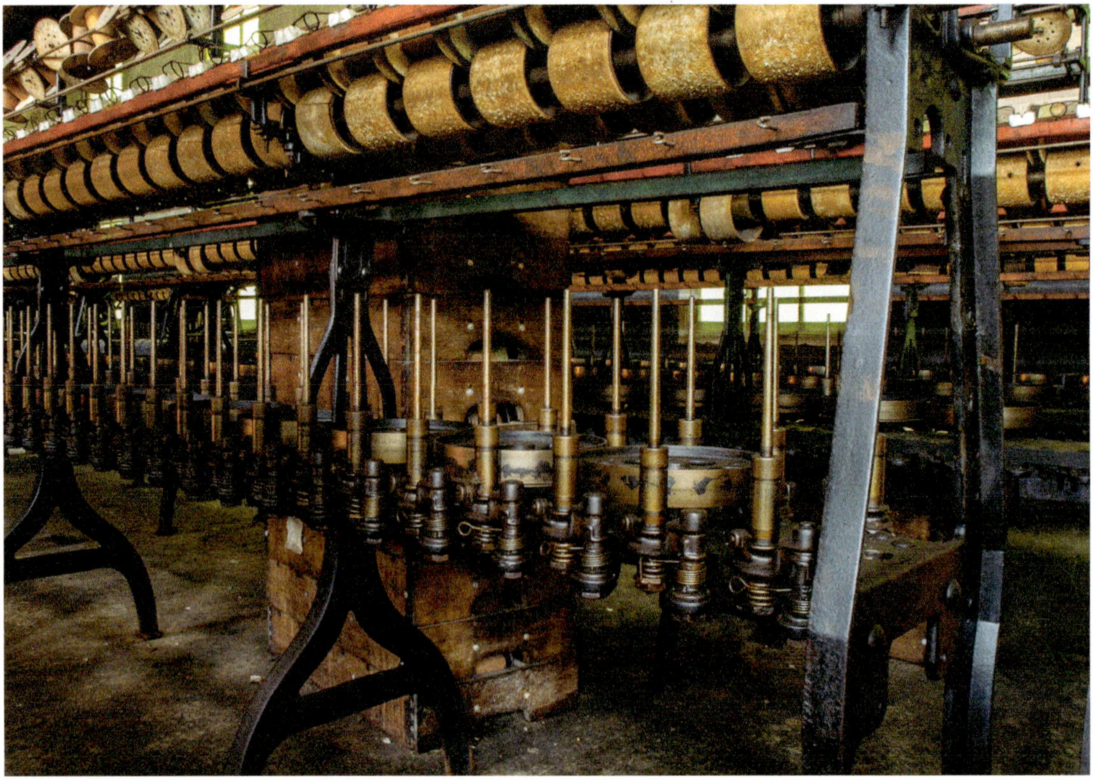

A winding machine looks poised and ready to continue its work.

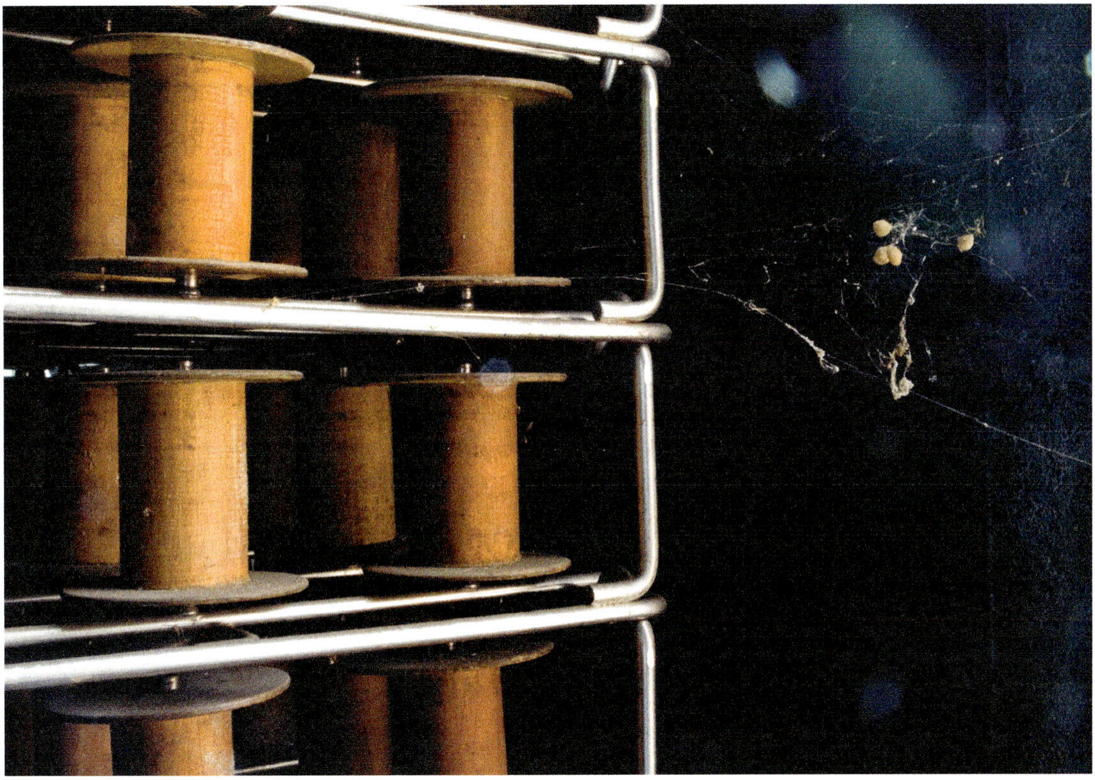

A spider web claiming a stack of spools for its own delicately spun web.

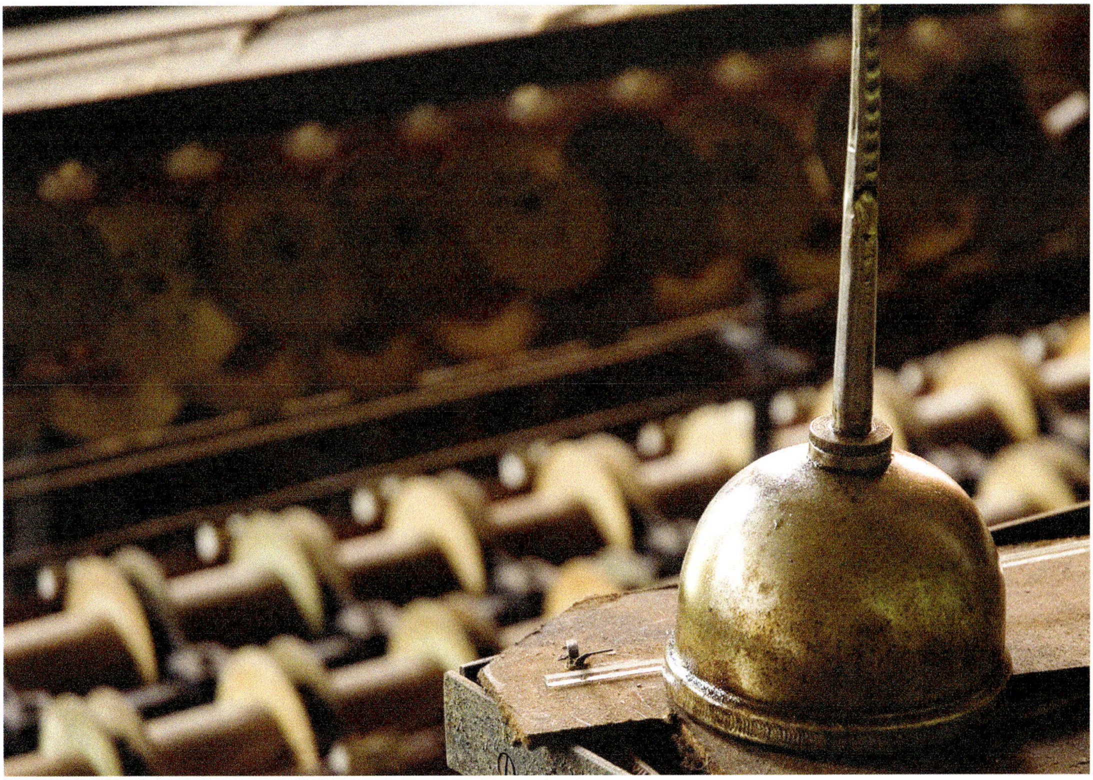

A vintage oil can, used to oil the winding machines.

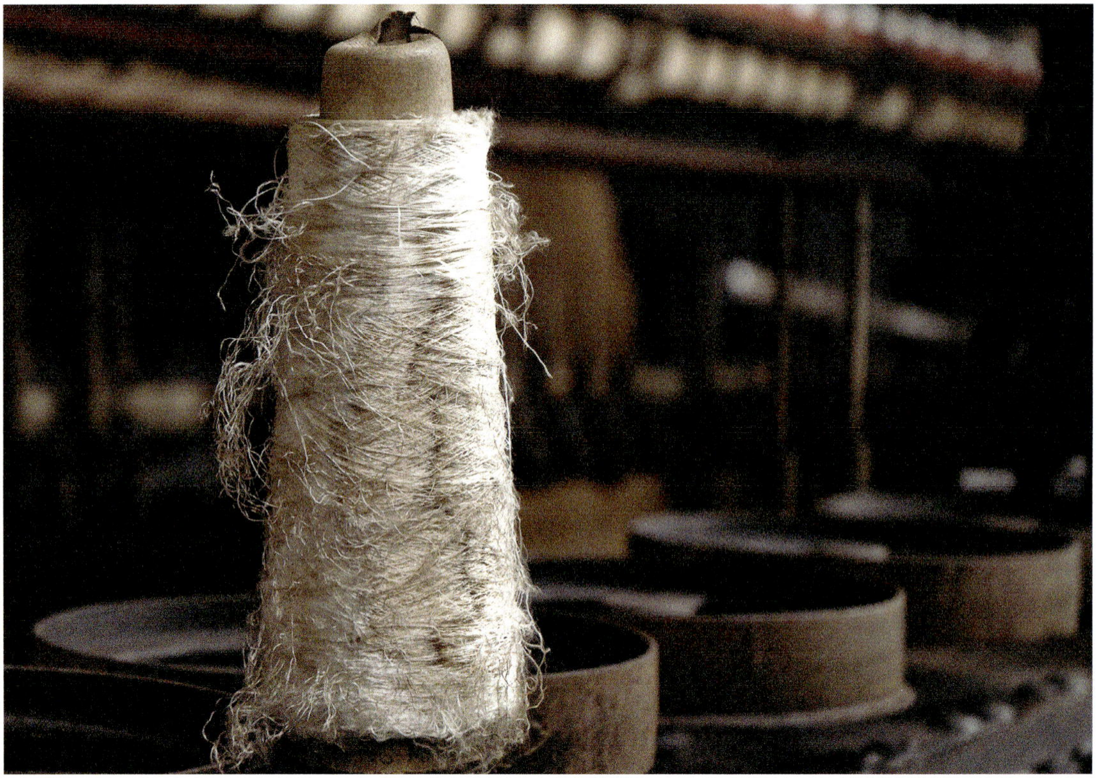

Silk, once white and freshly spun, now dirtied with dust and grime.

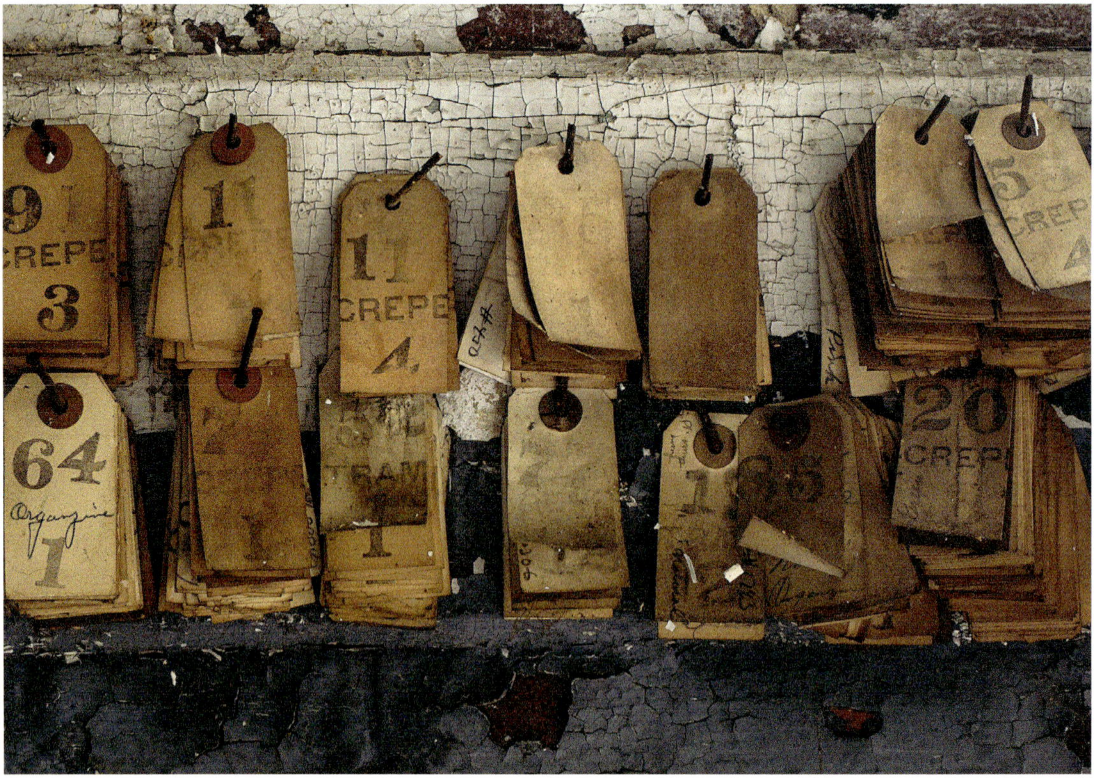

Faded labels adorn a wall.

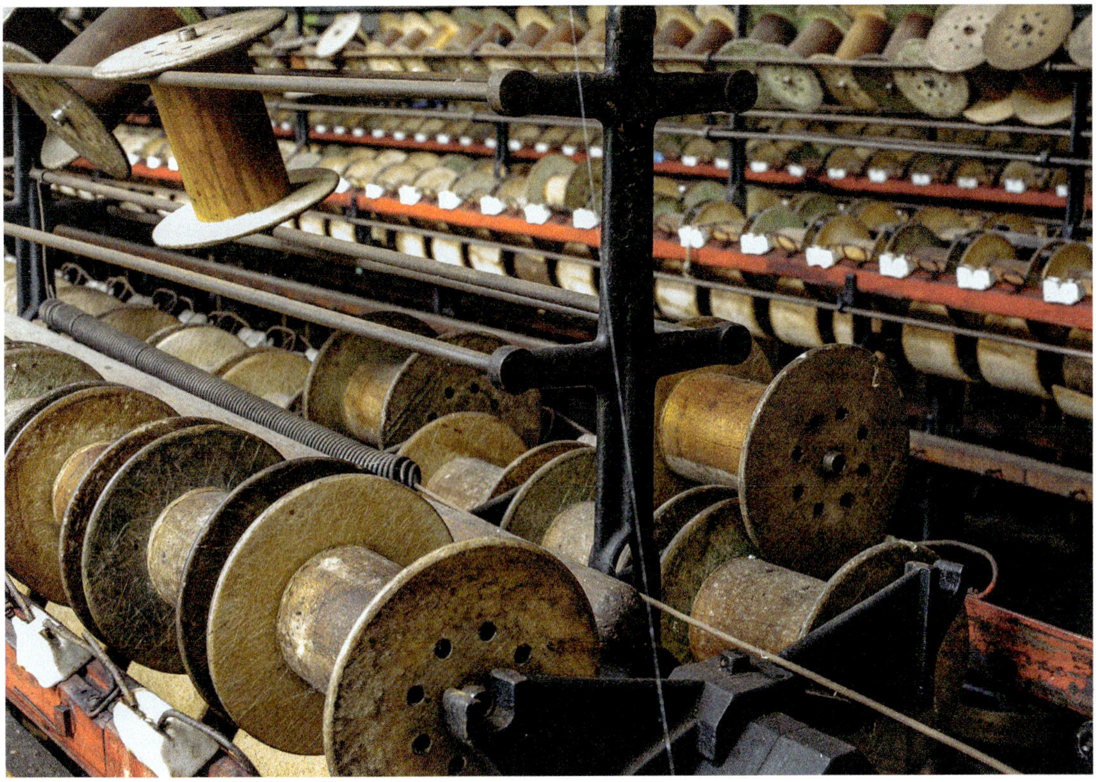

Spools or bobbins, just as they were left, waiting for silk that will never come.

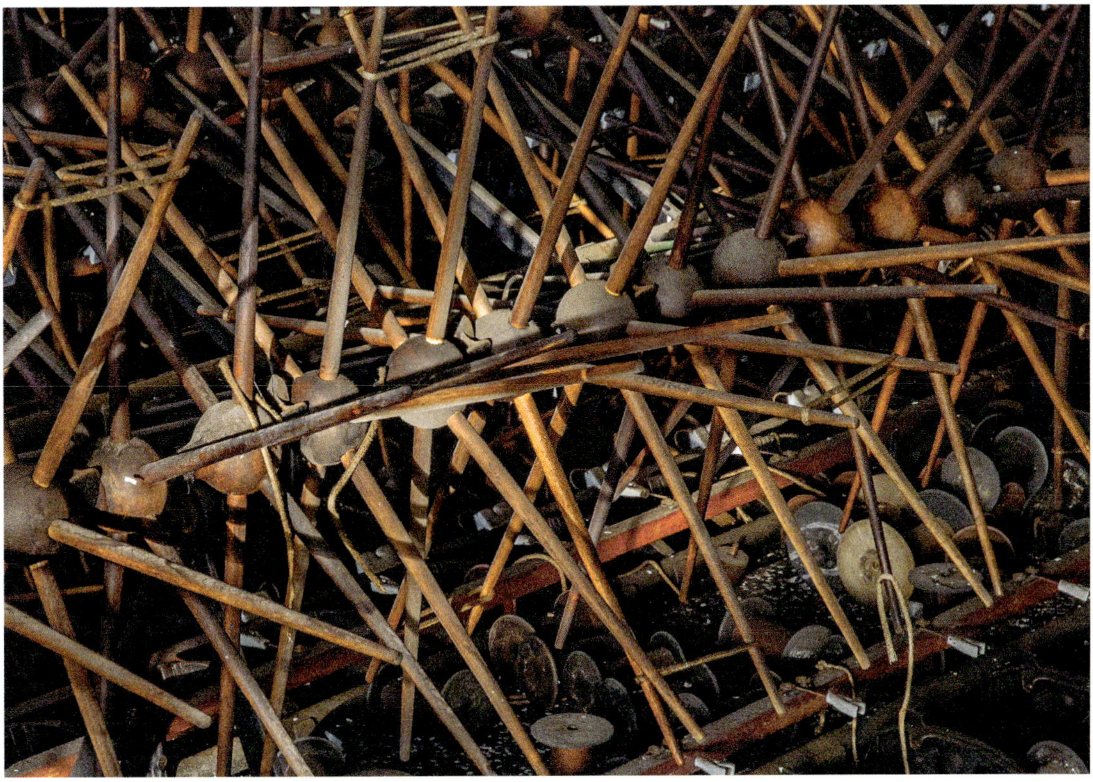

Winding reels or swifts lit by the afternoon sun.

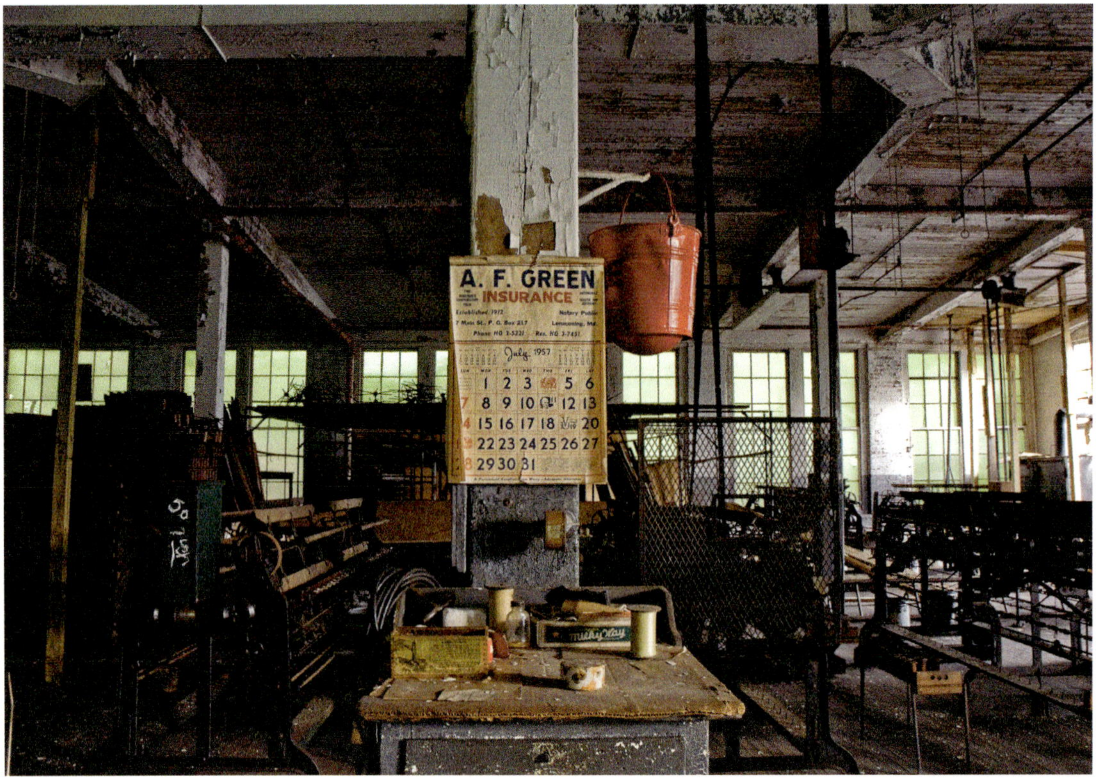

A supervisor's work station with personal belongings and a 1957 calendar showing the month the mill ceased operations.

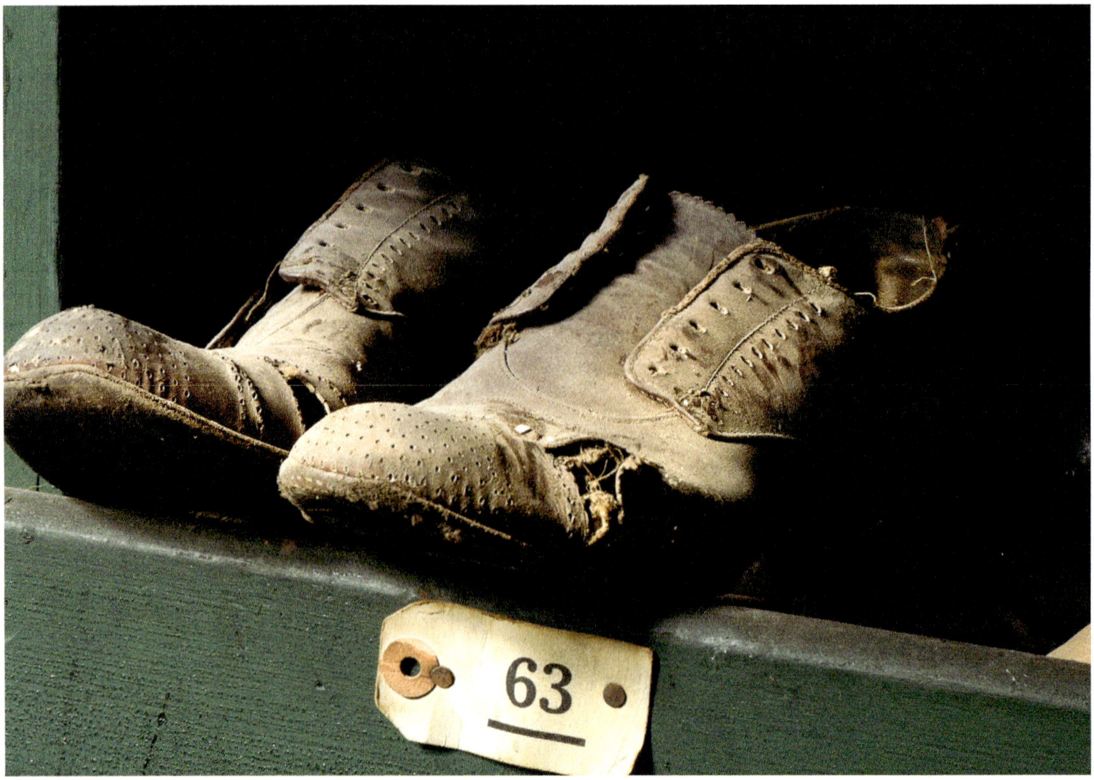

A worker's leather shoes.

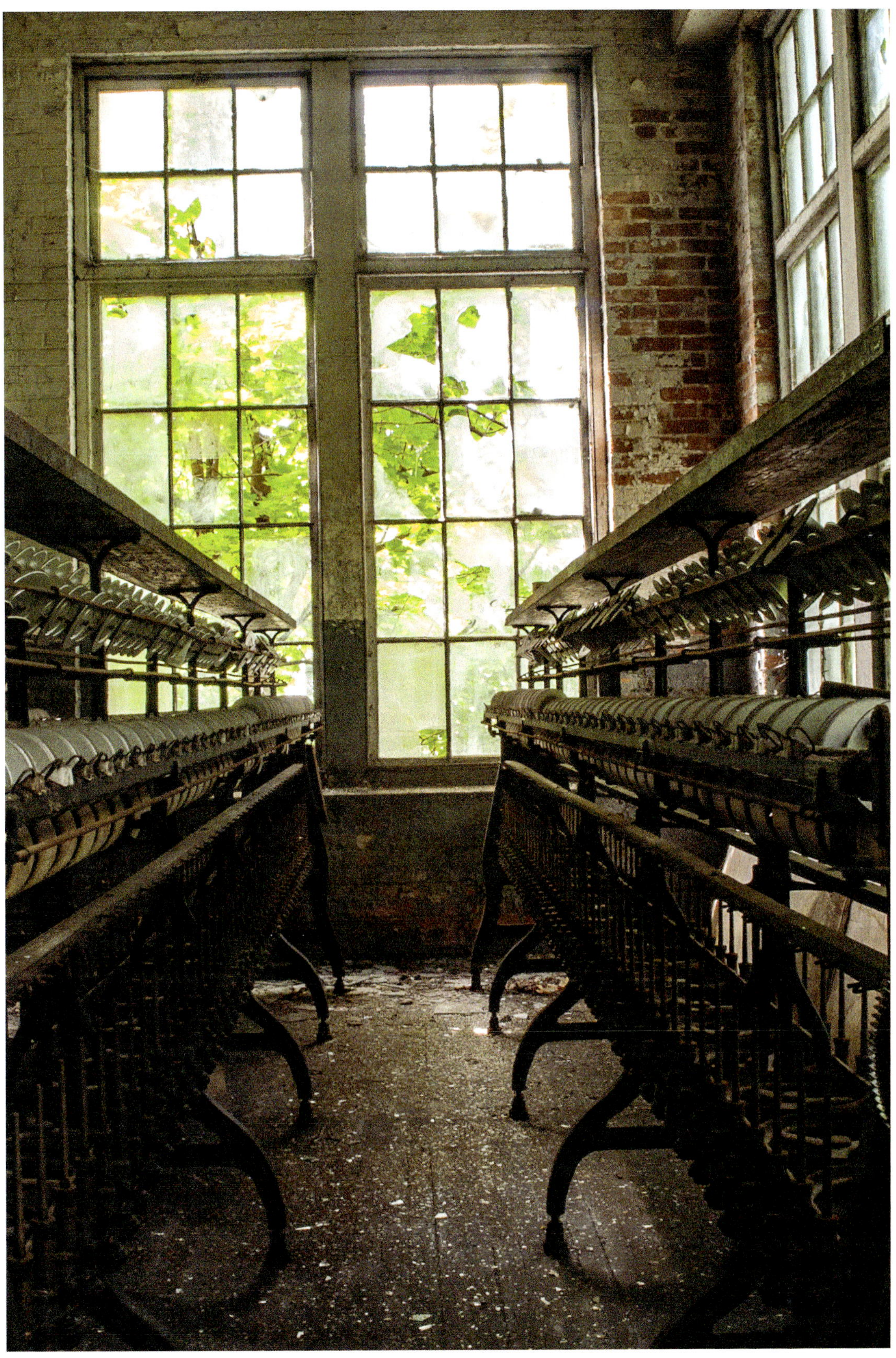

Broken windows are allowing mother nature to take her toll on the wooden floor and the precious part of history inside.

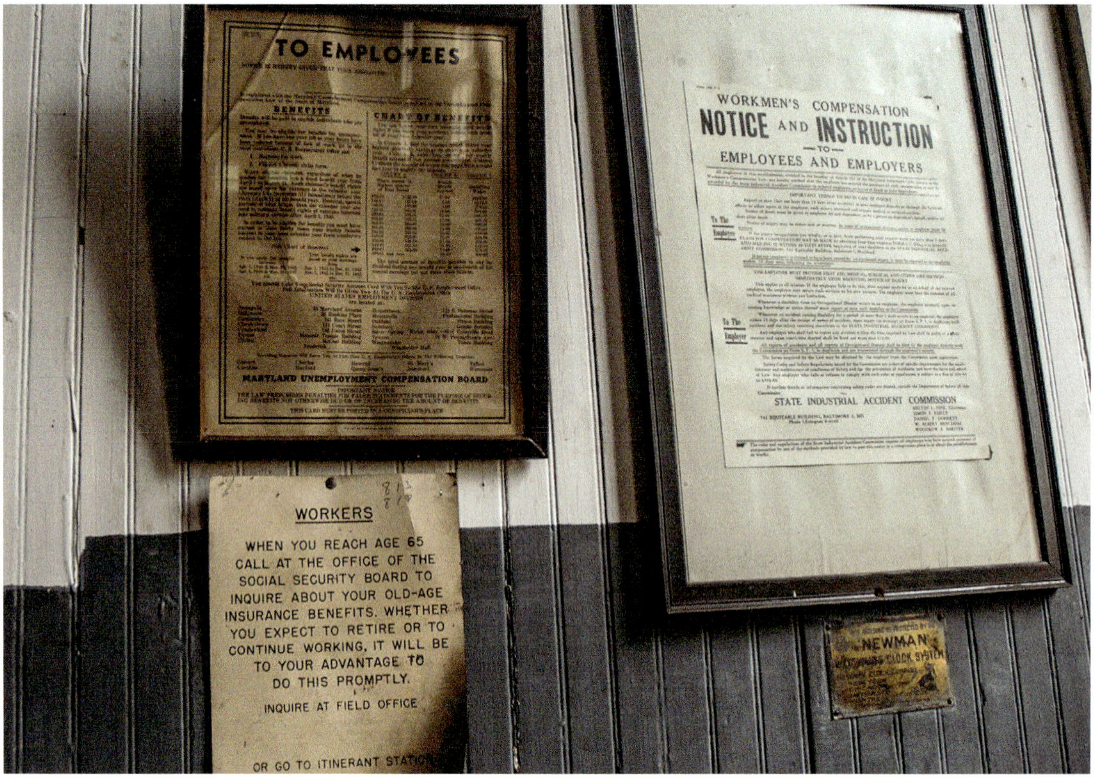

Pertinent employee information posted on a factory floor wall.

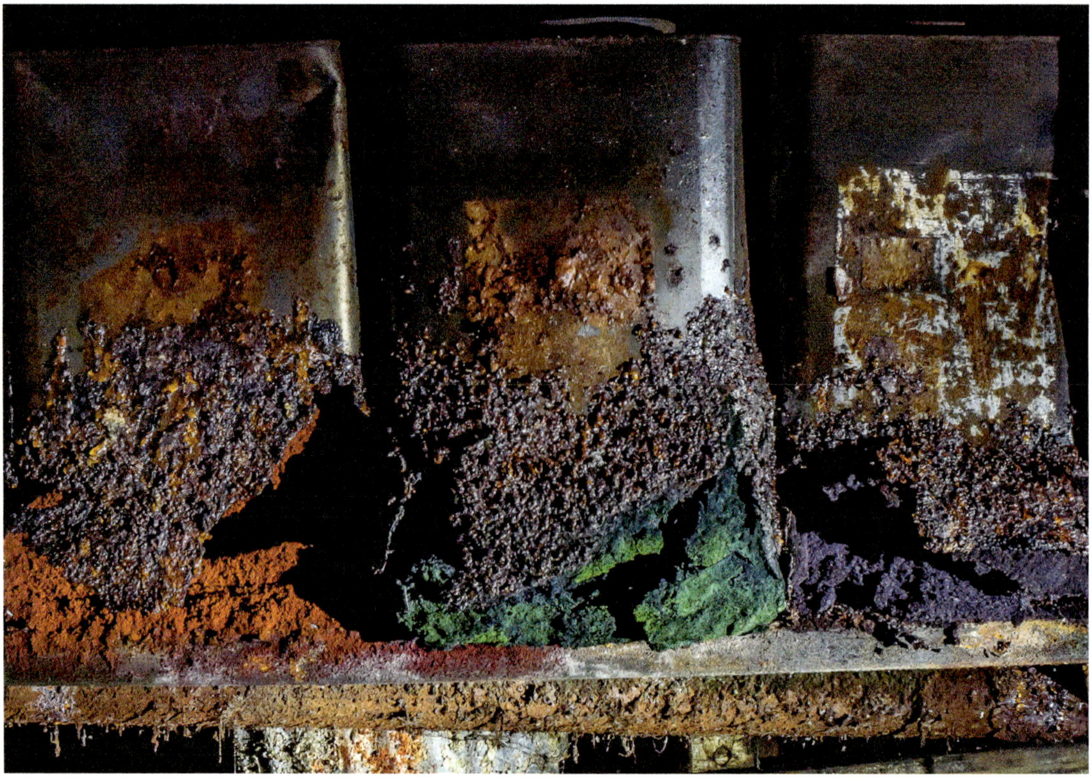

Tins of dye, rotting and exposing their powdered contents.

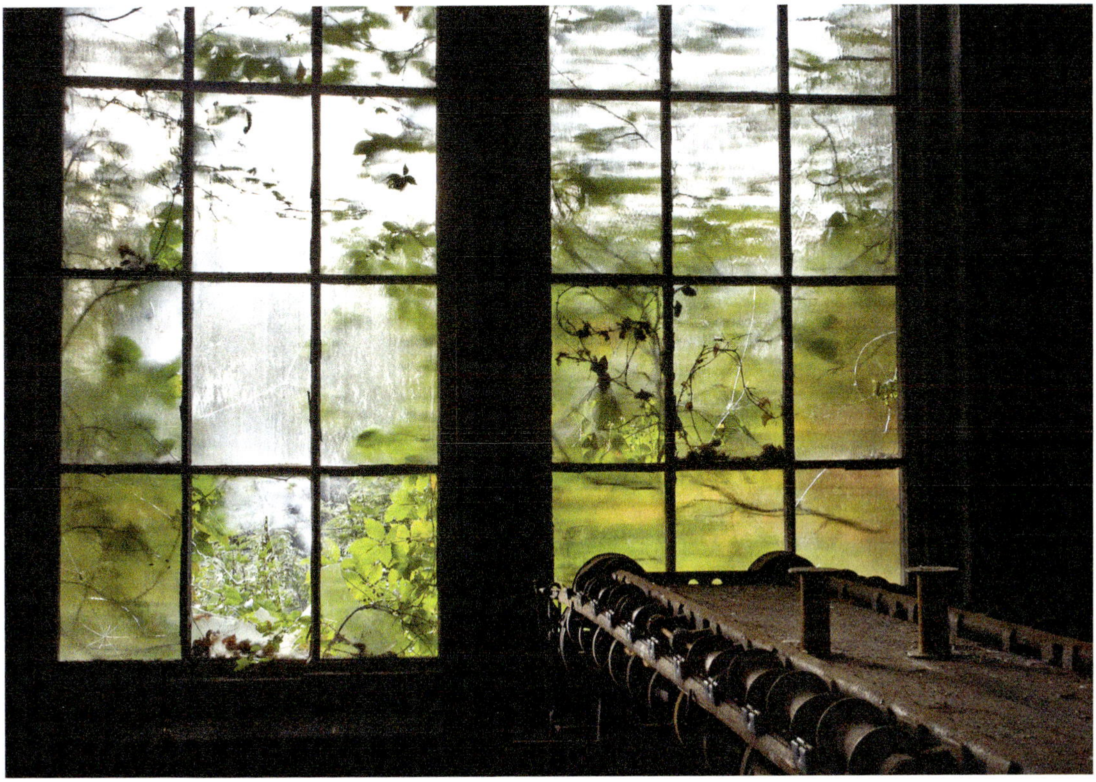

Two abandoned spools watch the lush overgrowth threatening to invade the mill through broken windows.

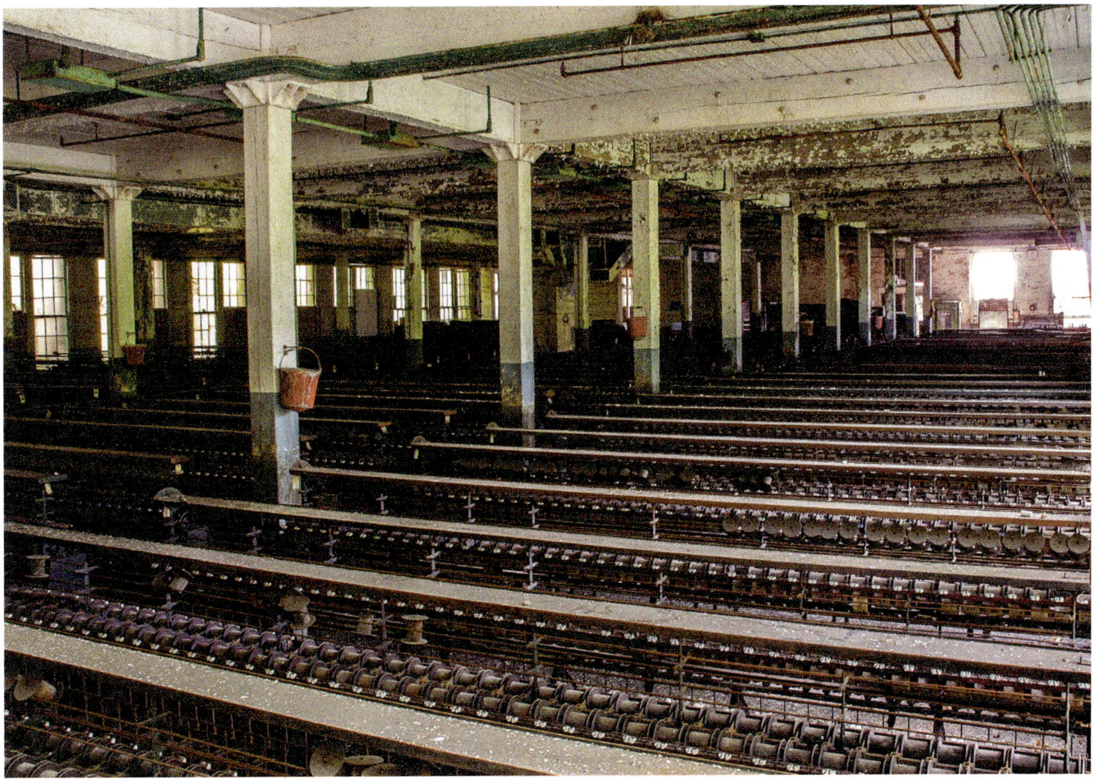

Fire buckets were placed at the end of each aisle, today they hang in place catching water from the leaking roof.

BIBLIOGRAPHY

Amoss, M., "Baltimore Observed: Encounter, Storybook Ending." *Urbanite* Dec. 2007: "Baltimore Architecture: Then and Now." Maryland Historical Society. Retrieved, 6 Apr. 2008, from www.mdhs.org/library/baltarch/Page4.html

Barnhardt, L., "Officials continue probe of plant fire." *Baltimore Sun* June, 25 2003. B1+. Howard County Historical Society

Baughman, J., "Hopes for abandoned mill site to become part of Patapsco Valley State Park." September 12, 2013. Retrieved from, NewsBank, April 4, 2018

Boo, K., "Forest Haven Is Gone. But the Agony Remains" *Washington Post* Mar. 14 1999 A01; "Residents Languish; Profiteers Flourish." *Washington Post* Mar. 15, 1999 A1

"Brewing…a major industry." Achievement May 1957. Baltimore: H.W. Buddemeier Co. Maryland Historical Society.

"Business plus Beauty."*Motography* Oct. 7, 1916, Vol XVI, No15. Retrieved from Library of Congress Apr. 14, 2018. ia600207.us.archive.org/24/items/motography162elec/motography162elec.pdf

Chalkley, T., "Harbor Next" *City Paper* [Baltimore] 25 Jan. 2006. Retrieved, 5 Apr. 2008, from www.citypaper.com/news/story.asp?id=11385

Clark, M., Clark's Elioak Farm. Retrieved, Mar. 30 2008, from www.clarklandfarm.com/

Davis, A., *Flickering Treasures* (Johns Hopkins University Press 2017), Retrieved Apr. 5, 2018 from, books.google.com/books?id=rrkyDwAAQBAJ&printsec

Distelrath, A., "John F. Wiessner & Sons Brewery Baltimore MD." *American Breweriana Journal*. Mar–Apr. 2003. Retrieved, Apr. 6 2008, from, www.americanbreweriana.org/history/wiessner.htm

Drooker, A., *American Ruins* (New York: Merrell, 2007)

Erlandson, R. A., "Company town is far from run of the mill." *Baltimore Sun* Nov., 21 1991. C1+ Howard County Historical Society

Failing, A., Degyansky, E., Jewell, C., Sallerson, A., Whetzel, D., and Lewis, M., *The Lonaconing Silk Mill History 1907–1957*. Retrieved Apr. 14, 2018, from Western Maryland Historical Library, digital.whilbr.org/

"Famous 'eye-con' set to watch over downtown Baltimore skyline–starting October 21" Brewers Hill. Retrieved Apr. 5 2008, from www.brewershill.net/news.html

Fritze, J., "Brewery project turns a corner." *Baltimore Sun* Jan. 12 2008

Gilfilan, M., Howe, K., Schlatter, E., Fitch, S. *Gone: Photographs of Abandonment on the High Plains* (University of New Mexico Press, 2002)

"Great Power Station: Consolidated Gas Electric Light and Power Company's New Plant." Notes on Electric Service June 1906. Retrieved from Baltimore Museum of Industry, baltimusindustry.pastperfect-online.com/35171cgi/

Haga, D., *Urban Atrophy*. Retrieved November 2007 from urbanatrophy.com

Hagberg, D. "John F. Weissner & Sons Brewing Company." Baltimore Antique Bottle Club. Feb 2005. Retrieved Apr. 4 2008, from www.baltimorebottleclub.org/newsletter.htm

Headley, R. K., *Motion Picture Exhibition in Baltimore: An Illustrated History And Directory of Theatres* (North Carolina: McFarland & Company, 2006)

"Jacob Tome Institute Circular of Information 1898." Port Deposit the Original Mayberry, Online Maryland Village. Retrieved, Mar. 10, 2008, from www.portdeposit.com/History/Jacobtome_JTI.htm

Jensen, B., "A Beer to Call Your Own." *City Paper* [Baltimore] Jan. 16, 2002

Kaltenbach, C., "Demolition work at Mayfair Theatre to begin today." *Baltimore Sun*, Aug. 29, 2016 Retrieved April 2, www.baltimoresun.com/entertainment/movies/bs-md-mayfair-20160829-story.html

Kelley, W. J., *Brewing In Maryland from colonial times to the present* (Baltimore: W. J. Kelley, 1965). Maryland Historical Society

Kiehl, S., "Show may go on at the Mayfair." *Baltimore Sun* Feb. 3

Kipp, J., Welcome to the Enchanted Forest. Retrieved Mar. 28, 2008, from www.theenchantedforest.ellicottcity.net/

Lake, M. *Weird Maryland* (New York: Sterling, 2006)

MacKenzie, M., *American Ruins: Ghosts on the Landscape* (Minnesota: Afton Historical Society Press, 2001)

Manigault, M. D., "Factory fire under investigation." *Columbia Flier* June 26, 2003 Howard County Historical Society.

Milford, M., "Displacing the Ghosts of Students and Sailors." *The New York Times* Mar. 12, 2000. Retrieved Jan. 2, 2008 from query.nytimes.com/gst/fullpage.html?res=9506E1D6

Mirabella, L., "Westport renewal rules are readied; Urban design agency to receive proposed guidelines today; Shoreline project dubbed "Harbor West." *Baltimore Sun* May 25, 2005

Motts. M. (alias) Opacity. Retrieved November 2007 from opacity.com

Newman, J., "Abandoned Mill is a Photographer's Dream–But for How Much Longer." *The Huffington Post*, June 4, 2015. Retrieved from www.huffingtonpost.com/joe-newman/abandon-mill-is-a-photogr_b_7511666.html

Owens, J., and Whig, C., "Future of Prized Tome memorial Hall Uncertain after Fire" Bainbridge Development Corporation, Oct. 3, 2014. Retrieved from www.bainbridgedevelopment.org/single-post/2014/10/03/

Peirce, J. W., *A Guide to Patapsco Valley Mill Sites: Our Valley's Contribution to Maryland's Industrial Revolution* (Indiana: Author House, 2004)

Pelton, T., "Haunting symbol of neglect; Forest Haven: Ruins of a D.C. mental institution in Anne Arundel County are a magnet for young ghost- hunters, arsonists and vandals." *Baltimore Sun.* Dec. 3, 1998, 1A. ProQuest. Apr. 8, 2008 www.proquest.com/; "Hoyer assails D.C. over Forest Haven; City not a good neighbor in Anne Arundel, he says" *Baltimore Sun.* Dec. 4, 1998, 7B. ProQuest. Apr. 8, 2008 www.proquest.com/

Reddy, S., "Sale of old brewery OK'd." *Baltimore Sun* May 17, 2007

Reimer, S., "Authorities investigate fire at former Bainbridge Naval Station." *Baltimore Sun*, Sept. 21, 2014. Retrieved Apr. 5, 2018 from www.baltimoresun.com/news/maryland/harford/bs-md-cecil-fire-20140921-story.html

Richards, K., "Buildings not empty after all." *Baltimore Sun.* Aug. 26 1994, 1B. ProQuest. Apr. 8, 2008 www.proquest.com/

Sceurman, M., and Moran, M. *Weird U.S.* Retrieved Jan. 5 2008, from www.weirdus.com/stories/MD03.asp

Sherman, N., Websites America, The Enchanted Forest History Retrieved Mar. 30, 2008, from www.websitesamerica.com/websitesamerica/Nostalgia/EF-Pages/EF-History.htm

Shorto, R., "An Economic Moment, Frozen in Time." *The New Yorker*, Aug. 11, 2016. Retrieved Apr. 14, from www.newyorker.com/business/currency/an-economic-moment-frozen-in-time

Stevens, M., "Brimstone Brewing Company-Rekindling Brewing Traditions on Brewery Hill." *Brewing Techniques* Sept. 1997

Thomas, Parkway Theatre Cinema Treasures. Retrieved Apr. 2, 2018 from cinematresures.org

Tyler, Urban Eden. Retrieved Nov. 2007, from urbaneden.ws

Williams, R. S., The Glenn Dale Hospital Mission. Retrieved Apr. 5 2008, from gdhospital.tripod.com/index.html

Zumer, B., "Devastating, Port Deposit's mayor says of fire that destroyed iconic Bainbridge building." *Baltimore Sun*, Sept. 23, 2014. Retrieved Mar. 13, 2018 from www.baltimoresun.com/news/ph-ag-bainbridge-fire-0924-20140922-story.htm